THE ARAB GULF ECONOMY IN A TURBULENT AGE

The Arab Gulf Economy in a Turbulent Age

Hazem Beblawi

CROOM HELM
London & Canberra

ST. MARTIN'S PRESS
New York

©1984 Hazem Beblawi

Croom Helm Ltd, Provident House, Burrell Row,
Beckenham, Kent BR3 1AT
Croom Helm Australia Pty Ltd, 28 Kembla St,
Fyshwick, ACT 2609, Australia

British Library Cataloguing in Publication Data

Beblawi, Hazem
 The Arab Gulf economy in a turbulent age.
 1. Persian Gulf States – Economic conditions
 I. Title
 330.953'6053   HC415.3

 ISBN 0-7099-3215-4

C C.

All rights reserved. For information, write:
St. Martin's Press, Inc., 175 Fifth Avenue, New York, NY 10010
Printed in Great Britain
First published in the United States of America in 1984

Library of Congress Cataloguing in Publication Data

Beblawi, Hazem, 1936-
 The Arab gulf economy in a turbulent age.

 Includes index.
 1. Persian Gulf Region–Economic conditions.
2. Persian Gulf Region–Foreign economic relations.
3. Petroleum industry and trade–Persian Gulf Region.
4. Economic history–1971-   . I. Title.
HC415.3.B43 1984 330.953'6053 83-40505
ISBN 0-312-04700-2

Printed and bound in Great Britain

CONTENTS

To Dina, Karim and Salma

PREFACE

My interest in the phenomenon of oil surplus funds goes back to the early seventies. In June 1973, a few months before the so-called first oil shock, I chose as a topic for my presentation before the annual meeting of the Egyptian alumni of the National Institute for Management Development: 'Perspectives for Oil Surplus Funds', Alexandria, San Stefano, June 1973 (reproduced in the Egyptian periodical 'International Policy', *Al Seyassah Al Dawliya*, July 1974). A subsequent long sojourn in Kuwait and later developments in the oil market increased my interest in the subject as well as broadening my outlook.

I first met David Croom at Exeter during a symposium organised by Exeter University, the Centre for Arab Gulf Studies, on 'Oil Revenues and their Impact on Development in the Gulf States'. I contributed to that symposium a paper on 'The Gulf Foreign Investment Coordination'. David Croom suggested, and I agreed, to publish with Croom Helm that paper along with other studies on the Gulf economy in a new volume. The present book is the result.

The volume includes papers published, though slightly adapted, over the last two years (1981-3), to which I added a substantial introductory essay, as well as a background essay on Kuwait. After an overview of the Gulf economy in the introduction, Part One outlines the international financial context while Part Two surveys some Gulf problems and Part Three concludes with the Kuwaiti example.

I have been greatly helped in the preparation of this volume by many people. I cannot acknowledge my debt to all those who contributed to the process of forming my thinking by their comments and criticism. I would like only to express here my thanks to Raid Fahmi with whom I had the pleasure of co-authoring a paper appearing in this volume. I am also grateful to the editors of the *Arab Gulf Journal, Finance and Industry* and Westview Press to reproduce here material previously published by them.

**INTRODUCTION:
AN OVERVIEW**

1 ARAB ECONOMY IN A TURBULENT AGE

Introduction

For years to come the oil price increases in 1973-4, and again in 1979, will be looked upon as a turning point in recent international relations. They have even been labelled 'the Oil Revolution', rather like 'the Industrial Revolution'. Later developments may, however, prove that it could be a premature judgement and the whole thing might turn out to be no more than another episode of history, magnified under the weight of the moment but fading away as its memory recedes.

This can by no means be true for the Gulf states. Whatever would be the final assessment, the 'oil shock' makes a milestone in the history of the Gulf states, thus promoting them from relative remoteness to the forefront of international finance and politics. Suddenly, peripheral countries are called upon to assume a world central role to maintain the world economic and financial health. The establishment of a 'new world economic order', an old dream, came for a while very close to realisation. Such a gigantic enterprise cannot, however, be undertaken by small countries. Soon, the financial pre-eminence of the Gulf states was overshadowed by their economic, political and military shortcomings. Even the 'new oil order', which was taken for granted, was now seriously undermined, and the all-powerful OPEC came to face enormous problems from within and without. The contrast between the core and the periphery did not fail to manifest itself in the oil showdown.

The oil shock coincided with, or perhaps resulted from, major changes in the world economic and financial setting. The breakdown of the international monetary system and the near failure of economic policies helped to magnify the impact of the oil price increases. Increasing world interdependence is accompanied by decreasing economic understanding. National political assertiveness is growing amid a more interdependent world while unregulated categories, such as the Euro-markets, are plaguing economic policies. Confusion and uncertainty are — and no wonder — the lot of our times.

3

The Oil Shock; Relative Prices or Income Redistribution

Early at the beginning of the century the oil barrel cost about $1.2 in the US. By 1970 it was only $1.69 (Ahmadi, Kuwait) — a remarkable stability with no parallel in recent history. In the last decade the official oil price went up to $34, reaching more than $45 in spot markets in overheated periods. This is the oil shock, or rather the two oil shocks of 1973-4 and 1979.

In fact, since late 1970, oil prices timidly started to move up with the Tehran Agreements. On 16 October 1973, while the crossing and the counter-crossing of the Suez Canal and the Golan Heights hypnotized the world politicians and public opinion, six Arab OPEC members (OAPEC) met in Kuwait and increased posted oil prices from $3.01 to $5.12 per barrel. The oil price increase was blended with a systematic monthly reduction of oil production and selective embargo measures. Stunned by surprise, the spot market reacted nervously, prices reaching more than $20 per barrel. On 23-24 December 1973, OPEC met in Tehran and increased the posted price to $11.65 while Arab embargo and production cuts continued — very cold news for Christmas and the New Year. The change was sudden, unexpected and grave. It was aptly called the first oil shock.

After a series of inconclusive annual increases in oil prices, the Iranian Revolution offered another opportunity for a second oil shock. From $13.34 in January 1979, oil prices reached $26.00 by January 1980 in successive OPEC meetings. It would, however, be a great mistake to think that oil price increases in the seventies were the result of the whims and eccentricities of some oil producing countries. The oil price rises reflected increasing scarcities in oil supply. In fact, the growth of oil consumption began to exceed the growth of additions to reserves. It is reported that by 1968 the State Department had sent word by foreign Governments that US oil production would soon reach the limits of its capacity. In 1970 US domestic oil production peaked and began to decline. The situation in most other countries was hardly any better. Moreover, economists have insisted, long ago, on the need to increase prices of exhaustible resources in an effort to rationalize their use in the economic system.[1] Rather than increasing over time, nominal oil prices were kept constant and eventually declined (1959) in a world of general price increase. Relative oil prices in fact went down instead of going up. They were thus bound to increase. The 'shock' was related to the suddenness of the price rise rather than to its trend; possibly also because it did overshoot.

The oil shocks implied two major changes: a change in relative prices and a change in world income distribution. By and large the price effect, because more apparent and immediate, drew most of the attention to the neglect of the perhaps more important distribution of income effect. Though both are operating and mutually reinforcing, it is always analytically useful to distinguish the two effects. While it is usually the price effect that dominates the rest, in the OPEC case it is probably the redistribution of income and the subsequent impact on macro-categories that have had far-reaching ramifications.

Rising Energy Prices

The shift from cheap and abundant energy to higher prices and scarcity has been the dominant feature of the seventies. The oil price increases since 1973, the so-called energy crisis, spectacularly attest to this point.

It seems, however, that it was not merely an energy crisis, but actually a total economic crisis. Economic activity, after remarkable sustained growth, slid or plunged; unemployment scored peak records, unknown since the Great Depression; inflation soared to unprecedented levels, at least in living memory, thus giving rise to stag- or slumpflation; productivity gains slowed down with negative signs in some years; trade figures declined, while resuscitated protectionism is once again in vogue; international indebtedness looms largely in the fate of developing countries, undermining the financial system.

To what extent were oil price rises accountable for such a depressing picture? In the aftermath of the oil shock, it was the fashion to attribute all or most economic evils to oil price changes. Like most emotional generalization, the statement, though possibly partially justifiable, is overly distorted. The oil prices eventually triggered new economic forces which, combined with economic policies within the institutional set-ups, contributed to the final results.

Manifestly, OPEC oil imports and imports generally are vastly exaggerated overall. In the United States the domestic content of the inclusive gross national product (GNP) is over 90 cents per $1 of goods sold for home demand or exports. The percentage of imports from OPEC to GNP moved from 0.3 per cent in 1973 to 1.6 per cent in 1979[2] — a very negligible trickle indeed. Oil imports are more substantial in Western Europe and Japan, but still a very minor element in their gross national product (GNP). Total oil imports of OECD countries from OPEC and other sources are estimated at $180 billion in 1979 against a total gross domestic product of around $6,500 billion, a mere 2.7 per cent.[3]

Such a minimal price-level bite of oil imports from OPEC can hardly substantiate a simple cost-push inflation argument. A more subtle case focuses on the role of oil price because of its strategic nature on the one hand and its impact on expectations on the other.

Prices, we are told in general equilibrium models, are set in an interdependent manner where every price affects and is affected by other prices. Some prices however, are dominant thus influencing the rest of prices more than others. Prices tend to be determined, in the final analysis, by the cost of production. The fact that various inputs are variably used in the productive system accounts for the nonuniform effect of a particular commodity's price on the rest of the economy. Energy prices in industrial countries and food prices in less developed countries are examples *par excellence* of such dominant prices.

With the exception of labour, no other input is as widely used in the productive system in industrial economies as energy. It follows that energy prices have a dominant effect cutting across the rest of the economy. Other fuel prices would sympathize with oil prices and, more importantly, other product prices, with varying lags, would follow suit. Of course, one might think that only a disarrangement in relative prices takes place with little or no change in the general price level. However, this is not so, since there always exist downward rigidities in some nominal prices. The realignment of relative prices will usually be accompanied by a substantial rise in the general price level. The case is stronger when the initial change affects a reference price like energy prices. Product price increases can hardly keep wage rates unaffected. The stage is set for a wage-price duet. The total impact of the oil price increase is, thus, far more important than the initial price rise. Sympathetic price rises in other fuels and throughout the productive system would lead to wage-price spiral and accordingly a general price increase.

The concern with energy prices in modern economies is only matched by the obsession of classical economists with food prices. The history of the Corn and Anti-Corn Laws in England attest to this point. English corn laws originated in the Middle Ages, limiting or prohibiting the export and import of corn. High prices during the Napoleonic Wars and later in the first half of the nineteenth century led to the establishment of the Anti-Corn Law League in Manchester in 1839. The *raison d'être* behind this movement was clearly to prevent food prices from rising, thus providing a basis for low wages and improved competitiveness. The share of food (corn in particular) in labour consumption and accordingly in the wage bill can hardly be overestimated. The repeal of the Corn Laws thus became the touchstone of the British industrial economy of the time. With the Peel Act in 1846 in the aftermath of the Ireland potato-rot cheap corn became one of the principles of British economic policies.

The parallel between food prices in the early stages of industrialization and energy prices in present-day industrial societies is very suggestive indeed. In both cases we are not simply faced with a commodity price, but rather with a reference price on which the whole price system is virtually founded. Because of their pervasive use throughout the economic system, food prices in the first case and energy prices in the second determine respectively the price level.

Nineteenth-century agricultural economies are not historical curiosities. They are to a great extent variations of the present-day less developed countries (LDCs). Two different types of economies are juxtaposed; the industrial or developed countries (DCs) and the less developed. The first type is sensitive to energy prices and the second to food prices and also to energy prices.

It was the fate of the world economy in the early seventies to witness simultaneously both the food and the energy crises. Food prices soared in 1972 only to be followed by the oil shock in 1973. Both rich and poor countries were plunged into price orgies, and a new era of higher inflation was thus inaugurated due to the increase in reference prices: food and oil.

Changes in oil and food prices are supply shocks affecting the cost of production. This does not mean, of course, that the oil shocks did not produce various secondary reductions in aggregate demand; in fact they did. It remains true, however, that the oil price increases are supply-side changes which would have required a component of supply management.[4] An expansionary fiscal and monetary policy would have been effective in cancelling out the decline in aggregate demand that resulted from the increase in the price of oil. There was a point, in these circumstances, to pursue an accommodative fiscal and monetary policy provided it was made clear that such a policy was not accommodating inflation but rather acting to cushion the economy against the reduction in demand resulting from the oil price increases.

It is significant to notice that, precisely at this juncture, most countries resorted to stringent monetary policies. In the US, real M_2 fell by 3.4 per cent between the end of 1973 and that of 1975.

Monetary policy was, for the first time, on M_1 target. It seems that the 'Fed' decided to pursue an M_1 strategy at the wrong time in an effort to vindicate the Friedman dictum: 'Central bankers are not to be trusted'. The situation in other industrial countries was hardly any different. Monetary policies thus exacerbated a deteriorating situation with no frontal attack on the supply-side inflationary pressures.

To add insult to injury, OPEC taste for theatrical decisions on price increases during their over-publicized semi-annual ministerial meetings created a fertile ground for permanent price rise expectations. It is the merit of the rational expectation doctrine to introduce information and reactions to its knowledge to the economic body theory. Economic agents attempt to anticipate future policies and accommodate their actions to it. It is true the theory originated in the context of the behaviour of economic agents with regard to domestic monetary and fiscal policies. Rational expectation is, however, a general postulate to account for economic behaviour *vis-à-vis* all economic policies – national or foreign. OPEC decisions to increase oil prices are already discounted in private agents' behaviour and fully reflected in their costing. OPEC, in turn, is confirmed in the belief that oil price increases are designed to offset the growing inflation. A new vicious circle has already trapped the economic system.

Important as it may be, the price effect falls short of absorbing the total impact of the oil shock. Oil price increase is not an act of God, the way a harvest failure or an earthquake is; there is no net loss but rather a transfer of income from oil consuming to oil producing countries. The way in which the oil proceeds are used affects the final outcome.

New Savers

More important than the change in energy relative prices is, perhaps, the transfer of wealth from oil consuming to oil producing countries and the subsequent change in the macro-aggregates' behaviour.

From its pre-oil-shock level of about one per cent of the gross domestic product (GDP), oil cost absorbed about five per cent of the GDP.[5] The oil import bill rose from \$28 billion in 1970 to \$535 billion in 1980, an increase of almost twentyfold over the decade. In 1970 the oil trade represented seven per cent of the world trade and reached 21 per cent ten years later.[6]

Notwithstanding the latent economic need for price increases of exhaustible resources, a dramatic redistribution of world income took place at short notice. On the face of it nothing seems to have changed in the underlying economic forces to warrant such a major change. The world resource base, the technology available and tastes have not undergone any sudden change before and after the oil shock. By and large, the world economic system continues to enjoy the same resource base and to apply the same known technology in order to satisfy the same final demand; only the share of oil producing countries in world produce has risen spectacularly with the oil shock. The change in the balance of power between the oil consuming and the oil producing countries (OPEC) made it possible for the latter to appropriate a bigger share in the world income. A *coup d'état* in the world economic order allowed a group of small countries, holding a vital commodity (oil), to levy an oil tax on the oil consuming countries.[7]

The principal oil exporting countries, mainly in the Arabian Peninsula and the Gulf, are very thinly populated and already enjoy a relatively high per capita income. It is axiomatic that a redistribution of income in favour of a high per capita income group would, *mutatis mutandis*, increase the propensity to save. With the oil price increases in the 1970s not only have some income recipients increased their share but more fundamentally, this was accompanied by an increase in the world propensity to save. The emergence of new savers – the oil producing countries – is probably the most significant change in recent economic developments.

Saving is a passive act of non-consumption; it is a leakage in the economic circuit. But saving is also a claim on economic resources – that is, savers hold financial assets.

By virtue of its passive aspect, it could be argued that unless matched by parallel spending, saving is deflationary. This was the Keynesian message and it was at the basis of the underconsumption theories of the nineteenth century. However, as holders of financial assets – and hence entitled to earn financial returns on their holdings – savers affect the cost structure of the economy. An increase in the returns on property titles would call for a corresponding increase in wages and the price level is pushed upwards. Inflation is thus not unrelated to the increase in financial assets – usually debt – following the emergence of the new savers.

Contrary to the conventional wisdom, recession and inflation can go together, as growth and price stability can be a perfect match. Without a deliberate increase in investment to match the new savings, stagflation seems to be a natural outcome. In other words, with the increase in the world's savings (read: the world's debt) only inflation or growth can sustain the world's ability to service its debt; inflation would be blended with recession, as growth could support price stability.

The emergence of the new savings following the oil price increase (the oil tax) cannot be dissociated from its impact on global expenditure patterns in the world. The pattern of using the proceeds of this new tax reflects its nature as an oil-rent tax. The rentier nature of the tax collector will not fail to make itself felt.

The increase in OPEC's share of the world income permitted boosting their domestic spending spectacularly, both in consumption and investment. However, because of the limitation on their domestic absorption capacity, excess savings remained unabsorbed domestically and resulted in huge balance-of-payments surpluses. A new phenomenon of oil surplus funds, the so-called petro-dollars, became a new feature of the world economy. These are excess savings taking the form of new financial assets held by OPEC surplus countries, especially the Gulf oil states. More important than the increase in oil prices is, perhaps, the emergence of the oil surplus funds – i.e. new savings funds affecting balance of payments. Thus, as new savings aggregates emerge in the world economy, a disturbing factor to external equilibria is introduced into world relations.

Placement, Not Investment

Rarely has an economic measure affected the world economy as the oil price increases have done. Only a world macro-model can help fix ideas. The oil price increases, it has been said, have introduced a new world income distribution pattern, thus increasing the world propensity to save.

It is perhaps the great merit of Keynes to have helped build macro-models and emphasize the importance of the *ex post* equality between savings and investment. This is an accounting equality or rather identity, which holds true for every economic system regardless of the economic forces behind it. One need not be a Keynesian to use this accounting identity as a tool for analysis. Whatever determines savings and investment, there must be at the end of the day an equality between realized savings and realized investment. Theories may and do differ as to what influences both investment and savings, but all agree that the equality must hold *ex post* between them.

With the oil shock, the world economic system had to accommodate the new savings (oil surplus funds) with the iron accounting equality savings-investment. Economic forces should operate in such a way as to reconcile two facts: the emergence of new savings and the maintenance of the accounting equality of savings-investment. Later development in this volume will show that three possible scenarios can logically satisfy the previous requirement – that is, in the face of the emergent oil surplus funds there could be:

(1)   a parallel increase in the rate of real investment in the world;
(2)   nominal dis-savings elsewhere in the world to offset the increase in OPEC's savings; or
(3)   an increase in financial assets, giving rise to increased nominal investment.

A combination of elements from different scenarios is always possible and, indeed, likely.

Experience has shown that the third scenario represented, to a great extent, the world response to the increase in the world's savings (petro-dollars). This does not preclude sporadic increases in real investments (specially within OPEC countries themselves), nor a few cases of transfer of property titles (dis-savings) to OPEC surplus countries. It remains true that, by and large, the rate of investment has not shown any perceptible increase with the emergence of the oil surplus funds. In fact, real investment rates were showing signs of slackening. Also, the transfer of wealth in the form of property titles was the exception rather than the rule. On the contrary, financial assets, particularly debt instruments (deposits, CDs, bonds, bills, notes, loans, papers, etc.) soared dramatically in the aftermath of the oil shock.

From an individual point of view, there exists a wide range of investment opportunities to choose among; be it venture capital, stock (new and old), bonds, bills, deposits, real-estate, loans, etc. They differ in risk and liquidity and accordingly in return, but hardly anything more. However, from the economy's point of view it makes a great difference to buy, for example, a new stock, thus contributing to the addition of a new production unit, or to buy an old stock hence just exchanging financial assets (money for stock). We have therefore to distinguish between two kinds of transactions on financial assets according to their effect on the productive system of the economy – that is, between investment and placement. By investment is meant the use of finance to add to capital goods, and, the term placement (derived from the French) will designate the purchase of titles and shares which does not add to the productive capacity of the system. Whereas investment adds to the productive capacity of the economy, placement adds only to the financial assets.

It seems to us that oil surplus funds were used, to a great extent, for placement rather than for investment. The real question here is, then, how could the equality of *ex post* savings and investment be brought about in this placement case. The increase in financial assets – particularly debt instruments – in the world economy triggered various economic forces which ultimately increased the nominal investment, that is in value terms, to match the increase in OPEC's savings. By the same token, OPEC's savings underwent a continuous erosion until their virtual disappearance in 1978 after the first oil shock, and again in 1982 after the second shock.

To understand the working of the economic forces to bring about the required *ex post* equality in the 'placement case', it is helpful to recapitulate our assumptions:

(1) No major reallocation between consumption and investment – that is, the old structure remained, by and large, unchanged following the oil shock.

(2) OPEC's new savings were not accompanied by nominal dispossession of wealth – that is, there were no nominal dis-savings. OPEC's financial assets were largely added to, not subtracted from, the total stock of financial assets.

(3) In time of crisis, confidence is seriously affected and nominal interest rates (financial yields in general) rise rather than decline. The circumstances in which oil prices increased were perceived as a major crisis.

It follows that OPEC's savings increased both the stock of financial assets and the nominal absolute value of returns on them, i.e. property earnings. This, however, cannot be the end of the story. One of the most amazing economic facts is that the average mark-up of prices over unit labour costs has remained so remarkably constant over the modern industrial economic history. The constancy over time in the average mark-up is, probably, the most substantive empirical law in economics.[8] An increase in property earnings cannot, thus, change the share of wage (reciprocal of the mark-up) in national income. The only way out will be a corresponding absolute increase in wages that can maintain the constancy of our empirical law. Inflation is already in the picture. With it, the nominal value, though not the real, of investment is increased and the accounting equality of *ex post* savings and investment is assured. While artificially magnifying investment in money terms, inflation is also eroding the value of savings – that is, the accumulated financial wealth of OPEC. A reverse income distribution movement is already at work. It took about a four-year cycle to undo via inflation what OPEC has done via oil price increases. Inflation is not the result of the oil price increase, it is rather a counter-offensive to neutralize the redistribution of income effect of the oil shock. This was not an inescapable fate; it is in the logic of the placement case. But why placement and not investment? Ironically, it was a search for security.

The Mirage of Security

In a monetary economy, contrary to a barter economy, savers are usually different agents from investors and accordingly are subject to different motivations. It is rare that the same economic agent combines both the savings and investment functions. Intermediation between savers and investors is normally realized through financial institutions against various types of financial assets. It is the crucial role of financial institutions and assets to channel surplus funds from savers to investors. A more efficient financial system helps achieve better allocation for investible funds along with maintaining higher growth for investment.

Neither entrepreneurs nor investors, OPEC surplus countries, as latecomer savers, looked for financial markets to place their savings in. It never occurred to them, nor had they the required expertise, to invest directly. Prudent, conservative and risk-averse savers would attach higher premium to secure, efficient and well-known financial institutions. OPEC surplus countries were no exception to this pattern of behaviour. By no means revolutionaries, OPEC surplus countries, mainly the Arab Gulf states, followed a conventional course of action by placing their surplus funds with the best-known world financial institutions.

The skewed nature of the private international financial institutions resulted, however, in a bias towards investment opportunities in developed countries (DCs), rather than to those available in less developed ones (LDCs). Though active worldwide, most private international financial institutions are only investment-conscious of opportunities within developed countries (OECD countries) and rarely so in the less developed. Their interests in, and knowledge of, the less developed countries are mainly, though by no means exclusively centred around the government's needs and thus balance of payments support. Local investment opportunities in less developed countries are hardly the concern of international financial institutions. That is, the so-called world financial market is heavily weighted against investment opportunities in the less developed countries. On the other hand, financial institutions in less developed countries are either absent from the international markets altogether, or lack sufficient credibility to attract OPEC surplus funds.

It follows from the above that OPEC savings' placement with the international financial market amounts to an implicit, though crucial, choice; that is, a choice to place its savings with developed countries rather than with the less developed. The question then arises as to whether or not such a choice would enhance real investment. This is a fundamental enquiry into the determinants of investment decisions.

It is generally accepted that the lack of investible funds (savings) inhibits investment in less developed countries. The availability of new savings would facilitate, but not guarantee, additional investment. Classical economists' emphasis on the importance of savings as the prime mover of economic growth stems from that fact. This is by no means the case in mature economies; investment is not necessarily held back because of insufficient savings. It is the insufficiency of demand, as perceived by the market, that constrains investment in most mature economies. One of the major innovations of Keynes is his treatment of investment as an exogenous variable independent of savings. To Keynes, 'a fresh act of savings' means a net reduction in effective demand. Future demand implicit in the behaviour of savers is not an effective demand to which investment would respond. This is due to producers' failure to pick up any 'signals' that could tell them where to re-employ the resources released from the production of consumer goods.[9]

The contrast between classical economists (supply siders) and Keynesians (demand management) exhibits a structural difference between less developed and more developed countries on the one hand, and a change in emphasis from savings to investment as a strategic economic policy instrument on the other. To a classic, savings' decision is what matters; available investment opportunities will compete for the resources thus released. To a Keynesian, it is the other way round. Investment decision is far more crucial; once it is taken savings will, eventually, be forthcoming. In developed countries the problem is not primarily one of availability of finance; it is a problem of demand.

Injecting new investible funds (OPEC's savings) in developed countries through international financial institutions would not, by itself, increase investment. It is not because financial resources happen to be available that investment will be boosted. Nothing seems to augur a change in effective demand towards more capital goods.

Moreover, OPEC's savings were not, to be sure, voluntary savings acquiesced to by oil consuming countries to finance new investment opportunities; they are forced savings imposed on the system. If the proceeds of such forced savings are reinjected into the system, they will be immediately absorbed with little real change to restore the previous state; *status quo ante*. Add to this a general environment of uncertainty and confusion hardly conducive to new investments. OPEC's savings were the result of a major disturbance in world economic relations associated with political tension in the Middle East (Arab-Israeli wars, Iranian Revolution); not particularly bright prospects for new investments.

In these circumstances it is not hard to understand that OPEC's new savings produced a surge in financial assets without much effect on real investment. The increase in financial assets (mainly debt instruments) increased property earnings and a chain reaction mechanism was triggered to bring about inflation, as has been sketched out earlier. With inflation, the value of OPEC's accumulated wealth underwent an insidious erosion process.

Paradoxically, OPEC search for security by placing their savings in the most robust financial institutions instigated a more menacing danger to these same savings. Shying away from the hazards of investment in the Third World to the more secure advanced countries brought about a much more redoubtable danger: inflation.

OPEC Forgot the Third World; they did not Forget OPEC

Placing OPEC's savings in developed rather than developing countries does not preclude an enormous effort by OPEC countries to assist less developed countries. It remains true, none the less, that OPEC's aid policy is part of its foreign politics — the aid diplomacy — and not an integral part of its investment strategy. Substantial as they are, OPEC's aid remained a small fraction of OPEC's savings which largely remained placed with the financial institutions in developed countries.

OPEC's surplus funds, it has been said, were not only an addition to world savings, but also a disequilibrium factor to balance of payments. The disregard for the less developed countries in OPEC's placement strategy proved to be only temporary and apparent. Through surplus-deficit dynamics OPEC found itself intricately bound to an indebted Third World.

OPEC's appropriation of a large share in the world income coincided with low absorption capacity in major oil producing countries; Arab states in the Gulf and Arabian Peninsula. It is because of their low absorption that OPEC's new savings took the form of balance of payments surpluses, i.e. external disequilibria. Had all the oil producers been high absorbers, such as Nigeria, Indonesia, Mexico, Venezuela, etc., the problem would have largely been reduced to a case of transfer of wealth among nations. The situation has been greatly complicated with the low absorbers. The redistribution of income gave rise to new savings which in turn gave rise to balance of payments disequilibria. Never before had balance of payments known similar huge imbalances in such short periods in peace time.

Much as nature abhors a vacuum, the economic system hardly tolerates disequilibrium, and this is particularly so with external imbalances. Unless maintained by design or tolerance (financing), economic forces would eventually come into play to correct for the imbalances (adjustment). A judicious mix of financing and adjustment is always needed in situations of imbalances. It remains true, none the less, that it can hardly be imagined to sustain indefinitely a balance of payments' deficit through financing only. In the parlance of economic theorists, balance of payments has a stable equilibrium − that is, an imbalance cannot be sustained indefinitely; readjustment is sooner or later inevitable. The ability to readjust varies, however, between countries. One way for measuring economic development is the ability of the economy to adjust; the more the economy is developed, the easier for it to readjust to new and unforeseen situations, and vice versa. Developed countries' ability to adjust is not only confined to restructuring their internal economies to cope with and eventually absorb imbalances; but they have a wider ability to shape the external environment to their advantage. The latter aspect is usually known as the 'dominance effect' of the more developed economies on the rest of the economic system.

With oil surplus funds' imbalances a huge financing problem faced the world economy; the so-called petro-funds recycling problems of 1974-5. Soon after a smooth harbouring of the financing problem, an adjustment process was underway in the developed countries. Efforts to reduce dependence on oil imports took place with different lags in most industrial economies; be it through conservation or substitution. However, conservation and substitution are longer term adjustment and require large investment and institutional costs. Side by side with these real efforts for readjustment, financial arrangements were also taking place. It has been mentioned earlier that OPEC's placement policy helped initiate an inflationary process. Inflation is a powerful instrument to erode these same surpluses as well as to diffuse them among nations. Inflation in developed countries was soon transmitted to the rest of the world thus giving rise to a new balance of payments structure.

Exported inflation from developed countries was not confined to OPEC imports but was extended to the rest of the non-oil developing countries. After the early deficits following the oil shocks, OECD succeeded in recovering a virtual global balance in three to four years from the initial disturbance. The less developed countries had thus to bear the brunt of the OECD readjustment effort. Though their share in oil imports had now shown any rise after the oil shocks the non-oil developing countries have seen their balance of payments deficits increasing more than proportionately. Imported inflation from the industrial countries helped bring about a deterioration of their terms of trade. With the shift of balance of payments disequilibria to the LDCs, OECD countries reached global equilibrium in 1978 and again in 1982. What they lost in oil prices *vis-à-vis* OPEC, was gained in increased manufactured exports prices to the LDCs. The counter-part deficits to OPEC surpluses were thus almost shifted to non-oil developing countries.

With increasing deficits, the non-oil developing countries' needs for financing grew immensely. The international financial market, commercial banks in the first place, were more than ready to provide the needed finance to the LDCs.

Failing to use the petro-dollars to increase real investment in the DCs, the international financial market was prompt to provide finance for balance of payments support in the LDCs. LDCs deficits thus needed to finance their imported inflation from the advanced industrial countries. For non-oil developing countries, 'on a terms of trade basis', affirms the Managing Director of the IMF, 'the cumulative loss incurred in the seven-year period 1973-9 was one of the order of $80 billion' — one should add at least as much for the second oil shock. 'Thus, the current account deficit of the LDCs has also been raised considerably by the general inflation in countries which export manufactures.'[10] It comes thus as no surprise to see that the LDCs debt soared dramatically from less than $70 billion in 1970 to about $480 billion in 1980. It would be unfair to attribute the whole of the increase of the LDCs external debt to financial mismanagement, though it cannot be totally excluded. It was more symptomatic of our times, times of generalized inflation. The LDCs were, no doubt, the least prepared to insulate themselves from such contagious inflation. It is to be noted here that it is the world banking system, situated in the advanced countries, which introduced the LDCs to the capital market. The same financial institutions that received OPEC's savings were extending loans and credit facilities to the LDCs. In a world of growing financial interdependence, the ultimate debtors of the OPEC's savings are the deficit countries in the LDCS; the fate of some is intimately related to the economic health of the others. The Third World emerged at the end of a long chain as the partner of OPEC, though a very weak partner indeed.

An Indebted Third World

Total accumulated financial assets owned by major OPEC surplus countries, almost exclusively in the Gulf area, are estimated at about $350 billion by 1982. Total disbursed external debt of developing countries is projected at $626 billion as of the end of 1982.[11] The present surge in international lending to the LDCs is less than a decade old. Until the early 1970s, the LDCs had only limited access to international capital markets and only official sources were available to supply them with external financing. The surge in bank lending to LDCs began in the aftermath of the first oil shock in 1974-5 and then accelerated with the second shock 1979-80 amid the unfavourable environment of much higher interest rates. 'Banks in which OPEC members placed a large portion of their suplus,' states Mr Rimmer de Vries of the Morgan Guaranty Trust before the subcommittee on International Economic Policy of the Senate Foreign Relations Committee, 'were encouraged to recycle these funds to mitigate the higher oil prices' recessionary impact on the world economy'.[12] The parallel between the surge of OPEC surplus funds on the one hand and LDCs increased indebtedness on the other cannot fail to strike observers. Not only had the two phenomena appeared simultaneously, but the same banks were instrumental in bringing them about.

The increase in LDCs' needs for external financing was hardly related to any rise in their share of oil imports, which remained relatively insignificant compared with OECD's share. Rather, a number of oil exporters — Mexico, Venezuela, Ecuador, Indonesia, Nigeria, Algeria, Egypt, etc. — figure prominently among the heaviest borrowers of the LDCs. In fact, these countries stood to benefit a great deal from the oil price increase were it not for the change in the general economic context that followed. Also, in spite of all their shortcomings, it would be a curious coincidence to believe in a sudden generalized collapse in management or a brisk surge in the degree of corruption in these countries to warrant the monumental increase in their external debt.

The correlation between the emergence of the new surplus funds and the increased indebtedness could conceal a true causation. Awash with new money from OPEC surplus countries, banks and private financial institutions failing to find a favourable investment environment in the developed economies, found the prospects of lending to the higher strata of the LDCs quite tempting.

Since, as has been mentioned earlier, the surge of new financial assets (OPEC savings) would unleash inflation in the absence of increased real investment, the stage is set for general inflation. However, inflation is only transmittable in as far as it is receivable.

More elaborate less developed countries, i.e. middle-income and newly industrialized groups, are more integrated in the international economy and thus more sensitive to world prices. They have also better access to the world capital market. It is no wonder then that imported inflation from OECD countries hit the higher income groups among the LDCs harder. More expensive imports were made easier and even pleasant by the preparedness of the banks to lend to the newcomers to the capital markets. These countries are the real victims of world inflation though they were not always seriously hit by direct oil price increases; some even benefited from the rise. Because more integrated in the world economic system though also more vulnerable, the higher income group of the LDCs became the softest underbelly and thus bore the brunt of the indirect effects of the oil shocks. They were, and are, however, the most promising elements in the Third World.

The New Economic Order: a Dream?

Reshaping the international order became for the better part of the last decade the major claim of the poor nations,[13] as well as the concern of the more detached international politicians.[14]

The special irony is that the crucial element in the search for a New International Economic Order consisted of a claim for a massive transfer of resources from the rich to the poor nations. On the face of it, this seems to have been partially achieved. A substantial transfer of resources has taken place from the rich industrial countries to developing countries (OPEC), and then a great deal of these resources were rechannelled to the rest of the LDCs through the capitalist banking system. Yet the poor nations remained as poor as they were, or almost. Moreover, not a few among them ended with a huge debt burden which threatens to compromise their future prospects. However, this is only a façade .The transfer of resources from the rich to the poor remained in most cases more apparent than real. True, there was an enormous surge in financial flows to the LDCs, but it is doubtful whether there was any perceptible increase in the transfer of real resources to the LDCs. The need for massive transfer of resources to the LDCs remains as pressing and imperative now as it was before — perhaps even more so now.[15]

Can there be a role for OPEC countries in the establishment of the New Economic Order? It would have been asking too much to expect that OPEC surplus countries (the Gulf states in particular) would assume alone the whole responsibility of reshaping the world economic order by investing their newly earned additional oil revenues in the less developed countries. This is also idealistic.

It could be argued, however, that such a policy can also serve the best interests of OPEC countries themselves. Apart from being a disinterested act of generosity, investing OPEC surplus funds in the LDCs could also be a calculated act of mutual benefits. History does not repeat itself, it is true, but the circumstances in which OPEC surplus funds emerged could have warranted a new form of a Marshall Plan. Without underestimating the formidable underlying obstacles, there was also a grave misconception of the potential benefits accruing to OPEC countries from investing directly in the LDCs. OPEC-LDCs solidarity is questioned in most OPEC surplus countries and for good reasons. It is true that there exist political and moral considerations to support such solidarity. Economically, however, no such justification seems to prevail. Hence the need for an intellectual effort to provide an economic case for OPEC-LDCs partnership. Only a two-way partnership can justify a sustainable flow of investment funds from OPEC to the LDCs, thus relating the New Economic Order to the New Oil Order. Such an analytical argument was, however, conspicuously lacking among most OPEC investors.

OPEC's new savings, it has been shown, cannot be maintained in real terms without a parallel increase in real investment. Here comes the crucial role of the LDCs as a potential partner for OPEC new savers.

Given structural demand limitations for real investment increase in developed countries, capital-hungry less developed countries could provide much-needed investment opportunities to match OPEC's available finance. This sounds too simplistic, since investment in the LDCs is not only a question of finance; institutional and material short-comings are too well-known to warrant any further comment. However, there remains a difference between developed and developing countries in regards to OPEC surplus funds. In developed countries, investment will not increase without a change in the demand structure. The avail-ability of OPEC finance cannot by itself bring about such a change. In developing countries, on the contrary, investment may increase with OPEC finance; no further need for a structural change in demand is required. It is not far-fetched, then, to assume that a transfer of real resources from OPEC to the LDCs can help increase investment in the world. OPEC new savings would be matched by LDCs new investment. The picture can be made still rosier. Increased investment in the LDCs would imply growing capital goods imports from developed countries, hence increased trade. Developed countries could have increased their capital goods exports to compensate for their higher oil bill (trilateral-ism). The world as a whole would become more thrifty, yet more capital accumulation would be forthcoming. We would witness a higher growth path for the world economy. The oil tax would thus be trans-formed into a development tax levied by OPEC and used to increase investment in the LDCs. Developed countries would, no doubt, have to reduce, momentarily, their real consumption in order to match OPEC new savings.

This, of course, is in an idealized world. Real life is far less attractive. Less developed countries, it will be remembered, are disappointingly mismanaged, lacking skilled labour, and deficient in infrastructure. These are enormous problems and cannot simply be removed by a stroke of the pen. However, the alternative proved to be as depressing, if not more so. Such an alternative, it has been shown, promised very little increase, if any, in real investment in developed countries, OPEC savings thus dwindled year after year under the pressure of inflation. The Third World, which was denied direct investment by OPEC, had to borrow heavily from the same oil funds to cope with rising prices. An OPEC role in the establishment of the New Economic Order is, of course, not risk- or trouble-free. The stakes were, and are, probably worth the while.

Finally, even a hypothetical OPEC role in the establishment of a new order cannot have impact unless it helps transfer massive resources to the LDCs. Huge as they were, OPEC surplus funds fell short of the LDCs capital needs. They risk being wasted ineffectively if thinly distributed all over the Third World. It is only by concentrating investment on a particular region that tangible results could be brought about. Since OPEC surplus countries are mainly Arab states in the Gulf and the Peninsula, a privileged region for a concentrated investment programme could ideally have been the Arab region. An Arab regional development plan thus appeared, in theory, most promising. This remained, however, only in theory. In reality, the overall context did not seem conducive to development. Restructuring the world economic order requires far more than the availability of finance; rather it is a question of bold leadership.

The Core and the Periphery

In all social systems including the international system, two classes appear: a class that rules and a class that is ruled. A variation of the same concept under the new label of the centre (or the core) and the periphery has gained increasing recognition in economic and political literature to characterize these two classes. The international economic system has thus its ruling (the centre or the core) as well as its ruled (periphery) classes. The former sets the rules of the game, the latter has to comply more or less passively. OPEC oil price increases in 1973-4 and again in 1979 were in a way a defiance of the established order, yet stopped short of bringing about a complete reversal.

OPEC surplus countries in the Arab Peninsula and the Gulf have acquired enormous financial power. They remained, none the less, politically, economically and militarily vulnerable and dependent. For one thing, apart from oil prices – and even here later experience showed how divided OPEC is – the Gulf states are fragmented among tiny political entities. Saudi Arabia by far the larger partner, is still a small country with a population of five to seven million, more than 30 per cent of its population is imported from neighbouring countries. The percentage of expatriates in the other Gulf principalities varies between 60 per cent (Kuwait) and more than 80 per cent (United Arab Emirates). Though very rich in per capita income, the Gulf states rest on alarmingly lopsided economies, with oil revenues representing more than 90 per cent of the budget sources, 95 per cent or more of exports. It is true that the oil sector's share in the GDP of some Gulf States (Kuwait) turns around 70 per cent, but it is also true that this is more an accounting device than a true representation of facts.[16] This is far from being a healthy economic state of affairs. Security issues are not any more comforting and they loom menacingly over the stability of the region. Over and above territorial conflicts, claims and counter claims, differences in ideologies, etc., the extreme wealth and the strategic position amount to an invitation for trouble. In Saudi Arabia, for example, oil is conservatively valued in current dollars at $5 trillion,[17] a very tempting prize for an outside power and/or an internal political group. The region as a whole is not lacking in foreign powers and/or internal groups with political and economic interests in the Gulf states. Against these odds, the Gulf states' military strength is only token and next to zero in combat test. A clear or concealed defence support from outside powers seems inevitable.

The establishment of the Gulf Cooperation Council (GCC) in 1981 was a step to bring together the Gulf states and prepare the ground to join their forces in the economic, political and military spheres. This remains, however, a first step, and a long way is yet to be covered before speaking of a new political, economic and military reality. A long history of fragmentation, feud, personal rivalry and at times mistrust, cannot be eliminated miraculously by the stroke of a GCC. Things are moving in the right direction, no doubt; yet there is still a long way to go. In spite of some efforts to establish some Gulf financial institutions, investment decisions of the petro-surpluses remain, essentially, an individual state prerogative. For all practical purposes, there is no Gulf foreign investment problem, but as many problems as there are states or more (in the case of the UAE, at least two independent investment policies, hardly co-ordinated, are those of Abu Dhabi and Dubai).

The contrast between individual and common interests is a recurrent topic in economic and political writings. It has often been suggested that if everyone in a group of individuals or states had some interest in common, then there would be a tendency for the group to seek to further this interest. Nothing seems to support this opinion, either in logic or in practice. It has been shown, on the contrary, that in many circumstances a rational individual or state should act against the common interest in order to maximize his or its own self-interest.[18] In the particular case of massive investment in the LDCs, particularly in the Arab region, though justifiable on a collective scale encompassing all the surplus funds of the Gulf states, it is not necessarily so for each country behaving independently. The risks and hazards of investment are too high for one country alone, even though not beyond the collective means of the Gulf states taken together. Also the impact of investment and hence the benefits grow more than proportionately with the increase in the amount invested. In these conditions investment in the Arab region, or in any other region, while promising within a collective context, is extremely risky if undertaken by a single country acting independently. What is good for each and every country acting independently does not always serve the common interest of a group of countries acting collectively.

Given the fragmentation of the Gulf states on the one hand, and their basic vulnerabilities on the other, it is very difficult to envisage them in any central role to reshape the world economic order or part of it.

Moreover dependence on the industrial developed countries for economic, political and defence matters would even turn the newly acquired financial wealth of the Gulf states into a conservative force to preserve the *status quo*. This conservative instinct is, actually, engrained in the Gulf by temperament as well as by an absence of any ideological militancy of the political regimes in power. Changing the *status quo* is a defying enterprise. As Machiavelli pointed out in another context:

> There is nothing more difficult to arrange, more doubtful of success, and more dangerous to carry through, than to initiate a new order of things . . . Men are generally incredulous, never really trusting new things unless they have tested them by experience.[19]

In the aftermath of the Second World War, two different examples for changing the economic order took place. The USA and USSR, with varying degrees of success and effectiveness, helped introduce new economic orders. The USA, empowered with economic and military might, introduced the Marshall Plan to reconstruct Western Europe and with massive investment in Japan, the Free World came into existence. The USSR with its ideological and military rigour established, behind an iron curtain, a socialist empire. In both cases, the USA and USSR had to play a pivotal role in the new order thus established, a very powerful incentive for the establishment of new orders — 'selective incentives' in the parlance of Olson.[20] The Gulf states, on the contrary, not only lack the economic, military and ideological requirements, but even worse, have no pretence to play a central role in a new order brought about by their financial might. Their potential role in building economic power in the Arab region or any other LDCs' region would be more self-liquidating than self-realizing. A judicious application of massive investment by the Gulf states in the rest of the Arab region would, more likely than not, bring about a shift in the centre of gravity in Arab politics from capital-rich centres to labour- and nature-rich centres — that is, the reverse of selective incentives, a not particularly exciting perspective. What was needed is probably more than pure imagination, it takes an act of heroism, in a Greek sense. This is hardly a role any country or group of countries is willing to assume, least of all rentier economies.

A Rentier Economy

In a celebrated passage, Adam Smith separated rent from other sources of income; wages and profit. 'Rent', it is to be observed, 'enters into the composition of the price of commodities in a different way from wages and profit. High or low wages and profit are the causes of high or low price; high or low rent is the effect of it.'[21] A long tradition of hostility and mistrust was, thus, born in the economic profession against rent and rentiers. Classical economists — Malthus apart — and later Marx have few kind words for rent and rentiers (mainly landlords). Rentiers were assaulted by both liberal and socialist economists as unproductive, almost anti-social, sharing in the produce without, so to speak, contributing to it. 'The rise of rent is always the effect of the increasing wealth of the country and of the difficulty of producing food for its augmented population. It is a symptom, but it is never a cause of wealth.'[22] A rent, it is to be remembered, is not merely an income for the landlords but generally a reward for ownership of all natural resources. 'Mines, as well as land, generally pay rent to their owners and this rent, as well as the rent of the land, is the effect and never the cause of the high value of their produce.'[23]

The general perception of a rentier was that of someone who, although he does not participate in the economic activity, receives nevertheless a share in the produce — and at times, a handsome share. In this stereotype analysis, a rentier is a member of a special social group who does not earn his income; he is merely apportioned a nice slice of the produce. This, of course, is a caricature, but there is always somewhere deep in the subconscious of the social observer a doubt as to the legitimacy of the rent — a feeling which is shared by liberals and radicals alike. Far from being an attack against property as such, it is rather an uneasiness about the social function of the rentier group in the economic process. The contrast between such a stereotype rentier and Schumpeter's entrepreneur is striking as well as instructive. Dynamic innovator, risk-bearer, Schumpeter's entrepreneur is almost the antithesis of the rentier. Though both are backed by private property, the contrast is almost total. Agent and promoter of progress and development, the entrepreneur à la Schumpeter is almost the opposite of the rentier. A possible reason for this latent hostility of the economic profession towards rent is that it is a reminder of Nature's avarice not of Man's ingenuity. It is 'the difficulty of production', asserts Ricardo, that 'raises the exchangeable value of raw produce, and raises also the proportion of raw produce paid to the landlord for rent, it is obvious that the landlord is doubly benefited by the difficulty of production. First, he obtains a greater share, and, secondly, the commodity in which he is paid is of greater value'. Or to put it differently, rent is the result of producing under conditions of increasing costs rather than constant or even decreasing costs. It is only human to resent conditions of increasing costs with all that goes with it.

In modern economic analysis, an efficient allocation of resources would call upon rent as much as other factor prices. No value judgement is implied; rent is an economic price like any other price. There remains, however, an important reservation on the social function of the rentier though not on the economic rationale of the rent. The discussion of a rentier economy is thus concerned with a social group of rentiers rather than the economic significance of rent as a price. A rentier economy is referring, after all, to a special behaviour and spirit.

Rent, it is to be remembered, is not a special peculiarity of some countries, it is, rather, a general phenomenon known in all economies. In as far as there remain differences in natural resources, endowment, human talent, knowledge, location, etc., there will always be rent paid or imputed. The difference between countries is, however, one of magnitude. While in most countries rent is only a small fraction of income receipts and pure rentiers are either non-existent or very few, the situation in the Gulf states is quite different; rent is, in fact, the dominant factor, whence the epithet 'rentier economies'.

Though technically not 'income', oil revenues are perceived in the Gulf states as property income accruing to the whole of society. Of course, a more accurate assessment would reduce the 'income' element in oil revenues to that part imputed to value added; the rest, that is the major part, being an exchange of assets or wealth (transformation of real asset – oil – into financial assets – foreign exchange). However, all this remains academic since oil revenues are perceived by governments and citizens as income and treated as such. In matters of behaviour, economic reasoning is of little help; only perceptions count.

No more than one to three per cent of total manpower is engaged in oil production, while adding 60–80 per cent to the GDP as conventionally measured. The very high contribution of oil in the GDP is not, of course, only the effect of a remarkably high productivity of oil labour, a rent element is, in fact, overwhelming. The fact that oil revenues are not directly related to enterprise and/or hard work, affects a large spectrum of behaviour and attitudes, both at government and individual levels. Oil revenues are perceived as windfall profits, a gift of God, *Al-Khair*. The age-old dictum linking reward to work is dramatically broken in favour of chance, opportunity, or rather accident. Another effect of the new frame of mind is the expectation of sudden wealth and quick profits. The fabulous wealth accumulated in so short a period made individuals impatient with a continuous, slow, gradual process of change. An oil rentier is so obsessed by the present moment that he is not interested in the distant future. 'In the long run we are all dead', the famous remark of Keynes, aptly describes a rentier mentality.

It is not my intention here to enumerate the various practices of a rentier mentality in the Gulf states. Examples abound in government policies as well as in individual behaviour. What is important here, is that this rentier mentality affects the perceptions of investment opportunities domestically and abroad.

Domestic 'investment opportunities' are usually trade, real estate and the new-found gold mine speculation in securities. Trade is securing a monopolistic position through agency and sponsorship for foreign brands. Profits are large and secure. Real estate, and later stocks, provided a fancy world for making fortunes through speculation. The money machine has finally been discovered in these speculative markets. The Kuwaiti stock market, its rise and fall, is a case in point in this unreal world. So-called productive or developmental projects with their longer-term horizon and risk element can hardly stand the competition of fast profits in trade and speculation.

'Investment opportunities' abroad could scarcely be any different from those at home. A rentier is impatient with long-term investment opportunity, particularly in developing countries with all the risks and uncertainties implied. Real estate speculation is always an attraction, as are quick profit projects. Developmental investments for the long run are not the oil investor's cup of tea.

However, it would be a distorted exaggeration to say that a rentier mentality was alone, or even largely, responsible for the failure to invest oil funds in the LDCs. The world economic system as a whole was hardly conducive to development. It looked as if it were designed to perpetuate waste and to encourage financial speculation.

Inadequate International Financial Environment

The emergence of petro-funds coincided with a deep crisis of the international financial system and a near failure of economic policies. The oil stock aggravated an already ailing situation to the point of almost total confusion.

The breakdown of the Bretton Woods' agreement in 1971 and the subsequent abandonment of the fixed exchange system could not have come at a worse time. For whatever may be the merits and demerits of the fixed exchange system, there is one thing that its proponents and opponents are agreed on, and, that is that a fixed exchange system favours capital movements among nations. It is even suggested[24] that the Bretton Woods fixed system was made more rigid than the founding fathers initially intended because of the unexpected rise in capital flows in the post-war period. It is almost axiomatic that periods of major capital movements are also periods of fixed exchange systems, be it a pure gold-standard or a degenerate version of it − e.g. the Bretton Woods' system and the present day EMS (European Monetary System).

In mid-1973 a floating exchange system was adopted by major industrial countries. A few months later, the biggest ever surge in balance of payments surplus (the petro-dollars) came to the market for placement. The result was inevitably dramatic changes in exchange rates which in turn helped fuel an international speculative environment. Short-term capital movements moved from one place to another making and breaking enormous financial gains. Short-term profits in foreign exchange markets overshadowed any eventual longer-term investment returns.

To the impeding effect of a volatile exchange system to capital investment flows is added the apparent abdication of all regulation over important segments of the international financial system. The emergence and then the growth of the Eurocurrency markets helped increase speculative trends, volatility in exchange and interest rates and, of course, reduce the effectiveness of domestic policies. It is true that the Euromarkets appeared long before the emergence of the petro-funds. However, it was only with the emergence of the petro-funds that the Euromarket became a serious rival, yet unregulated, market for lending and borrowing. The lack or inadequacy of discipline in the Euromarket helps explain some abuses as well as a bias towards short-term placement to the detriment of the longer-term investments.

Concurrently with these shortcomings and lacunae in international financial institutions, economic policies in the seventies suffered from basic inconsistency and hesitancy. Keynesian economics which characterized economic policies in the post-war period came under fire with the emergence of a new counter doctrine; 'monetarism'. Money supply figures became an obsession for a new aggressive brand of technocrats in central banks and administrations. Thatcherism and then Reaganomics testify to the ascendancy of this new trend. The abandonment of the fixed exchange rate system helped rehabilitate monetary policies as it downgraded fiscal policies. With money supply targets, interest rates showed wild variations unknown in recent times. The floating exchange system helped maintain interest rate differentials among nations. The monetarists' emphasis on the priority of the fight against inflation brought interest rates to new heights. Short-term interest rates overshot long-term rates; an inverted interest structure thus prevailed to the detriment of long-term investment.

Such an environment is hardly conducive to any long-term investment. In fact it encourages speculation and short-term placements. Petro-funds were naturally attracted by the prospects of high short-term returns from high interest rates and possible exchange rates' profits.

Short-term profits proved, however, to be also short-lived. High financial returns concealed the erosion of the underlying economic conditions through inflation and recession. No more than a decade after the first oil shock OPEC countries discovered to their dismay that the seventies will probably go down in history as the decade of missed opportunities. This is more so for the Arab Gulf states. One day OPEC opened their eyes on a third oil shock, a shock in reverse this time.

The Third Oil Shock

On 24 January 1983 almost a decade after the first oil shock, Ahmad Zaki Yamani, the Saudi oil superstar declared at the end of a Geneva OPEC meeting, 'There has been a complete failure, I do not see a bright future.' On 14 March 1983 OPEC could finally agree on quota production and a new marker price for the Arabian Light, cutting it from $34 to $29 — the first such cut in OPEC history. The 'oil glut' took over from 'energy and oil crisis' as catchwords in headlines and news media. From a seller market blended with all sorts of premiums, the oil market is becoming a buyer market with all sorts of discounts. OPEC production declined from its peak of about 31 million b/d in 1979 to less than 17 million b/d in 1983, thus reducing its share in oil trade from two thirds in the mid-seventies to less than 45 per cent in the early eighties.

All this sounds new and strange; the 'new oil order' seems to be threatened with a different oil shock, a reverse oil shock this time.

It is not easy to ascertain that the new situation represents a permanent state of affairs due to structural changes brought about by conservation and substitution. The world economic recession is, perhaps, responsible for a good half of reductions in oil demand. Economic recovery should, in fact, revive demand for OPEC's oil. More stable and especially more predictable prices could thwart or at least reduce expensive investment in alternative sources. The oil market setback is by no means permanent.

Oil producing countries have, no doubt, been affected by the softened oil market. They are more seriously affected, however, by their own policies in regard to oil pricing and the use of their oil revenues. Once the darling of bankers and other financial institutions, Mexico, almost bankrupt, went into the red. Brazil, Venezuela, Nigeria, Indonesia are hardly any better. The Arab Gulf states, also affected by the oil glut, are in much better shape. With small populations and huge foreign investment, the Arab Gulf states remain stoutly immune from imminent financial pinches. They have also the added advantage of possessing ample oil reserves compared with the rest of oil producing countries. A relatively long time horizon (70-100 years) extends before them for oil production, a rare chance to learn from past experience.

Past experience has shown that price policies are not separable from investment policies. External disequilibria — surpluses as much as deficits — are not sustainable without a deliberate strategy for long-term investment in recipient countries. The petro-funds, as savings funds, have to be matched by investment programmes.

Experience has also shown that developed countries do not increase their real investment rate simply because of the availability of financial resources. Real investment opportunities in developing countries, though immense, raise serious risk problems. They do not make sense, moreover, unless undertaken on massive scale in selected areas. The Arab region seemed a privileged area for Arab petro-funds.

The spectacular opportunity given to the Arab states in the Gulf to 'tackle their massive development requirements and build Arab unity on the basis of fruitful economic co-operations' has been dissipated in wasteful expenditures, both domestically and internationally.[25]

The present weak oil market is not, however, the final act. The so-called third oil shock is no more than a temporary setback. World demand for oil has no way but to increase, if not immediately then in the not-so-far future. The Arab Gulf states with their huge reserves of oil will be called upon to play a still vital role in the world economic order. Past experience is only relevant in as far as it helps improve our understanding of the environment around us. Without trial and errors, human experience loses its significance. The third oil shock is probably a necessary interlude or pause for yet another rebound. The experience of the two previous oil shocks can thus hardly be over estimated; hence the need for similar volumes.

Notes

1. H. Hotelling, 'The Economics of Exhaustible Resources', *Journal of Political Economy*, April 1931.

2. *Council of Economic Advisory*, Washington D.C., 1980, pp. 203–319.

3. OECD, *Economic Outlook*, Paris, July 1979, p. 58.

4. R. Solow, 'What to Do Macro-economically When OPEC Comes' in Stanley Fisher (ed.), *Rational Expectations and Economic Policy* (University of Chicago Press, 1980), p. 263.

5. Maurice Laure, *Reconquérir l'Espoir* (Julliard, Paris, 1982), p. 20; *The Economist*, 29 January 1983.

6. IBRD, *World Development Report* (Washington, D.C., 1981).

7. Ph. Heymann, B. Bertheloot, *Aujourd'hui et Demain: La Crise* (J.C. Lattes, Paris, 1974).

8. Sidney Weintraub, *Our Stagflation Malaise* (Quorum Books, Westpoint, Connecticut; London, England, 1981), p. 51.

9. Alex Leijonhuvud, *Keynes and the Classics* (The Institute of Economic Affairs, London, 1969), p. 37.

10. J. de Larosière, Address before the Economic and Social Council of the United Nations, Geneva, 4 July 1980; *IMF Survey*, 7 July 1980.

11. OECD, *Economic Outlook*, Paris, January 1983.

12. Rimmer de Vries, *World Financial Markets*, Feb. 1983.

13. Jan Tinbergen, *Reshaping the International Order (RIO)*, ed., A Report to the Club of Rome (E.P. Dutton & Co., New York 1979).

14. First Brandt Report, *North-South: A Program for Survival* (London, 1980).

15. Second Brandt Report, *Common Crisis, North-South Cooperation for World Recovery* (London, 1983).

16. Thomas Stauffer, 'The Dynamics of Petroleum Dependency. Growth in an Oil Rentier State', *Finance and Industry*, no. 2 (Kuwait, 1981).

17. W. Quandt, *Saudi Arabia in the 1980s* (The Brookings Institutions, Washington D.C., 1981), p. 14.

18. Mancur Olson, *The Logic of Collective Action* (Harvard University Press, Cambridge, 1971).

19. Niccolo Machiavelli, *The Prince* (George Bull Baltimore; Penguin Books, 1961), p. 5.

20. Mancur Olson, *The Rise and Decline of Nations* (Yale University Press, 1982), pp. 20–3.

21. Adam Smith, *The Wealth of Nations* (1776, Everyman's Library 412, London, 1960).

22. David Ricardo, *The Principles of Political Economy and Taxation* (1821, Everyman's Library, 590, London, 1962).

23. Ibid.

24. Tom de Vries, 'Jamaica or the Non-Reform of the International Monetary System', *Foreign Affairs*, April 1976.

25. Malcolm Kerr, 'Rich and Poor in the New Arab Order', *Journal of Arab Affairs*, Oct. 1981, p. 1.

PART ONE:
THE INTERNATIONAL CONTEXT

2 INTERNATIONAL FINANCIAL MARKETS: THE END OF STABILITY?[1]

The task of an international investment manager is no longer an easy one. The volatility and instability of the international money and capital markets are not made to comfort him. Gone are the days of relative stability, growth and, above all, reasonable predictability which used to characterize the 1960s. The 1970s were in many ways a complete reversal of the economic trends of the previous decade. The 1980s promise to be still more difficult than the 1970s.

I intend in what follows to sketch out an outline of major factors contributing to the transformation of the international economic scenery. First, the institutional framework for international financial transactions will be discussed; that is, the transition from fixed to flexible exchange rate systems. Secondly, the impact of increasing scarcities in food and energy will be dealt with. Finally, I shall dwell on the less and less controllable financial flows associated with the emergence of Eurocurrencies and petro-funds and their effects on national economies.

From Adjustable-Peg to Managed Floating

The fixed exchange-rate system established at Bretton Woods in 1944 came under heavy attack particularly during the 1960s. First, the system was criticized since its inception as failing to provide a built-in mechanism for adjustment.[2] The responsibility to maintain external equilibrium rested upon domestic policies, hence exposing national governments, more often than not, to the difficult choice between external and internal equilibrium. The system exhibited, as applied, basic incompatibility among three major elements: highly mobile capital flows among countries, a desire to use monetary policy for domestic macro-economic objectives of price stability and full employment and a commitment to maintain fixed exchange rates.

Secondly, a fixed exchange-rate system is conceptually based on the premise of the availability of a certain amount of international reserves. With the slow increase in the supply of gold and the reluctance to raise its price, the system was forced to rely on one of the key national

35

currencies — in the event the US dollar. What was conceived to be a sort of gold-standard system degenerated into a dollar-standard one. The predominant role of the US dollar provoked various reactions. Early in the sixties, Triffin drew attention to what came to be known as the 'Triffin Dilemma': that 'the growth of world reserves could not be fed adequately by gold production at $35 an ounce, but that if the United States continued to run deficits, its foreign liabilities would inevitably come to exceed by far its ability to convert dollars into gold upon demand and would bring about a gold and dollar crisis'.[3] To this basic instability is added that fact that some countries, in particular the France of de Gaulle, were vehemently against, if not jealous of, the benefits reaped by the *de facto* world central bank (the US) in terms of seigniorage rights. A large movement to convert dollar-holdings into gold thus ensued.[4]

Finally, the continuous deterioration in the US balance of payments deficit, particularly with the extension of the Vietnam war, aggravated an already very weak situation. The Nixon decision to suspend the convertibility of the dollar into gold in August 1971 brought a *coup de grâce* to the fixed exchange-rate system clearing the way to the floating exchange-rate regimes.

The rectification of this situation was legalized with the second amendment of the IMF Agreement, effective April 1978, whereby the international monetary system moved from a fixed exchange-rate to a flexible exchange-rate system.

It is, however, noteworthy to emphasize here that the change is one of degree rather than of complete reversal. The fixed exchange-rate system established by the Bretton Woods agreement was not absolutely fixed; it was, in fact, an adjustable-peg, although the IMF tended to be more rigid in its interpretation than was probably originally envisaged.[5] Also, the flexible exchange-rate system is not a pure floating; it is, actually, a managed floating system. The difference between the two systems, however, remains important enough to warrant differentiating them by the greater frequency of exchange-rate changes, by the larger share of the external adjustment burden that is assigned to the exchange rate and by the absence of a publicly declared target exchange rate[6] in the case of the managed floating.

Before spelling out the impact of the shift towards greater flexibility in exchange rates, it is revealing to note that this change coincided with the oil price shock in 1973–4 and the emergence of the petro-funds, hence the need for greater capital flows. The merits of the fixed exchange-rate system to enhance capital flows cannot be overestimated.

It is quite paradoxical that the abandonment of the fixed exchange rate took place precisely when the potential for capital flows became greater, a point I shall return to later.

Now I turn to pinpoint a few differences in the international environment due to the change towards more exchange flexibility.

Rehabilitation of Monetary Policies

It is generally maintained that under fixed exchange rates, an increase in interest-sensitive capital mobility will decrease the efficacy of discretionary monetary policy while increasing the efficiency of fiscal policy.[7] This has been argued, in particular, by Fleming and Mundell.[8] In fact, one would expect intuitively that, under fixed rates, an increase in capital mobility makes it more difficult for monetary authorities to influence domestic interest rates while a move to floating exchange rates will enhance the effectiveness of monetary policy.

With fixed exchange rates, domestic and foreign assets become more or less substitutable. The more they are perfect substitutes, the less one can speak meaningfully about a market-determined relative price between them. In other words, the more they are perfect substitutes, the less interest differentials can be sustained. In fact, when capital mobility is perfect and fixed exchange rates are maintained, there can be only one interest rate in the world. On the contrary, with flexible rates domestic and foreign assets become less perfect substitutes and thus relative returns (interest differentials) on assets can persist in spite of capital mobility. Interest differentials would then reflect exchange risks.

The transition from a 'fix-price' (fixed exchange) to a 'flex-price' (floating exchange) system, is not without impact on the mechanics of equilibrium and indirectly on macro-policy. Disequilibria adjustments take the form of price changes (exchange rate changes) in the floating system and stock variations (reserve movements) in the fixed exchange system.[9] The stock variations (international reserves) not only deny monetary authorities the right to use interest differentials as a policy instrument but also make it difficult for them to control their own money supply. In Germany and Switzerland, for example, it was found that it became increasingly difficult, in the late 1960s and early 1970s, to maintain a restrictive monetary policy while keeping both a fixed exchange rate and relative freedom for capital flows.[10] It was observed in Germany that a restrictive domestic monetary policy brought forth capital inflows, thus creating a pressure to revalue unless the Bundesbank intervened to support the dollar by offering more DMs. Private capital flows, thus, became a chief channel by which an excess supply or demand for money is eliminated. Comments by Mr. Emminger, then President of the Bundesbank, on the rationale for Germany to float in 1973 were very instructive: 'For countries like Germany and Switzerland . . . the main — or even the only — reason why they went to floating in the spring of 1973 was the necessity to regain control over their own money supply'.[11]

Money supplies of industrial economies other than the US were largely determined by their balance of payments.[12] Of course, it is assumed in this view — the lack of control over money supply under fixed exchange — that the monetary authorities do not resort to 'sterilization' of the increased international reserves. This assumption proved to be fairly valid in practice. Most industrial countries found it possible, but at times very difficult, to control their money supply under fixed rates. Within the industrial country group, control over the money supply was most difficult in Germany, Switzerland, Belgium, Austria and France and least difficult in Japan, the US, the UK and Italy.[13]

Though the integration of national financial markets continues to be a topic for debate,[14] it is argued that the scope of monetary integration is enhanced by a choice of the exchange-rate system. Fixed exchange rates seem to promote money market integration thus weakening national monetary and credit policies.[15]

Against this change in the institutional framework, a parallel change in the frame of mind is taking place. The Keynesian Revolution of the late 1930s seems to have completed its full circle. We are possibly living now with a 'monetary' counter-revolution.

Milton Friedman's new 'monetarism' is undoubtedly gaining more ground. First, the Federal Reserve of St Louis, then most of the research staff of the IMF and even the 'Fed' in Washington seem to follow one or another of the new monetarists' approaches.[16] With Mrs Thatcher at the head of the British government, monetarists seem also to have consolidated their position in the UK. Professor Friedman's influence is also on the rise with the new Reagan administration.

The sophistication and subtlety in the definition and measurement of the various aggregates of money supply — M_1 . . . M_2 . . . etc. — can only intensify the monetarists' grip.

To sum it up seems fair to conclude that the shift towards greater flexible exchange rates would rehabilitate the monetary policy and increase the possibility of interest differentials among countries. The revival of the new monetarist school among policy makers would make such an outcome more than a possibility; it is almost a certainty.

The previous discussion shows that there exists a strong drive for more uses of the monetary policy and interest rates differential among countries. The institutional as well as the intellectual environment is so much in favour of such a trend. This, however, does not imply that monetary policy under the flexible exchange system would be more effective, much less that the monetarists are entirely right. There is a greater chance to see more of monetarists' policies but their success is a different story.

Difference in Inflation Levels

The experience of the last two decades has not only shown a greater price stability during the 1960s than in the 1970s, but also a wider difference in inflation levels in the latter. Calculations of the standard deviation of inflation rates among industrial countries indicate greater dispersion of inflation rates under floating than under fixed exchange systems.[17] The standard deviation of the consumer-price-index inflation rates among the seven largest industrial countries (Canada, France, Germany, Italy, Japan, the UK and the US) increased from 1.6 per cent for the 1962-72 period to 4.4 per cent for the 1973-78 period.[18]

It is not easy to draw meaningful theories only from statistical correlations (correlation is not causation). However, it can be accepted that governments are subject to more discipline under fixed exchange than they are under the floating system. Under the former, there exists a commitment by national authorities to maintain the par value of their currencies. A country that inflates at a higher rate than its trading partners will, *ceteris paribus*, incur a balance of payments deficit, thus facing the risk of depleting its international reserves. For this reason a real commitment to fixed exchange rates and the determination to maintain adequate international reserves would lead to more discipline in the fight against inflation or at least to keep pace with other countries' rates of inflation. A devaluation would, of course, help decrease strains on an inflating country but it is also assumed that devaluations are less frequent under the fixed exchange system.

With floating systems, countries would feel less commited to any particular exchange rate. A country can maintain a higher rate of inflation than its trading partners, leaving it to currency depreciation to clear the foreign exchange market. The balance of payments constraint is eliminated or very much reduced under floating systems. Currency appreciations and depreciations help maintain countries' different levels of inflation unaffected by the balance of payments constraint.

We are not interested here in tracing the origin of inflation (external or internal) and/or discussing the insulating properties of the exchange system against various sources of disturbance. What is important here is that, regardless of the origin of inflation, with more flexible exchange rates we are more likely to see different levels of inflation among countries.

Revival of Speculation

In fixed exchange systems, it has been shown, the par value is maintained more or less stable and the market is cleared through changes in stocks (quantities), i.e. variations in official reserves. It follows that the stability of exchange rates should be coupled with the availability of an adequate quantity of official reserves. They are, moreover, functionally dependent — that is, the more exchange rates are kept rigid the greater the need for official reserves. Views could diverge about the impact of the fixed exchange system on speculation. Meade showed in the 1950s that the par value system combined with freedom of capital movement — contrary to the assumptions made at Bretton Woods — would increase 'riskless speculation'.[19] Under the adjustable-peg, exchange rates are not absolutely fixed, they are adjusted in the case of 'fundamental disequilibrium'. Meade maintained that private institutions are just as capable as the authorities in recognizing situations of fundamental disequilibria. Usually, because of bureaucratic and political constraints, monetary authorities delay their exchange rate adjustment (reluctant adjustment), thus giving private institutions and individuals ample time for riskless speculation. It is this possibility of riskless speculation that probably led, contrary to the intentions of the founding fathers of the IMF Agreement, to the extreme rigidity of exchange rates as implemented by the IMF management.[20]

At the other extreme, under pure floating the need for official reserves is brought to a minimum. The market is cleared through price changes, i.e. changes in exchange rates. However, there is less agreement regarding the impact of increased exchange rate flexibility upon the demand for private reserves.[21] Muchlup argues that a free market determination of exchange rates would produce specially large private foreign balances because increased hedging in forward markets by risk-averse foreign traders will produce profitable opportunities for speculators.[22] Others[23] argue that a system of floating rates drastically reduces the demand for foreign exchange by both official and private holders. Whatever the theoretical impact of the adoption of a flexible exchange system on total reserves, official and private, the timing of the abandonment of the fixed exchange system towards the floating system coincided surprisingly with the surge of the petro-funds which, for a variety of reasons, are kept to a large extent in short-term claims, hence fuelling the potential for speculation. Speculation is no more riskless than under the adjustable-peg; it could be very costly and, indeed, it is. A flexible exchange system would normally reduce international capital mobility but if it is superimposed on a situation of abundant liquidity, as happened in the aftermath of the oil price increase, it can only increase the potential for speculation affecting and getting affected by exchange rates.

To sum up, the change of the international monetary framework from an adjustable-peg (Bretton Woods) to a managed floating (Jamaica) helped increase world interest rate differentials, inflation level differences and speculation.

The End of Cheap Food and Energy

Classical economists — Ricardo, Malthus and their followers — emphasized in the late eighteenth and early nineteenth centuries the limits of Nature. The Industrial Revolution, which was then under way, helped to delay and push these limits and, instead, brought to the forefront the potentials of Man's ingenuity to overcome obstacles and open new frontiers.

The world population was only 2,000 million in 1930, reached 3,000 million in 1960 and now stands at over 4,000 million. It will reach 6,000 million or more at the turn of the century. That the world can face the increase in the demand for food does not seem to be an insurmountable obstacle. In the last 40 years alone, modern farming methods have doubled and even tripled yields per land unit for major food grains such as wheat, rice and corn. The real challenge resides, perhaps, in the dangerously skewed pattern of food production and distribution, with large surpluses in some countries and growing deficits in most of the less developed countries. Before World War II, every major region of the world except Western Europe was a net exporter of grain, the basic measure of food sufficiency. Today Africa, Asia and even Latin America are net importers of grains.[24]

Per capita food production in the LDCs rose marginally in the 1950s and 1960s and fell back in the 1970s. With the 1973-74 disappearance of large food surpluses in the United States and other countries and the resulting high prices, the LDC governments have learned that they can no longer count on continuing access to cheap sources of food.[25] For the LDCs the classics' grim warning is still with us.

The increasing cost of food for the LDCs is not another commodity price increase which will affect relative prices and the allocation of resources. It is rather a basic change in the structure of prices which could affect all prices, pulling up the absolute price level.

Classical economists were very apprehensive of any increase in the 'wage-bill' (food prices in particular) because of its impact on the general price level. Sraffa[26] in his effort to reformulate Ricardo's labour-theory of value, went into a long analytical argument to show that the cost of labour in terms of corn − note that corn is not one commodity but is in fact a 'basket' of food crops − can affect the whole price structure. Some Cambridge (England) economists would maintain that Sraffa's system with Kantarovitch's is the precursor to the formulation of the linear programming problem. Like a linear programming problem, price determination is solved with reference to a basic programme. Sraffa's work is, in fact, centred on an attempt to prove that corn prices constitute the basic programme to which all other prices are related. Food prices thus determine all other prices and Ricardo's labour theory is rescued. With continuously increasing food prices in the LDCs, it is not far-fetched to assume that they are moving towards an era of general price increases.

Developed countries, on the other hand, do not have a food problem, food is also becoming only a minor element in their consumer goods basket. None the less, they face a problem similar to the LDCs food shortage − that is, energy. In 1972, non-renewable energy sources supplied close to 98 per cent of the world energy consumption.[27] In 1968 the State Department sent word that United States oil production would soon reach the limits of its capacity. In 1970, some 111 years after the birth of the US oil industry, its domestic production peaked and began to decline.[28] The situation in other developed countries is hardly any better; in fact, it is worse. Europe and Japan depend almost completely on imported oil. Oil and natural gas are the preferred fuels worldwide, accounting for 75 per cent of the US energy consumption and for about 70 per cent of the world's energy consumption.[29] For the first time in history since its industrial uses, oil discoveries have lagged behind consumption. The first oil price shock, in late 1973 and early 1974, definitely marked the end of the era of secure and cheap oil. More than the action of OPEC, the oil price increase reflects a change in the industry's economics with the passage from easily accessible oil fields to less accessible ones. In the first phase, the cost of production was the main point of reference in oil prices while, in the second phase, the cost of substitution became more relevant for oil pricing.[30]

It has been found that in 1974 only 2.4 per cent of the US increase in prices could be explained by the oil price increase.[31] Similar conclusions have been reached in other OECD countries. Though the percentage may seem small, the importance of energy lies in its pervasive use throughout the economy; no other input is as widely used cutting across the whole spectrum of production processes. Like water and air to life, energy vitalizes the functioning of the economy, it powers the machines that make the country productive, the heating and cooking systems that make people comfortable, the lights that turn night into day, the motor vehicles, aircraft and railroads that make the world mobile, etc. Economically, the price and availability of energy affect rates of real growth, inflation, unemployment and the standard of living.[32]

To use the Sraffa system, it seems plausible to assume that energy prices are to the modern economy what corn prices were to the classical economy. An increase in energy cost would move the whole price structure upward and not only energy relative prices. Energy costs in modern economies, like corn prices in Ricardo's system, are the basis for other prices and any increase in these costs would trigger an upward price movement.

In a world of increasing food and energy costs, it seems that we are embarking on a more inflationary era due to fundamental scarcities in food and energy.

The Emergence of Eurocurrencies and Petro-funds

Though both the Eurocurrency and petro-funds phenomena owed their existence to different reasons, their interaction cannot be mistaken. The Eurocurrency market came into existence much earlier than the drastic increase in petro-funds after 1973. Its appearance was related to cost advantages available to offshore (Euro) banks. Different reserve requirements, special regulations – e.g. the famous regulation Q in the US – and possibly lower information costs due to the proximity of borrowers and/or lenders, were the main reasons for the appearance of the Eurobanks and Euromarkets.

It is, none the less, undeniable that the surge of substantial petro-funds in 1973-74 helped revive the Euromarket when its *raison d'être* seemed to be waning with the gradual elimination of the discriminatory regulations between domestic and Eurobanks. The mushroom growth of the Euromarket resulted, to a great extent, from petro-funds' recycling. Denis Healey pointed out that it was widely believed during the IMF meeting at Nairobi in the autumn of 1973 that the Eurocurrencies would soon disappear.[33] The injection of huge petro-funds gave the Euromarket a *sursis* enabling it to survive. From its level of $500 million or so in 1959,[34] the gross size of the Eurocurrency market surpassed $ one trillion in late 1979.[35] Moreover, the Eurocurrency market and petro-funds constitute two overwhelming external factors over which domestic authorities have little control. Though the impact of petro-funds by far outranks that of the Eurocurrency market, it is useful to discuss briefly the latter before turning to the former.

The Eurocurrency Market

The impact of the existence of the Eurocurrency market and its growth on global rates of inflation and national monetary independence is a matter of controversy.

The debate over the ability of the Eurobanks to create credit by analogy with the domestic commercial banks is no more topical.[36] Because the term 'deposit' is used to describe the placement of funds in the Eurocurrency market and also connotes the means of payment within a country, Eurocurrency deposits have often been considered a form of money, competing with each national currency.[37] The domestic commercial banks' multiplier seems to be an inadequate tool of analysis for Euromarkets. Eurocurrencies do not take the form of demand deposits and, indeed, as they always bear interests, are closer to time deposits. They are looked upon, moreover, as instruments of placing funds rather than as means of payment. Inflationary effects of the Euromarket are, perhaps, more indirect in nature. Through the increase in redundant liquidity, following the introduction of flexible rates, the Euromarket could be instrumental in propagating inflation.[38] It is also maintained that the Euromarket helps create private and official international liquidity outside the control of national or international authorities, thus making it more difficult to fight inflation.[39] By its nature, the Euromarket is an unregulated market. This is a major loophole against the strict implementation of national monetary policies. The Euromarket developed in such a manner as to subvert national constraints on credit.

It is also universally accepted that the growth of the Euromarket has increased short-term capital mobility. However, given the parallel developments in petro-funds and exchange systems referred to earlier, the existence and growth of short-term borrowing can only fuel speculation.

Finally, some economic and financial circles[40] always maintain an uneasy feeling about this unregulated market warning against the prospects of possible defaults and accordingly the potential for triggering financial disorder. Though this is by no means the general perception; it can only add to the uncertainty of the money and capital markets.

Petro-Surpluses and their Mode of Placement

It is worth emphasizing at the outset that the existence of the petro-surpluses raises genuine problems for the world economy, independently of the oil price increase. It should be made clear that the increase in oil prices does not necessarily imply balance of payments disequilibria nor the emergence of petro-surpluses. Though closely related, oil price increases and petro-surpluses are two different problems. Because it so happens that the major oil producing countries are sparsely populated with limited absorptive capacity, the oil price increase was accompanied by the emergence of the petro-surpluses. The coincidence of these two events should not lead to confusion between them; their effects are quite distinct. In what follows I intend to analyse the impact of the petro-surpluses and their uses independently of the oil price increase. This is a macro-analysis transcending the cost analysis of oil prices.

The validity of the whole macro-analysis is based on the premise that some variables are significant in affecting the behaviour of the economy. The petro-surpluses, as an economic aggregate, should then be sizable enough compared to other aggregates to justify a macro-analysis. Since the functioning of the economy depends, to a large extent, on 'flow' aggregates, it is very useful to compare the petro-surpluses with some relevant annual flows.

The petro-surpluses are, in fact, additions to world savings in the form of foreign financial assets. It is therefore only natural to compare the petro-surpluses with savings (or investment) aggregates in major countries. But petro surpluses are savings of a particular form, i.e. foreign financial assets; thus, they are liable to be transformed in the future, through exports, into real assets. Investment (savings) and exports are, then, appropriate aggregates for comparison.

In 1974, in the United States, the biggest economy in the world, private gross fixed capital (investment) totalled $205 billion and exports

$113 billion. In 1979 these figures were respectively $369 billion and $214 billion.[41]

The petro-surpluses reached some $60 billion in 1974 thus representing more than 30 per cent of the US private investment and 50 per cent of exports. It is true that the petro-surpluses tended to decrease in subsequent years to reach their lowest level in 1978 before rebounding again in 1979 in the wake of the Iranian Revolution. Estimates of petro-surpluses put them at about $45-50 billion for 1979 and at $100-110 billion for 1980.

Compared with appropriate aggregates in the biggest economy in the world, the petro-surpluses are not small quantities. Any change of similar magnitude is bound to have a substantial impact on the world economy. In fact, the American and the world economies would suffer from much smaller changes.

Having shown the relative importance of the petro-surpluses to the world economy, I shall analyze the new situation by using the Keynesian technique of the identity of *ex post* savings and investment.[42] This usage will be different from Keynesian models in at least two respects. First, the analysis will be applied to the world economy as a whole and not to a national economy. In a closed national economy there must be equality between realized savings and investment. This holds true for every case, since this is an accounting identity. Taken as a whole, the world economy is nothing but a closed economy to which the equality of saving and investment must also hold. Secondly and more importantly the mechanism used to bring about this equality will be different from the familiar Keynesian multiplier.

The starting point to the analysis is to recognize the nature of the petro-surpluses as additions to world savings. The oil price increase is, in fact, nothing more than a redistribution of world income in favour of OPEC countries brought about by the change in their terms of trade. This means an increase in the world propensity to save. OPEC surplus countries already had a very high propensity to save prior to the oil price increase in 1973-74. With the huge income rise, OPEC savings increased enormously after 1973-74. Given the limited absorptive capacity for investment, OPEC surplus countries' savings reflected themselves in the form of foreign financial assets − i.e., the petro-surpluses. In fact it is the other way round: that is, the increase in the oil consuming countries' deficit and accordingly their financial liabilities gave rise to OPEC savings.

I have dwelt at length elsewhere[43] on this issue, showing that the necessary *ex post* equality between savings and investment following the increase in OPEC savings (petro-surpluses) could be brought about by one of these scenarios:

1. There could be a parallel increase in the rate of real investment in the world (real investment scenario).
2. There could be dis-savings elsewhere in the world to offset the increase in OPEC savings (transfer of wealth scenario).
3. There could be neither increase in real investment nor dis-savings, but only an increase in financial assets (placement scenario).

The said study showed that the world economic development seems to suggest that the 'placement scenario' — the increase in financial assets — is probably the best description of the actual development. World real investments can hardly be said to have increased in the aftermath of the oil shock of 1973-74. Rather, world investments tended to slacken during the seventies.[44] It would also be an exaggeration to suggest that a major real transfer of wealth took place following the oil price increase. Both OPEC surplus and host countries seem to be quite discreet trying to minimize the handing over of property titles to OPEC surplus countries. Failing to raise real investment and/or effectuate dis-savings to match the increased OPEC savings (petro-surpluses), the deficit countries issued new financial assets to finance their deficits. OPEC surplus countries, on the other hand, were satisfied to hold new financial assets that are both credit-worthy and free of political animosity. The supply of the new financial assets was thus matched by increased demand from OPEC to hold them. OPEC new savings were thus the result of the increased financial liabilities of oil importing countries following the rise in the oil bill.

The spectrum of financial assets is very broad indeed. They include the all-liquid money and quasi-money, the less liquid securities and still more illiquid claims and debts. It is not easy to have a full survey of these assets, it suffices to refer to simple indicators for the increase in world financial assets following the emergence of the petro-surpluses: the Eurocurrency market and countries' indebtedness. These two indicators are, moreover, directly related to the petro-surpluses. In both cases, there was a sharp rise in their volume following the increase in OPEC savings.

Since we assume that the real capital stock has not undergone any major change with the issuance of the new financial assets, the capital stock is now owned (directly and indirectly, in equity and debt) by a wider class of owners. The new claimants to wealth are entitled to a nominal return on their assets equivalent to that of the 'old' owners of wealth. If it so happened, as in fact it did, that nominal yields on financial assets have not been depressed by the increase in the supply of financial assets, the cost of capital would also increase. A general increase in the cost of capital cannot go without repercussions on the whole economic system. Empirical investigations have shown, in fact, a remarkable historical constancy in the rate of profit, capital/output ratio and the share of profit.[45] With the constancy of these ratios, particularly capital/output, the increase in the value (cost) of capital would entail a corresponding increase in the value of output. A general price increase movement is set in motion.

Now prices are introduced into the picture. An increase in OPEC savings would call for the injection of new financial assets. Earning the same nominal yields as the old ones, the new financial assets would bid up the cost of capital, triggering, in turn, a general price increase. Nominal investment would thus increase. Hence, in reaction to the increase in OPEC's savings, there will take place a general price rise; nominal investment will also increase and the equality of *ex post* savings and investment is maintained. Here we find that inflation is built into the scenario. It is necessary in order to bring about an accounting equality between savings and investment. Short of increasing real investment and/or undertaking parallel dis-savings, the only available possibility to match OPEC savings was to increase nominal investment. OPEC's savings are *ipso facto* turned into nominal savings, thus losing their real value with continuous inflation.

The previous analysis of the impact of the petro-surpluses, it should be remembered, is different from the standard analysis attributing inflation to oil price increases. In our analysis, it is not the oil price increase *per se* that is responsible for inflation. Rather, it is the necessity to equalize savings and investment and the inability of increasing real investment and/or realizing open dis-savings that can explain inflation. In other words, ours is a macro-analysis of the petro-surpluses conducted via their effects on savings and investment.

I have tried to demonstrate elsewhere that the apparent contradiction between the last conclusion and the established Keynesian models on the effects of excess savings can be reconciled given the different nature of the savings function in each case.[46] In a Keynesian model savings are a function of the level of income while OPEC savings were and still are a function of the distribution of income. An excess savings over investment can be undone in a Keynesian model, by reducing the level of income (deflation). Excess OPEC savings over world investment can be undone by a reverse income distribution. Inflation could be instrumental in bringing about such reversal. The difference between the two models resides then in the nature of the savings function and the subsequent reactions to bring about the equality investment savings.

It must be emphasized that the previous outcome is not due to a deliberate policy by any country or group of countries. In fact, everyone is suffering from inflation. It is, perhaps, related to the preference of OPEC surplus countries to place their petro-surpluses in the industrial country group and the inability of the latter to increase the rate of their investment.

The industrial countries' inability to raise their real investment is a matter of structure rather than of policy. Without a drastic shift in effective demand towards more capital goods industries, it cannot possibly be envisaged that an increase in the rate of investment could take place. Paradoxical as it may sound, only the Third World, with its huge needs for capital goods, can bring about the necessary change in effective demand and make the increase in real investment feasible.

The limitation of the Third World for absorbing productively the petro-surpluses are too well-known to need any further elaboration. With all their shortcomings, developing countries seem to offer a good chance to transform the oil financial phenomenon into a real one by matching OPEC additional savings with increased real investment and not only new financial assets. The risks are huge in such an enterprise, as are the stakes. This is the OPEC surplus countries' dilemma; that is, secure and credit-worthy placement in the industrial countries would trigger inflation and ultimately erode OPEC savings on the one hand, real investment in the Third World has to face risks of poor management and political instability on the other hand. The choice is by no means easy. Given the prevailing economic and political constraints, it is more likely that the present mode of placement of the petro-surpluses would continue and that inflationary pressures would persist.

Conclusion

Having ventured on a quick *tour d'horizon* of major factors affecting the international financial environment, it is always useful to conclude with some policy recommendations. Rather than suggesting any recommendation, this chapter is organized in such as way as to provide a description of the present situation and explain the underlying factors responsible for its transformation. A valid description should, none the less, lead to a proper prescription and a diagnosis is only relevant in as much as it helps to indicate a cure. Without pre-judging what is good for the international community and what is not, the increasing instability in international financial markets, though possibly benefiting some participants, could also undermine the long-term foundation for a healthy development. In the light of the foregoing discussion, it is important to identify areas of possible action with a view to redressing the international situation. In particular, it should be made clear that not all the factors referred to earlier in the discussion have the same degree of determinism. There exists a difference in nature between changes in fundamental economics and those in the institutional set-up. The freedom with which a change can be introduced in the institutional set-up is far greater than in fundamental economies. However, we should not underestimate vested interests, balance of power, etc., which can pose formidable obstacles to any change in the institutional set-up. On the other hand, fundamental economics can always be transcended by major technical progress, new inventions and/ or changes in tastes which, in many cases, can prove to be quite dynamic and far from immutable. The distinction between the two categories remains, however, by and large valid.

Fundamental and institutional changes are, no doubt, potent and mutually interacting with continuous feedbacks. The unhappy timing of the adoption of a more flexible exchange system with the emergence of huge capital movements could only fuel speculation and increase foreign exchange risks. No foreign exchange policy can bring about equilibrium in this situation. The surpluses (and hence deficits) which emerged in global payments balances were 'unadjustable' in the short run. This is a structural imbalance.[47] The existence of the Euromarket with enormous funds circulating outside the control of national authorities reduces monetary discipline and increases uncertainty. Monetarists' policies aggravate, in the event, a monetary situation on which they seem to have little knowledge, let alone influence. The fact of continuous inflation and unstable and uncertain foreign exchange induces the oil producing countries to review periodically their oil prices to make up for the loss in real terms, thus triggering another wave of uncertainty. The extreme volatility of the financial markets inevitably makes authorities, institutions, investors, individuals, etc. overduly concerned with the financial aspects of the market to the neglect of the real aspects (e.g. increasing real investment opportunities in developed and less developed countries). All in all, we are caught in one of the most vicious of vicious circles.

It remains true, however, that the distinction between fundamental economics and institutional set-up could be instructive in view of any eventual reform. The increase in food and energy costs on the one hand and the structural imbalance in external current accounts on the other seem to represent a fundamental change underlying the world economy. In the present state of arts and tastes, food and energy are no longer cheap commodities. Also, the petro-funds as a new feature of balance of payments seem liable to continue in the future, at least for some time. These are two new developments with which we have to learn to live.

Apart from this, there seems to exist much room for changes and adaptability. Fixed versus flexible rates, monetarist versus demand and supply management, Euromarkets versus disciplined markets, financial placement versus real investment of petro-funds, etc., are all matters of policy, subject to trial and error. On the face of it, it appears that the world economy is probably passing through a transitional period which can be made much less painful if better institutional arrangements are agreed upon. Whether or not this could be made feasible in the near future is a matter of judgement.

Notes

1. First published in IBK Papers, no. 2 (Jan. 1981), Industrial Bank of Kuwait.

2. M. Friedman, 'The Case for Flexible Rates' in *Essays in Positive Economics* (University of Chicago Press, 1953).

3. R. Triffin, *Gold and the Dollar Crisis: The Future of Covertibility* (Yale University Press, New Haven, 1960).

4. R. Cooper, *The Economics of Interdependence: Economic Policy in the Atlantic Community* (Columbia University Press, New York, 1980).

5. T. de Vries, 'Jamaica, or the Non-Reform of the International Monetary System', *Foreign Affairs*, April 1976.

6. M. Goldstein, *Have Flexible Exchange Rates Handicapped Macro-economic Policy?* (Special Papers in International Economics, Princeton University, 1980).

7. T.D. Willet, 'The Eurocurrency Market, Exchange-Rate Systems, and National Financial Policies' in C.H. Stem, J.H. Makin and D.E. Logue (eds.), *Eurocurrencies and the International Monetary System* (Washington DC, 1976).

8. J.M. Fleming, 'Domestic Financial Policies under Fixed and Floating Exchange Rates', *IMF Staff Papers*, vol. 9, 1962; R.A. Mundell, 'Flexible Exchange Rates and Employment', *Canadian Journal of Economics and Political Sciences*, vol. 27, 1961.

9. J.R. Hicks, *Capital and Growth* (Oxford at the Clarendon Press, 1965).

10. Goldstein, *Flexible Exchange Rates*.

11. Ibid.

12. R. McKinon, 'Dollar Stabilization and American Monetary Policy', *The American Economic Review*, Papers and proceedings, May 1980.

13. Goldstein, *Flexible Exchange Rates*.

14. R. Aliber, 'The Integration of National Financial Markets: A Review of Theory and Findings', *Weltwirtschaftliches Archiv*, vol. 114, no. 3 (1978).

15. Cooper, *Economics of Interdependence*.

16. N. Kaldor, 'The New Monetarism', *Lloyds Bank Review*, July 1970.

17. M. Whitman, 'International interdependence and the US Economy' in W. Felliner (ed.), *Contemporary Economic Problems 1978* (American Enterprise Institute, Washington, 1978).

18. Goldstein, *Flexible Exchange Rates*.

19. J. Meade, 'The Case for Variable Exchange Rates', *The Three Banks Review*, Sept. 1955.

20. de Vries, 'Jamaica'.

21. J.H. Makin, 'Eurocurrencies and the Evolution of the International Monetary System' in Carl Stem, J. Makin and Denis Logue (eds.), *Eurocurrencies and the International Monetary System* (Washington DC, 1976).

22. F. Muchlup, *International Payment, Debts and Gold* (New York, 1964).

23. A.A. Walters, 'Floating Rates, World Liquidity and Inflation', *Euromoney*, July 1973.

24. D.C. Kimmel, 'Food and Agriculture: A United Nations View', *Economic Impact*, no. 32 (1980/4).

25. S. Wortman and R.W. Cumming, *To Feed this World: The Challenge and the Strategy* (John Hopkins University Press, 1978).

26. P. Sraffa, *Production of Commodities by Means Commodities: A Prelude to a Critique of Economic Theory* (Cambridge University Press, Cambridge, 1961).

27. R.G. Ridker and W.D. Watson, *To choose a Future* (John Hopkins University Press, 1980).

28. S. Stobuagh and D. Yergin (eds.), *Energy Future*, Random House, New York, 1979.

29. *US Oil and Gas Prospects to 2010*, A Report by the National Reserve Council USA, 1979.

30. J.M. Chevalier, *Le Nouvel Enjeu Pétrolier* (Calmann-Lévy, 1973).

31. H.A. Merklein and W. Hardly, *Energy Economics* (Gulf Publishing Co., Texas, 1977).

32. 'The Leverage of Oil' in *Great Decisions: 1980*, Foreign Policy Association, New York, 1980.

33. D. Healey, 'Oil, Money and Recession', *Foreign Affairs*, Winter 1979/80.

34. *The Economist*, 11 July 1959.

35. The Bank for International Settlements, cited in *International Herald Tribune*, 25 Feb. 1980.

36. M. Friedman, 'The Eurodollar Market: Some First Principles', *Morgan Guaranty Survey*, October 1969.

37. R. McKinnon, *The Eurocurrency Market*, Essays in International Finance, no. 125, Princeton University Press, December 1977.

38. Makin, 'Eurocurrencies'.

39. Willet, 'The Eurocurrency Market'.

40. In particular, *International Currency Review*.

41. IMF, *International Financial Statistics*, October 1980.

42. This argument has been developed in greater length in the author's study: H. Beblawi, 'The Arab Gulf States' Predicament: Individual Gains and Collective Losses', in M. Kerr and S. Yassin (eds.), *Rich and Poor States in the Middle East* (Westview Press, 1982).

43. Ibid.

44. IMF, *Annual Reports*, 1975, 1976, 1977.

45. N. Kaldor, 'A Model of Economic Growth', *Economic Journal*, 1957; L. Pasinetti, 'Growth and Income Distribution', in *Essays in Economic Theory* (Cambridge University Press, 1974).

46. Beblawi, 'The Arab Gulf States' Predicament'.

47. I. Frank, Ch. Pearson and Riedel, 'The Implications of Managed Floating Exchange Rates for US Trade Policy', *Monograph series in Finance and Economics, 1979* (New York University, 1979).

3 THE REAGAN PROGRAMME AND THE AMERICAN ECONOMY: AN APPRAISAL IN PERSPECTIVE[1]

'This is the worst state since the Depression', asserted Ronald Reagan describing the economic situation of the United States in the eighties, in his message to Congress on 18 February 1981. This may or may not be true. However, it seems that the general perception of the average American is not far from this diagnosis. The sweeping victory of the Republicans last November for the Presidency and in the Senate can only confirm this view. The polls were in fact a popular mandate for a change in the economic policy.

Probably not since the New Deal of Franklin D. Roosevelt has the American economic policy witnessed such a change in orientation. It is, thus, important to review briefly the evolution of the American economic policy and the present mood of the new American outlook.

I

The great Depression of the 1930s was so traumatic that the economic thinking of the whole capitalist world underwent a fundamental metamorphosis under its impact. For the United States alone, its dollar income was cut by half before the economy hit bottom in 1933. Total output fell by a third and unemployment reached 25 per cent of the labour force. The depression was no less catastrophic for the rest of the capitalist world. It is no wonder then the general perception was that capitalism is an unstable system which cannot be left to its own forces without endangering the very foundation of the system.

The orthodox economics preached that the best economic policy for the crisis was to leave it to market forces to cure the situation. Also, monetary policy, if properly handled, should be sufficient to keep things in order.

The election of 1932 was a turning point in the economic thinking of both the public and the administration. The government played a major role to redress the situation and has since been assigned a prime responsibility in maintaining an acceptable level of economic activity. The government is not only responsible for maintaining law and order as is usually accepted, but also to provide a high level of employment.

John Maynard Keynes provided a theoretical apparatus to salvage the foundations of capitalism and the ground for government intervention in the economic activity. The Keynesian revolution gained a wide acceptance in the economic profession and provided a badly needed justification for extensive governmental intervention.

Economic equilibrium is not necessarily maintained, asserted Keynes, at the level of full employment. Equilibrium can very well be realized at less than full employment. Also, money wages are rigid downward and cannot be relied upon to bring about full employment. To Keynes, 'Money does not matter'. Unemployment is, in fact, due to the insufficiency in demand. Only by increasing the effective demand can full employment be attained. Government spending particularly through public works can increase effective demand and accordingly employment. If the monetary policy is impotent, fiscal policy is the main policy instrument in the Keynesian medicine. Budget deficit is no more a sin, it is a deliberate policy to complement the insufficiency of the effective demand. The government is required now to undertake a systematic deficit in cases of insufficiency in the effective demand.

Roosevelt was inaugurated as President on 3 March 1933 and immediately launched a vast programme of spending; 'the hundred days of a special congressional session.' Though the New Deal was not the origin of the Welfare State, it definitely ingrained the idea of the Welfare State in the minds of the public. Keynesian economics on the one hand, and Welfare State on the other, helped to increase public spending greatly. From the founding of the Republic to 1929, spending by governments at all levels − federal, state and local − never exceeded 12 per cent of the national income except in times of war. Typically, federal spending amounted to 3 per cent or less of the national income. Since 1946 non-defence spending alone has never been less than 16 per cent of the national income and is now roughly one-third of the national income. Federal governmental spending alone is more than one-quarter of the national income.

The fact that the increase in government spending was related to its role as provider of the Welfare State, is very important for the understanding of the new tide of conservatism. The drive for the Welfare State probably reached its apogee with the 'Great Society' of President Lyndon Johnson, though, paradoxically, it was the Nixon administration which showed the highest government intervention.

After more than two decades of impressive performance, the US economy started to show signs of weakness. The dollar came under pressure in the late 1960s before suspending its convertibility into gold in August 1971. Productivity has dropped significantly since the 1970s. From 1949 to 1969, output per man-hour of all persons employed in private business — a simple and comprehensive measure of productivity — rose more than three per cent a year; in the next decade, less than half as fast; and by the end of the decade productivity was actually declining.

In the early 1970s an already overheated economy faced in 1973-74 the oil price increase, and the world economy plunged into the severest recession since World War II, but this time with inflation. The United States which was insulated almost during the whole of this century from inflation started to experience two-digit inflation.

Concurrently with these economic difficulties, the United States faced a series of political setbacks. After the traumatic Vietnam War, the US seemed to lose its edge in strategic armament. Suffice it to notice the increasing influence of the USSR in Africa (Angola, the Horn of Africa) and South Yemen, the fall of the Shah of Iran, the invasion of Afghanistan and possibly of Poland. Add to this the humiliation during the episode of the American hostages in Tehran. All these factors aroused the conservative instinct in the US. However, conservatism is not only an instinctive reaction, it has its body of thoughts and some of them are quite persuasive. The most influential figure in the economic but also political thinking is probably Milton Friedman. But there are other figures also, particularly as far as the economic reform is concerned. Laffer and the proponents of supply side are also important. To these we turn now.

II

The 'conservative radicalism' represents now the new tide in economic and political thoughts in the US and possibly in Western countries.

Inflation is, to this breed, the number one economic problem in the capitalist system. It might look inappropriate to quote Keynes to represent the conservative state of mind regarding the dangers of inflation. Keynes, however, aptly described these dangers; 'there is no subtler, or surer means of overturning the existing basis of society than to debauch the currency. The process engages all the hidden forces of economic laws on the side of destruction and does it in a manner which not one in a million is able to diagnose.'

On the face of it, three possible courses of action seem to be available to combat inflation. First, there is fiscal policy, secondly, price control, and, finally monetary policies. The fiscal policies have been too much advocated by Keynesian economists, but with little success. The Keynesian medicine which was quite effective in promoting economic activity during recession proved much less successful in the opposite situation. It was discovered that it is much easier to promote economic activity during recession by tax-cutting and expenditure increase, than it is to combat inflation through tax increases and expenditure cutting. In fact, public expenditure cannot be easily reduced as it is much easier to cut taxes than to increase them. Galbraith, a notable liberal economist of a marked Keynesian inclination, admits that 'if expenditures can be increased but cannot be reduced and taxes can be reduced but cannot be increased, fiscal policy becomes a one-way street. It will work wonderfully against deflation and depression but not very well against inflation'.

A generalized price control is resented by most economists, though not all (Galbraith in a recent book defends it). The general feeling is that price control can only work in exceptional periods like wars, but in general it is wasteful, very costly and could endanger freedom and democracy.

The monetary policies seem for the time being the only available means to contain inflation. The monetarists carry the day almost everywhere now. Milton Friedman is the apostle of the new creed. His ideas on the economic policy transcend, however, this narrow monetarism and cover a wider scope of the whole economic policy. His new book *Free to Choose* is not a best-seller in the US only but also in other western European countries.

The ideas of Friedman are so important in shaping the new American thinking that a few words on them seem in order. After his book *Capitalism and Freedom*, Friedman expands in his *Free to Choose* on the same topic with a very persuasive and lucid argument. This is probably the most systematic attack on the increasing role of government in recent times. The basic idea is simple enough. It has been said more than two hundred years ago with Adam Smith, when he attacked the Mercantilists for the excess of the government intervention. Friedman borrows from Adam Smith that an individual who

> intends only his own gain, is led by an invisible hand to promote an end which was not part of his intention. Nor is it always the worse for the society that it was no part of it. By pursuing his own interest he frequently promotes that of the society more effectually than

when he really intends to promote it. I have never known much good done by those who affected to trade for public good.

Time and again, Friedman asserts the waste and inefficiency in resource utilization in government intervention. Though the intentions could be good, invariably the results are disappointing, affirms Friedman. Misinformed and/or uninformed, bureaucrats are lousy managers. He also emphasizes the lack of incentive, or, better, the conflict of the bureaucrats' interests with the general interest. He defends the Director's Law: 'public expenditures are made for the primary benefit of the middle class, and financed with taxes which are borne in considerable part by the poor and rich.'

Friedman also contends that the increase in the government role is not confined to substituting public for private spending. It is rather a change from productive to non-productive spending. The increase in government spending is mainly an increase in transfer payments with the enlargement of the Welfare State. He also has serious doubts whether services of this Welfare State reach their objective. More often than not, bureaucrats are serving themselves. Or in the words of another writer of the same vein, Gilder, this resulted in a 'depleted capitalism' in which 'government bureaucracies proliferate to furnish the services that overtaxed business no longer can provide'. Moreover, by increasing the burden on the productive sector to support the Welfare State, the system is taxing work, risk-bearing and enterprise − i.e., the very basis of progressive capitalism.

Milton Friedman's advocacy for the free market has its political dimension. For him, the free market is the best guarantee for individual freedom and democracy. Increasing the role of the government is not only inefficient, it is also a menace to political freedom. Friedman is, of course, no naïve to overlook the imperfections of the market, but to him the imperfections of the government are far more serious.

It is important to see the new Reagan policies against this change in the intellectual and emotional background. Reaganomics is the product of a new faith, conservative radicalism. This faith is manifest also in a new book *Wealth and Poverty* by George Gilder and which received a very wide interest. Gilder tries to defend capitalism on a moral basis. To him 'it is the belief that the good fortune of others is also finally one's own' which provides the moral basis of capitalism. He also attacks the Welfare State because of the 'moral blight of dependency'.

In the same vein but more specifically related to Reagan's economic programme, is Arthur Laffer of Southern California. Laffer is the new champion of the supply siders. Rediscovering the old Fathers of the economic science is not the exclusive privilege of Friedman. Laffer also rediscovers J.B. Say, the French economist, and rehabilitates his Law 'that supply creates its own demand'. It follows that we should not bother ourselves with the demand, but only with the supply, and the demand will take care of itself. Incidentally, it was Keynes who first challenged Say's Law (if we overlook Malthus). Keynes claimed that it is the reverse of Say's Law which determines economic activity. Demand determines, according to Keynes, the level of income and hence the supply. It is here, in fact, that Keynes parted company from orthodox economics.

The opposition Say/Keynes can be put differently. In the relation between investment and savings, which is the exogenous variable and which is the endogenous? The Keynesians would claim that investment is the exogenous variable, and once it is determined, economic forces would generate the necessary savings to finance it. To Say and the classics, it is savings which determines the level of investment. To the Keynesian all the attention should be given to investment, savings will be available. To the classics it is the other way round.

It follows that Laffer and his followers recommend a policy centred around tax cuts. To them a tax cut, if properly implemented, would encourage people to work harder and save more. Therefore the focus of the policy should be to help enhance savings.

The supply siders' contention is criticized by Democrat economists (such as Walter Heller) as ignoring that 'common sense and arithmetic show that the jump in demand would be much bigger and faster than any conceivable jump in supply.' In fact, both views can be reconciled. In the history of economic thought, the classical view (supply side) represents the long run, while the Keynesian view (demand side) represents a shorter run concept. Thus the inflationary impact – in the short-term – of tax cuts cannot be excluded, though they might be anti-inflationary in a longer run.

The new supply siders are not prescribing a new neutral medicine; they are, in fact, part and parcel of the conservative trend. The increase in savings following tax cuts, will result in substituting private for public spending. It is a return of the ethics of work and thrift.

We cannot complete the new conservative picture without a few words on the new monetarism. Contrary to Keynes, the Chicago School led by Friedman declares that 'money matters'. Inflation is a monetary phenomenon arising from a more rapid increase in the quantity of money than output. The cure to inflation is simple to implement. What is needed is to reduce the rate of growth of the money supply.

In the light of the above political landscape it was natural that the Reagan economic programme during the election campaign included few basic elements:

(1) Tax cuts for both personal income and corporate taxes.
(2) Reducing the government role in the economic activity.
(3) Realizing a balanced budget by 1983.

It is revealing to notice here that budget balancing comes late in priority after tax cuts and public spending reduction. Republican tradition would have suggested first priority to a balanced budget. But the Reagan programme does not fit a traditional Republican one; it is a blue-print for a new society. Thus even a temporary increasing budget deficit is not really the issue. The deficit itself is no more than a sign of looseness. In the US the current budget deficit is no more than two to three per cent of the national income, while in Japan the current deficit is above six per cent of its national income. Germany's budget current deficit is about two per cent of its national income. Yet both Japan and Germany, in spite of the difference in the size of their budget deficit have had lower inflation than the US. Friedman seems to be persuaded that tax cuts are good under almost any circumstances, even if accompanied, by a temporary deficit. 'If the tax cut threatens higher deficits,' asserts Friedman, 'the political appeal of balancing the budget is harnessed to reducing government spending rather than to raising taxes.' This is the path that President Reagan proposes to follow.

III

Having surveyed the evolution of the American economic policy and the present state of mind of the new administration, we can proceed to have a closer look at the figures of the Reagan Programme. It is very important, however, to keep always in mind the fact that Reagan's economic policy is based as much on facts as on faith. The Treasury Secretary Mr Regan almost shocked the Joint Economic Committee of the Congress when he informed them that 'the economic assumptions and forecasts built into the recovery plan were not based on a model but a subjective view of the administration's economists'. The members of the Joint Committee seemed disturbed by that relevation. In fact, they should not have been. The Reagan programme in an act of vision where there is a great deal of faith as well as facts and figures.

The Reagan programme is a complete package of tax cuts and government spending reductions. The programme, if enacted by the Congress, would have its impact on the fiscal year beginning next October.

The document forecasts a real growth rate for the economy of 4.2 per cent in 1982 and a sharp reduction in inflation to 8.3 per cent in 1983 and 5.5 per cent in 1984. The budget would be balanced by 1984. Specifically the programme calls for:

(1) A $44.2 billion cut in personal and business taxes to take effect, Congress willing, on July 1 this year. This would produce a $6 billion tax cut in the present year. This would include personal income cuts of 10 per cent per annum over the next three years, thus bringing tax-rate scale of 14.70 per cent down to 10.50 per cent by 1984. Also is included the accelerated business depreciation allowance. The new system would allow most capital equipment to be written off in a maximum of 10 years.

(2) An as yet largely unspecified schedule of relief from government regulation.

(3) Cuts in the rate of growth of federal spending by removing $41.1 bn off the budget proposed by President Carter for the fiscal year 1982.

(4) An increase of $7.2 bn in defence spending.

The deficit in the fiscal year 1982 will come on top of an estimated $42.5 billion, about $6 billion more than President Carter's deficit. Later figures suggest a still higher deficit.

The proposed reduction in public spending was a compromise between the demands of the right-wing conservatives and the partisans of liberal thought, thought with a definite bent to the right. The Roosevelt New Deal programme was left intact. Proposed reductions in public spending were concentrated on the more recent and more unpopular government growth. Spending on what was called the 'truly needy' (including old-age pensions, veterans' pay, basic unemployment benefits and similar social services) will continue to be financed on the present lines.

Obviously the first obstacle facing the Reagan programme is to have it enacted by Congress. The administration prefers to have the programme discussed in the Congress as a package. The Democratic members in the Congress maintain a different view of the subject. The

Democrats still have majority in the House of Representatives. However, the probability is high to have the Reagan programme by and large accepted by Congress.[2]

Another problem facing the implementation of the programme, even if the Congress passes it, is the coordination between the 'Fed' and the Administration. Theoretically, the 'Fed' is independent of the President, but in fact, the President is not altogether incapable of influencing the 'Fed'.

The real challenge to the Reagan policy is that it is based on untested assumptions. Whether the supply will respond to incentives as hoped by Reagan advisers is a matter to be seen. Still very crucial is the patience to be accorded to the Reagan administration to provide results and its determination to persist in their conviction. The supply siders' economics is by definition longer-term policy. The immediate impact of tax cuts would eventually be increasing rather than decreasing inflation. Mrs Thatcher — the iron lady — proved to be determined to pursue her policy in spite of the increasing malaise in the employment sector. Whether Reagan will be as tough as Mrs Thatcher, remains to be seen. Finally there is the question of expectation. It was held that among other things, expectations helped to increase inflation. Will President Reagan inspire a more stable economy? Another question mark! The credibility of the programme is a condition for its success.

Notes

1. Paper originally prepared as an IBK News Letter, March 1981 and reproduced in *Finance and Industry*, no. 2 (1981), Industrial Bank of Kuwait.

2. The Congress has approved President Reagan's Tax Cut Program, 30 July 1981, with 25 per cent tax cut over three years starting October 1981.

PART TWO:
ARAB GULF PROBLEMS

4 THE PREDICAMENT OF THE ARAB GULF OIL STATES: INDIVIDUAL GAINS AND COLLECTIVE LOSSES*

Introduction

It is no longer a matter for debate that the international economic order, inherited from the Second World War, is becoming more and more obsolete. The issue to be considered here is the extent to which the new order can be related to an emerging new Arab order.

The increase in oil prices in the wake of the war of October 1973 was acclaimed by most of the Third World as a turning point in international economic relations, and this has even been seen as the first major change undertaken by small countries since the age of Vasco da Gama.[1] Indeed, the Organization of Oil-Exporting Countries (OPEC) — a group of mostly small countries — has successfully imposed on the industrial West a redistribution of world income to the benefit of its members. Thus it is not surprising that in the minds of many developing countries a new era has started and the long-ignored 'have not' nations have at last found a place in the sun. To some extent this view has also been shared by OPEC countries; the seventh Special Session of the United Nations General Assembly was, in fact, convened on the initiative of the late President Boumedienne of Algeria to discuss the establishment of a new international economic order.

Now, only a few years after what is probably 'the largest shock per unit of time that the world economy has ever seen',[2] observers in the Third World and elsewhere are less exuberant, and euphoria has given way to a more sober assessment. The OPEC countries too, no less than the others, have discovered that behind a treacherously simple façade, reality is far more complex and involved. Almost everyone but OPEC has been studying the new situation thoroughly. Members of the Organization for Economic Cooperation and Development (OECD) were particularly interested in recycling oil funds with minimum disruption of economic activity and short of reversing the trend of oil price increases.[3] The Third World was — still is — preoccupied

* A slightly modified version of a chapter included in *Rich and Poor States in the Middle East*, (ed.) M. Kerr, S. Yassin, Westview Press, 1982.

with the increased external debt. OPEC countries alone seemed to be quite content with their action on prices, as if other problems were not their business or else could be settled in a matter-of-fact fashion. Later experience showed that the investing of oil funds is anything but a matter-of-fact business; what appears to be conventional common sense may turn out to be utter nonsense. Things are by no means clear.

My intention in this chapter is to discuss the problem of the investment of oil funds from the perspective of OPEC's self-interest. An explicit formulation of the problem and of the underlying assumptions is, nevertheless, expedient in clarifying OPEC relationships with developed and developing countries.

The Problem

As a first approximation OPEC surplus countries face two problems in their relations with the rest of the world; these may be called, respectively, the energy problem and the financial problem. Although they are intimately related, it is useful to look at them separately.

The level and the value of oil production are major policy issues facing OPEC countries. Financial considerations are no doubt prominent among those influencing the level of oil production. There are, however, other important factors − technical, political, economic, etc. − that affect OPEC countries in their production and price policies, and these include among others production-reserve ratios, availability of energy substitutes (actual and potential), domestic absorptive needs, world demand, and political stability in producing and consuming countries.

In the prevailing circumstances, given any realistic level of production, some OPEC countries will realize balance of payments surpluses. With small populations, very limited domestic absorption, large reserves and oil production capacity, some OPEC countries are unable to spend their oil earnings domestically with any degree of efficiency. The largest share of the oil revenues goes to four small countries in the Peninsula and the Gulf − Saudi Arabia, Kuwait, the United Arab Emirates (UAE) and Qatar − and also to Libya. These countries are 'far too small to absorb more than a fraction of the money pouring into their treasuries'[4] and will always have a financial problem, namely the proper use of their financial surpluses.

My analysis will be confined to this financial problem, assuming that the energy problem has been settled one way or the other. This is, by and large, a problem for the Arab Gulf states. In the following discussion I shall use 'OPEC surplus countries' and 'Arab Gulf states' interchangeably.

It has been suggested that economic analysis would gain increased insight, once the emphasis is laid on the assets as the central analytical concept.[5] This is more so in the case of the oil producing countries. What is usually referred to as the huge income of OPEC is a misnomer. From OPEC's viewpoint there is no income earned; there is only an exchange of assets. OPEC countries are, in fact, transforming their real asset (oil) into foreign exchange. Broadly speaking, assets are of two types. First we have the real or tangible assets which consist of producers' and consumers' goods of all kinds. Secondly there are the financial assets, which are certificates, ownership shares, and promises to pay.[6] Since every financial asset creates liabilities of equal value, it is the real assets which are the ultimate wealth. Financial assets are in fact nothing but claims on the real assets. The value of any financial asset resides, in the final analysis, in its ability to be converted into a real asset. Financial assets then are deferred real assets.

From the foregoing it is easy to define a guiding principle for the asset management of the Gulf states. These countries should follow a conservation policy, understood in the larger sense, for their various assets. Applying this to the management of the financial problem, the criterion for the foreign investment of the Arab Gulf states should, then, be the maintenance of, if not the increase in, the value of their financial assets. This can be done only if the financial assets maintain their value in terms of real assets; that is, if financial assets are hedged somehow against inflation. From the economic point of view, what matters is not the accumulation of financial assets *per se*, but the implicit deferred transfer of real assets involved. This is a problem similar to the one known to students of international economics as the 'transfer problem'.[7]

We can now define the 'self-interest' of the Arab Gulf states in the context of the financial problem. It is ultimately to sustain the long-run economic viability of these states, given the transient nature of the oil. This can be accomplished by preserving for the future the value of the accumulated financial assets in terms of real assets. To define any country's self-interest by one objective is oversimplified, if not simplistic. None the less I think that the relevance of this narrow definition remains quite valid. In spite of the fabulous affluence observed in certain circles in the Gulf states, everyone, without exception, is haunted by the fear of the post-oil era. The viability of these states after the oil is perhaps the most legitimate and pervasive concern of the population in the area. The 'defective telescopic faculty' defined by Pigou is probably reversed in the Gulf area. Under the tranquil surface there is a panic for survival.

Having defined the scope of the problem (that is, the financial problem of the Arab Gulf states), and the criterion for their self-interest (that is, the maintenance of the real value of the financial assets), we now need to identify the possible options available to them in relation to this problem.

I shall not investigate every possible alternative. Rather, I shall limit myself to a high level of aggregation, namely the option between investing oil funds in developed or in developing countries. In real life things are never presented in this simplistic manner of either/or, but there exist many possible combinations. Also there are practical limits, at least in the short run, which make this option academic rather than real. Less developed countries (LDCs) are simply not prepared, in the short run, to absorb the totality of the oil funds. Much ink has been poured into the pinpointing of various bottlenecks in developing countries. Many bottlenecks, real as they are, could be alleviated in the medium term – as I shall explain later – with proper development effort. They are no more than 'quasi-bottlenecks'.[8]

OPEC has, of course, many political, cultural and moral affinities with developing countries. If OPEC countries were isolated politically from the developing countries, they would be extremely vulnerable in a world composed predominantly of oil importing countries.[9] My purpose in this study is, however, to see if there is also an economic case for OPEC solidarity with the LDCs. It is not only from an enlightened moral concern, but also from an enlightened self-interest that I approach the problem. The quest for a new international economic order is intimately related to the consolidation of the new oil order.

The Magnitude of the Problem

In a subject such as the new Arab wealth, loaded with political emotions and involving the mass media, nothing is easier than exaggeration. A proper assessment of the real impact of oil funds has a direct bearing on the method of analysis. In fact the validity of the whole macro-analysis is based on the premise that some variables are significant in affecting the behaviour of the economy; that is, it is based on the faith that there exist few strategic variables that cannot be dealt with by the traditional marginalist method. The absolute value of any economic aggregate has no meaning *per se*. It is only through comparison with other relevant aggregates that we can form an idea of its significance. The choice of comparison-aggregates is not an arbitrary act.

There are two concepts of oil funds which need to be kept separated in our minds: a 'stock' concept and a 'flow' concept. Both are important and they are, moreover, interdependent, since the 'stock' concept is nothing other than the cumulative value of previous 'flows'. It is always useful, however, to keep the two concepts distinct for the purpose of proper analysis.

Two major increases in oil prices took place after a remarkable stability in the oil market. From its price of $1.2 at the beginning of the century, the oil price rose to about $1.6 a barrel in the late 1960s. The Tehran Agreement in September 1970 paved the way for oil price changes. The first round of major increases began, in fact, with the October 1973 war. Since the quadrupling in 1973-74, oil prices remained relatively stable up to 1978. A second round of price increases was triggered off by the Iranian revolution. Oil prices increased in a series of steps throughout 1979, roughly doubling by December 1979.

Oil funds have been compared with the accumulated financial capital in the United States. 'The total financial capital of the Arab oil countries at that time [1980] should thus be about 3-4 percent of that of the United States'.[10] And accordingly, 'the Arab oil funds will be large, but the United States is financially larger'.[11] That the Arab oil funds are only a negligible fraction of the financial assets of the United States, much less of the total tangible wealth, is a fact that no one, I think, would dare to challenge. After all, this is a comparison between a 'stock' accumulated over two centuries with another 'stock' piled up in less than a decade. The Arab oil producing countries are in fact extremely poor in their resource endowment, except for oil, and even this is only for the time being. It could never be claimed that the Arab wealth could compare in a meaningful sense with the wealth of any OECD country, let alone that of the United States. The comparison is nevertheless useful for other purposes. It refutes all allegations of an eventual risk of Arab money controlling the host OECD countries. In this respect, three to four per cent is really insignificant even if we do not take into account the lack of Arab know-how to make such control effective.

But to conclude from the foregoing that oil funds are only marginal to the functioning of the world economy is equally misleading. The functioning of the economy depends to a large extent on flow aggregates. It is much to the point here to compare oil funds with the major annual flows. Although Bent Hansen, for example, concedes that the gross private savings in the United States were 'about $250 billion in 1974' and oil surplus funds in the same year 'about $60 billion', he concludes that such a 'comparison with annual flows also dwarfs the oil-fund accumulation'.[12] This is almost one quarter of the savings of the biggest economy in the world. A change of this order in American savings cannot leave either the American economy or the world economy unaffected. In fact world economic stability would suffer from much smaller changes.

Oil surplus funds are additions to world savings in the form of foreign financial assets, a fact about which I shall have much to say later. But for the time being, this is sufficient to suggest a comparison with aggregate flows like savings (or investment) and exports. Being an addition to world savings it is natural to compare these oil funds with savings (or investment) aggregates in major countries. But they are savings of a particular form; that is, they are foreign financial assets. Therefore they should be transformed in the future, through exports, into real assets. Thus investment and exports are appropriate aggregates for comparison. Table 4.1 shows American exports and private investment during the seventies.

Table 4.1: United States Exports and Private Investment during the 1970s (in $ billion)

Year	1970	1971	1972	1973	1974	1975	1976	1977	1978	1979
Exports	53.9	56.0	62.5	87.5	113.0	129.0	141.7	150.6	175.9	214.3
Private Gross Fixed Capital Formation	137.0	156.3	178.8	202.1	205.7	201.6	233.0	281.3	329.1	369.0

Source: International Monetary Fund (IMF), *International Financial Statistics*, December 1977; April 1980.

The choice of American aggregates for comparison is based not only on the fact that the United States is the leading economy in the world, but also because there existed strong reasons to believe that it might become 'the major intermediary in the process of investing the Arab oil funds',[13] an assumption confirmed to a great extent by subsequent experience.[14]

In 1974 the annual flow of oil surplus funds (some $60 billion) represented more than 50 per cent of American exports and Arab funds alone represented more than 40 per cent. The oil funds were some 30 per cent of American private investment in the same year. These are not small quantities. Any change of such magnitude is bound to have a substantial effect on the world economy. It is true that the oil surplus funds tended to decrease in subsequent years from their peak of $60 to $65 billion in 1974, and their downward trend continued to some $5 billion in 1978. With the Iranian revolution and the subsequent oil price increases in 1979, a second round of the oil shock took place, with oil surpluses boosted to about $45 to $50 billion in 1979 and projected surpluses of $110 to $120 billion for 1980.[15]

The continuous decrease in oil surplus funds in the first round (1974 to 1978) was in fact the result of economic forces that were caused, at least partly, by policies of oil fund investment. Without a different strategy for oil fund investment for this second round, inaugurated in 1979, there is no reason why the final outcome should be any different from that of the previous round.

The following analysis of the world economy will be undertaken in a macro-framework inspired by the Keynesian model. The differences are, however, quite substantial. First, the savings function used here differs from the Keynesian function in that savings are a function of the distribution of income and the level of income. The effect of the redistribution of world income is, in fact, paramount in the case of oil price increases. Secondly, the analysis of the adjustment mechanism will make wider use of the interaction stock/flow concepts – i.e., financial assets and investment and savings flows. Thirdly, though the world economy taken as a whole is no more than a closed economy, international relations none the less complicate the picture. In particular, the surplus-deficit balance of payments' relationships bring to the forefront equilibrating forces in a manner different from that known in a closed national economy.

The analysis in this chapter will be mainly confined to the first round extending between 1974 and 1978; a period long enough for economic forces to work out the necessary adjustment to the new situation.

In the following pages I propose to study the basic option of oil fund investment in developed or in less developed countries in two stages. To begin with I shall depart briefly from major constraints to make an economic case for investing these funds in the LDCs. Following a method cherished by most economists, that of 'partial analysis', I assume other things to be equal and take it, in the first part, that the long-run economic interests of oil surplus countries are paramount. This will help us fix our ideas. It is much easier to proceed by successive approximations. In the second stage I can relax this single-minded approach by introducing more realism. This part will consist of a discussion of major social and political constraints on the optimization of the problem facing the Arab Gulf states.

An Economic Case: Investment in the Less Developed Countries (LDCs)

The Conventional Wisdom

Accumulating financial assets for a limited period, no matter how long, while being terribly lacking in other resources and know-how, suggests that the Arab surplus states have essentially to be conservative investors. This seems to be the only rational investment policy and the least troublesome. What is needed is simply to maintain the *status quo* with the minimum possible disruption to the system. This is the conventional wisdom.

OPEC and OECD Complementarity. On the face of it, OECD countries seem to offer OPEC surplus countries a wide spectrum of advantages that LDCs are unable to match. The complementarity of OPEC and OECD countries has in fact been pointed out by several authors[16] and various levels of complementarity have been distinguished.

> There is a mutual dependence based upon oil trade: the two sides now represent respectively more than 90% of all imports and exports . . . There is a mutual dependence based on trade outside of oil: the OECD countries are the major suppliers of food, consumer goods, capital goods, arms and modern technology, and the OPEC countries provide important export markets for OECD countries . . . There is a mutual financial dependence; the OECD countries are dependent on the recycling of OPEC financial surpluses and several of the most important OPEC countries have increasing financial interests in OECD countries . . . There is a mutual political dependence created by the situation in the Middle East.[17]

The implications of this approach are clear. OPEC countries gain enormous economic benefits by investing their surplus funds in OECD countries as opportunities there for investment are greater, technology is available, credit-worthiness is much higher and more secure, and markets are highly organized. The situation in the LDCs is almost the opposite. The various inadequacies of the economies of the LDCs are too well-known to need any further elaboration. It is, then, only fair to say 'that any large scale recycling scheme . . . to less developed countries soon would be faced with demands for lower interest rates, moratoria and so forth that would challenge the very principle on which all these schemes are based, i.e., loans at commercial rates.'[18]

There is of course no denying the great and badly needed political leverage that OPEC countries can obtain from investment in the LDCs. However, this political advantage should be weighed against the economic advantage that OPEC countries obtain from their investment in OECD countries. The trade-off between these considerations would in all probability indicate some mix of oil fund investment in both OECD and LDCs with the OECD getting the oil funds primarily for economic reasons, the LDCs for political reasons.

In broad lines, this is the commonsense reasoning and, to a great extent, it represents the dominant attitude to the financial problem in OPEC surplus countries. Of course, there is a general recognition of the need for greater efforts for development in the LDCs. But it is recognized also that the development of LDCs is a very long, hazardous process. It is a task that OPEC cannot handle, and the safest investment opportunities remain in the OECD countries. In other words, sound investments for OPEC countries are somewhat different from development aid for the LDCs. Aid for development is a meritorious undertaking and there has been genuine aid-giving by OPEC countries to LDCs. But as a senior American government official has remarked, OPEC's attitude towards developmental investments in the LDCs is seen by them

in a somewhat different category than their investment funds. They see [it as] a contribution to the development process, to political stability in their part of the world — and I am referring to Arab countries — in that light [sic], rather than as part of their funds on which they are going to have to draw in the late 1970s and 1980s, as they develop.[19]

The rationale behind this conventional wisdom rests with the implicit famous assumption of *ceteris paribus*. In particular it is assumed that oil funds cannot change the economic situation; that they are mere additions to the world economy and make no qualitative change. Hence OPEC surplus countries face pre-established options to choose from, and these options themselves are independent of the pattern of investment given to these oil funds. In other words, the conventional wisdom deals with OPEC financial problems in a marginalistic fashion, in the same way as an individual behaves under perfect conditions: a 'price taker' rather than a 'price maker'. The irony of the situation is that while OPEC countries have understood the limits of 'price taker' behaviour in the area of oil pricing they have been led — or rather misled — by the same price taker behaviour in the financial arena. What makes a great deal of sense from the viewpoint of an individual engaged in prudent financial management may prove to be extremely harmful in the aggregate. This has a name in logic: the 'fallacy of composition'. I shall discuss at greater length the conflict of common and private interests in the second part of this study.

To enforce the argument let us pursue this kind of calculus to see how far it can lead us astray. It was the fashion among economists in the aftermath of the oil shock in 1974 to come up with projections for future oil funds. More often than not these were based on the assumption of 'other things being equal'. It was an exercise in futility, a fallacy of arithmetics. Financial institutions and professional economists in the West — the World Bank, United Nations agencies, the OECD, banks, governmental offices, investment companies, etc. — came up with their projections for future oil funds and their recommended policy in this regard.[20] The degree of sophistication varies from one study to another but all were more or less based on the assumption that everything could be handled by the partial analysis of supply and demand. The underlying world economic structure, it was assumed, remained basically the same.

The Fallacy of Arithmetics. Without the hindsight of later developments, let us imagine the process that OPEC surplus countries would follow in trying to work out their own projection with the benefit of the conventional wisdom.

We are in 1975. The OPEC countries, particularly in the Gulf area, have realized unprecedented financial surpluses. Aware of the seriousness of the problem, let us imagine that the governments of these countries have asked a 'dummy' group of experts to work out a probable scenario for their future financial surpluses. Being good economists, well trained in the profession, our distinguished imaginary team would, in all probability, start by making the obvious — though unrealistic — assumption of 'other things being equal', in particular by conducting the whole exercise in real terms, in 1974 prices.[21] The inflation factor could be introduced later, and the necessary adjustments would be easy to calculate. Thus, the team has cleared its conscience. After making this devastating assumption, our team would proceed confidently to make reasonable assumptions about the relevant variables to our problem. The techniques used for the projection could be quite sophisticated, such as the use of various elasticities and regression analysis in econometric micro-models, or crude and simple methods.

The results alter very little with the refinement of techniques used; it is the reasonableness of the assumptions that matters.

The purpose of the whole exercise is to show the futility of the conclusion no matter what reasonable assumptions are made, once inflation is eliminated. This is similar to demonstrations known to mathematicians as *reductio ad absurdum*. In these circumstances it is no use refining too much the technique of projection once the fundamentals are inadequate. I shall assume that the team uses very simple methods, and we shall now see what 'reasonable' assumptions could be made:

Accumulation of financial assets. In 1973 oil surpluses amounted to some $5 billion. In 1974 they were $60 billion. At the beginning of 1975, what would be the reasonable assumptions about the yearly addition to financial assets? It might look reasonable *at the time* to assume that OPEC countries would be able to add annually some $40 billion to their financial assets.[22] As a matter of fact, in retrospect, the OPEC countries realized in the following two years surpluses ranging between $35 and $45 billion, in spite of the tremendous increase in public spending and the magnitude of their aid to the Third World.

The OPEC surpluses are the difference between total receipts and total expenditures. Many factors affect the development of receipts and expenditures. Receipts are primarily determined by oil prices and production levels. More refined methods would work out different cases for demand elasticities for oil in consuming countries. However, increased refinement is not always synonymous with increased realism. Given the structure of the oil market (a seller's market for OPEC) and the tendency for exhaustible resource prices to increase over time[23] it is not altogether unreasonable to assume that the OPEC receipts will continue to increase. On the expenditure side, it is important to note that a large part of investment expenditure in the Gulf area was made in large infrastructure projects which, in most cases, are expensive import-intensive and — at least in the medium term — once-for-all projects. Thus it is not inconceivable that domestic expenditure would, after the initial increase, tend to stabilize at a lower level.[24]

With these considerations in mind the figure of $40 billion as an annual average financial surplus would seem easily justifiable. To assume constant equal annual financial surpluses is no doubt unrealistic; however, for the sake of the simplicity of exposition let us assume that this is a reasonably approximate average.

The time horizon for financial surpluses. To estimate the life cycle of oil is a difficult task. Available estimates for the Gulf states vary from 30 to 100 years. Let us assume that our team would take the conservative estimate of 15 years. It is absurd to think that output would continue steadily on the same level during the whole period and then stop suddenly. But since it is more likely that oil will still be flowing after 1990, it is simple to limit the time horizon to 1990 with constant output to that date. So it is assumed that oil will be forthcoming during the whole period to end completely by 1990.

Investing oil funds in OECD countries. Following the conventional wisdom, our team would recommend that, as conservative investors, OPEC countries should place their financial assets in secure investment opportunities in the Western industrial countries and preferably in the United States. It is maintained that the American financial market is a huge one and that the oil funds can accordingly 'be accommodated completely in the American financial system without serious upheavals.'[25] Later experience, in fact, confirmed this assumption, with the OPEC surplus countries – particularly the Saudis – showing a striking preference for the American market.[26] Hence it is perfectly in order to emphasize the American market.

Since OPEC investments in the United States, or more generally in OECD countries, are motivated by the vast investment opportunities available it is natural that our team would expect to realize a handsome return on these investments, which we can assume would be at around 6 per cent.

Repatriation of the OPEC yields after 1990. As rentiers, OPEC countries are accumulating financial wealth to draw upon when the oil runs out.[27] Since our hypothetical team has set 15 years for financial surplus accumulation let us assume that OPEC surplus countries will start to consume eight per cent annually of their accumulated wealth; that is, they will be living on their yields rather than eating up their capital. This means that these countries would become rentier economies, living on the fruits of their past accumulation.

These are the assumptions of the imaginary scenario undertaken by a dummy group of experts in 1975. On these assumptions, OPEC countries would be accumulating some $1140 billion in 1990. This is a huge amount of money. But such a reputable institution as the World Bank in one of its estimates advanced the figure of $1206 billion for 1985, not for 1990.[28] The figure of $500 billion was very much quoted in the wake of oil price increases for 1980[29] and it is not very much out of tune to expect it to have doubled in a decade.

The transfer of only a reasonable annual yield on this accumulated wealth (eight per cent) would amount to something like $91 billion annually in the early nineties. This is a kind of debt service of which host countries, particularly OECD countries, should assume the burden. With the assumption that American exports increase from 1974 onward by 6 per cent annually in real terms, this means that the debt service for OPEC financial wealth would represent the equivalent of 30 per cent of American exports in the early nineties. This is hardly an acceptable burden. A substantial reverse capital outflow to OPEC surplus countries should, then, take place precisely at the end of the oil era. The recipients of oil funds in the seventies and eighties would, beginning in the nineties, have to maintain a persistent surplus current account to service OPEC financial assets.

Fundamentally it is a country's overall level of savings relative to investment that determines its current account. Underlying the sustainability of current accounts surpluses is an assessment of the sustainability of the consumption patterns.[30] Servicing previously accumulated OPEC financial assets without increasing the future potential for savings would amount to a reduction of real consumption. This is supposed to take place after the cessation of oil flows from OPEC to oil importing countries. The higher the financial burden, the more difficult it is to enforce it. In fact, a going concern is the most effective guarantee for enforcing one's financial claims. If the oil consuming countries cannot decrease their real consumption to pay for the oil imports and add to their future wealth while the oil is still forthcoming, it will be extremely difficult for them to do so after the oil depletion. The future needs of the present oil surplus countries do not seem to offer sufficient motivation for the oil importing countries to reduce their real consumption in the future, precisely when there is no longer any going concern among them. The heavier the financial burden, the less likely that it will be honoured. Only through increasing the world's future propensity to save by adding to its wealth could OPEC financial assets be serviced without reduction of future consumption.

The moral of the imaginary exercise above does not lie in any particular figure or assumption. In fact there is ample room for changes in these assumptions. But even then the result will remain the same. What is wrong is the belief that oil funds are just more finance looking for investment. Investment opportunities are not given before and independently of the use of the oil funds; on the contrary, they depend on the way oil funds are used. Oil funds being major additions to world savings, it is only by analyzing the underlying forces of investment and consumption that we can draw any meaningful conclusions. The basic flaw in the preceding scenario is not with figures but with the mode of thinking. Oil funds are not simply arithmetics of quantities to be added, multiplied, compounded . . . and so forth. Oil funds represent a structural change in the world economy, and without analyzing this structural change, any attempt at understanding it is as doomed to absurdity as is our imaginary exercise.

The Dilemma of OPEC Savings

Increased World Propensity to Save. Sparsely populated and already enjoying high per capita income before the oil price increases in 1973-4, OPEC surplus countries have a very high propensity to save.[31] The oil price increase is, in fact, nothing more than a redistribution of world income in favour of OPEC countries, brought about by the changes in their terms of trade. This means an increase in the world propensity to save.[32] The fact that the increase in world savings is related to income redistribution is of paramount importance to the understanding of the new situation created by the oil price increases.

The standard practice in macro-analysis, following Keynes, is to relate savings to the level of income. It is maintained that savings are a function of the level of income. Many refinements to the savings/consumption function are available, such as introducing the permanent rather than the actual income,[33] or the relative alongside the absolute income, among independent variables.[34] Even the 'distribution of income' factor is used, but it is also affirmed that 'these distributional effects are commonly exaggerated by observers.'[35] In any case, these refinements are very often relegated to the background, and we are left again with savings and the level of income. A notable exception to this practice is to be found in the Cambridge School (England),[36] in whose models distribution of income has always played a prominent part. The Cambridge School is, however, concerned with long-run growth models:[37] the relationship of distribution of income (as between profits and wages) and the growth of the economy. In the OPEC case we are witnessing an immediate (and rather abrupt) change in income distribution with the result of an increase in savings without a corresponding increase in income (it actually declined). This would call for a new line of thought for the problem.

Savings-Investment Equality. I shall analyze the new situation by using the Keynesian technique of the identity of *ex post* savings and investment. Keynesian economics might be greeted now with more protest than acclaim. This is one thing, but the use of the specifically Keynesian apparatus of thought is another. It has in fact embraced the modern system of national income accounts, and has, accordingly, a general applicability.[38] Keynes himself used it to account for income (employment) changes (through the multiplier), while Kaldor, for example, accommodated it for a theory of income distribution in a growth model.

Whatever determines the *ex ante* savings and investment, there must be *ex post* equality between realized savings and investment. This is an accounting identity. In a closed economy there must be equality between realized savings and investment. International relations complicate the picture without altering any of its essentials. Taken as a whole, the world economy is nothing more than a closed economy.

It has been shown that oil funds add substantial flows to the world economy aggregates. They are, moreover, injected into the world economy and not confined within the political boundaries of their initial owners. It may therefore be best to deal with these funds through a macro-framework for the world economy as a whole. This macro-analysis gives a spurious air of neatness and simplicity to a real situation far more intricate and complex. It has, none the less, the merit of bringing to light the whole situation and allowing us to see the whole wood rather than just the single trees.

Possible Responses to Increased OPEC Savings. If the savings-investment equality must hold *ex post* in all cases, theories differ among themselves as to the way the economy would respond to an *ex ante* change in either of them. There is no doubt that OPEC countries have increased their savings after the oil price increases in 1973 and 1974. Yet every saving it matched, *ex post*, by a parallel investment. Three logical scenarios can then take place in the face of the OPEC savings increase:

(1) There could be a parallel increase in the rate of real investment in the world.
(2) There could be dis-savings elsewhere in the world to offset the increase in OPEC savings: i.e. no change in the net position of the world.
(3) There could be neither increase in real investment nor dis-savings, but only increase in financial assets, with real investment

remaining unchanged.

Let us call the first scenario 'the investment case', the second 'the distribution of wealth case' and the third 'the placement case'. These labels need little explanation – for this purpose we need only to understand the French term *placement*, as distinguished from 'investment'. By placement I mean the purchase of titles to debts or shares; that is, the purchase of financial assets. The term 'investment' can then be confined to the use of finance to add to capital goods.[39] Whereas investment adds to the productive capacity of the economy, placement adds only to the financial assets.

It is not necessary that only one of the above scenarios should take place as a result of OPEC's new savings. A combination of elements from different scenarios is always possible, and is even more likely to happen. It is useful, however, to analyze each case separately in order to emphasize the different outcome from each.

Scenario 1: The Investment Case. This is a very interesting case, since it represents the ideal outcome for OPEC countries and the world at large. It implies some temporary sacrifices during a transitional period for resource allocation. There will be a real response to the increase in the world propensity to save. The allocation of resources between consumption and investment will be shifted in favour of investment. Thus the immediate effect of the oil price increase would be a reduction in consumption equal to the increase in OPEC's savings. However, there is no reason why the decrease in consumption would be distributed equally among various countries. It is likely, though not necessarily so, that this would be distributed somewhat in relation to oil imports.

This is the true meaning of the assertion that oil price increases imply the transfer of real resources. The issue is not the transfer of real resources from oil importing countries to OPEC as is usually maintained:[40] rather it is the reallocation of resources from consumption to investment. What is important is not who foregoes resources and to whom they go; rather it is to what uses resources are allocated. It is natural, none the less, that the oil exporters would have substantial claims on the additional investment (in ownership and/or debt).

The reduction of real consumption in this case need not be permanent. With a higher rate of capital formation the world would grow richer, and previous consumption levels would accordingly be resumed and even surpassed in time. The world economy would move to a higher growth path.[41] The transition to this new path would inevitably imply some distortions in prices, employment, and so forth, before full adjustment could be accomplished. The important aspect about this case is not to visualize the final outcome but to identify the mechanism for bringing it about. Here we find that economists would differ in their appreciation of the economic forces capable of achieving this result.

Interest rates versus effective demand. The neo-classical versus neo-Keynesian debate is a longstanding one and it is easy to recognize its traces in almost every policy issue. In our specific problem the neo-classical could only be brought about by a change in relative capital price, the rate of interest. Economists nurtured in the Keynesian tradition would claim that only a change in effective demand could enhance the real investment.

Bent Hansen, otherwise a Keynesian, seems to think that the neo-classical mechanism would do the trick as regards problems of our kind. He argues that investing oil funds in OECD countries and in particular in the United States would, under reasonable assumptions, affect the credit market in such a way that it 'would generally tend to be easier. *Real investment* would tend to increase because the desired long-term real capital stocks tend to increase with *lower interest rates* [emphasis mine] ',[42] Thus the increase in world savings following the emergence of OPEC surpluses would mean that 'interests would fall just sufficiently to induce that amount of real investment'.[43]

This argument assumes that the rate of interest is not a monetary phenomenon dependent on the policies of monetary authorities. To put it differently, it is assumed that 'the monetary system operates in such wise as to interpret and not to distort the influence of real forces', that is 'the rate of interest depends on the demand for and supply of investable funds; behind the former stand the forces of productivity, behind the latter those of thrift'.[44] More serious is the implication in this approach that investment is a demand for capital, itself a productive factor employable in the economy according to its relative price as compared with the prices of other factors of production.[45] If one accepts this representation, the traditional thesis which assumes the dependence of investment on the rate of interest naturally follows.

The second approach, in a Keynesian vein, would portray investment as independent of the propensity to save. It is the effective demand, with all the structural ingredients that it embodies, that determines the investment function. A shift in effective demand towards more capital formation would be necessary to bring about an increase in real investment. Here it is worth emphasizing that underlying the apparent difference between the neo-classical and the neo-Keynesian approaches is a deeper policy recommendation. In the neo-classical approach no structural change is needed; financial markets with their ordinary instruments (interest rates) would be sufficient. Hence OECD countries with their highly organized financial markets would be the proper place to invest oil funds. Following the neo-Keynesian approach there is no guarantee that the market forces would bring about the necessary changes in effective demand. Hence, OECD countries by the simple fact that they have better financial markets are not necessarily the best market; LDCs with vast potential investment opportunities might be the answer to the required change in effective demand.

In any case, following this scenario, there would be a parallel increase in real investment to match the increase in OPEC savings. Real consumption has to be curtailed, at least in the early stages. Financial assets would in all probability increase proportionately to the increase in real investment. 'With real investments running at a higher level, a continued inflow of oil exporters' funds might thus take place without further increase in the price of financial assets.'[46] It is by no means necessary, according to this scenario, that general prices should increase if the curtailment of real consumption is brought about by appropriate policy measures. There might be one-time changes in prices to bring about the necessary reallocation of resources, but there would not be any inherent need for continuous price increases.

Scenario II: The Distribution of Wealth Case. In this case there will be no net change in the global situation; there will be only a redistribution of wealth. This scenario corresponds to a great extent to the general popular feeling in the wake of the oil price increases. The mass media at this time cried wolf, and exaggerated stories about an eventual Arab takeover of the Western economy made headlines. This was a time when one could read articles about how many years or months it would take Saudi Arabia to purchase General Motors or even all the Fortune 500 corporations. A minority share in Krupp purchased by Iran, a Kuwaiti purchase of some real estate in South Carolina, Libya's investment in Italy's Fiat, and similar transactions gave support to such fears.

In any case this scenario assumes that the increased wealth of OPEC countries will be accomplished by the impoverishment of the oil importing countries. The former will save more and the latter less; that is, the increased OPEC savings will be offset by the other's dis-savings.

The allocation of resources between investment and consumption will remain, by and large, unaffected; only the holders of claims on wealth will change. OPEC surplus countries will have more financial assets, the rest of the world less. But to assume that there would be no real change, and that only the holders of financial assets would alter, is an extreme simplification. Some alterations in industrial allocations are conceivable and even likely with the change in holders of assets. There is no reason to suppose that the latter would necessarily perpetuate the 'old' demand. However, the main feature of this case is that the overall allocation of resources between investment and consumption will remain unchanged regardless of the change within each of them. The world as a whole would be neither richer nor poorer; only the distribution of wealth would change.

If real consumption, savings and investment aggregates remain unchanged as suggested by this scenario, so would the volume of financial assets. There is no reason why the rate of flow of financial assets would increase in this case, neither is there any inherent reason why general prices should change. There is only a change in the holders of the financial assets.

Although the outcome of this scenario is simple to conceive, it is difficult to think of a mechanism that would bring it about. What is needed is a mechanism whereby oil importing countries would finance their oil deficit by handing over financial claims on their domestic wealth to oil surplus countries; that is, liquidating part of their wealth in favour of OPEC countries. A similar mechanism was at work in the fifties and sixties in the relationship between the American economy and the rest of the world. During most of that period the United States had a favourable trade balance, though the overall balance of payments was in deficit. The American dollar was — and still is — the principle international reserve currency: these two factors account for the ability of the United States to finance its major overseas investments — i.e. the transfer of wealth to the United States.

There are, however, at least two basic differences between this American example and the OPEC case. First, American foreign investments were carried out gradually over a long period, while the OPEC phenomenon is an abrupt one. A difficulty with the OPEC situation stems to a large extent from the suddenness of its appearance.[47] Had the increase in OPEC wealth taken place gradually over the last 25 years (at three per cent annually for example), the world accommodation to this transfer of wealth would have been smooth. Second, and more important, American foreign investments usually took the form of a technology-management-finance package, whereas the OPEC savings are pure finance without any element of technology. This accounts partly for the hostile reaction to OPEC finance in most host countries, particularly the OECD countries.

In view of these features of the new OPEC riches, it is hard to conceive of a situation where a substantial sellout of existing securities and/or of newly issued ones to OPEC countries could take place without creating a major disruption in financial markets and affecting the underlying confidence in it. This is a situation that most oil importing countries would resist. OPEC countries, for their part, would be extremely reluctant to accept it either. They have shown a great deal of discretion in these matters. Therefore we believe that this scenario is very unlikely to take place, not only because it is difficult to think of a smooth mechanism for bringing it about but particularly because all interested parties are opposed to it for various reasons. Thus the most publicized scenario for the aftermath of oil price increases is, in fact, the least likely to occur.

Scenario III: The Placement Case. In the previous two cases financial assets were introduced in the system only indirectly. The world economy adjusted to the new situation of increased propensity to save through changes in real aggregates; in the first case the increase in real investment, and in the second the redistribution of wealth. Financial assets followed the real adjustments. They increased proportionately to the increase in real investment in Scenario I, and remained constant — if in new hands — in Scenario II. The basic fact in these two scenarios is that there exists a direct relationship between real investment and the flow of financial assets, which remains constant in both.

The characteristic feature of the new scenario is that this relationship is broken. Financial assets would increase independently of real investment and would set the economy in motion. Financial assets are therefore introduced directly into the picture as a result of the increased OPEC savings, and other adjustments would follow. Thus in this scenario the reactions to OPEC savings are mainly financial rather than real. Here we assume that the overall allocation of resources between investment and consumption remains by and large unchanged after the oil price increases, and that there is no apparent dis-saving in other parts of the world following the OPEC savings increase.

This opens a new chain of reactions through the behaviour of financial assets. In the face of increases in the oil import bill and the emergence of a trade deficit on one hand, and the reluctance of all parties to transfer wealth to OPEC or to change consumption patterns on the other hand, the deficit countries would issue new financial assets. OPEC countries on the other side would be desirous of holding the new forms of wealth that were credit-worthy and did not create political animosity. Hence the supply of new financial assets would be matched by a new demand from OPEC to hold them.

Now everything seems in order. OPEC countries would increase their savings and hold a preferred form of wealth. The deficit countries would minimize the real transfer of resources (from consumption to investment, or from oil-consuming to OPEC) and finance their deficit by issuing new paper. But this cannot be the end of the story – there must be something missing. OPEC's savings seem to be increasing without a corresponding increase in investment or an off-setting by dissavings. This is impossible. What is left out is the behaviour of costs and prices in the new situation.

The increase of financial assets held by OPEC countries means a corresponding increase in the financial liabilities of deficit countries. If OPEC countries choose to increase their savings in the form of new financial assets this means that they intend to own them – i.e. to receive a reasonable return on them.[48] Since we assume that the real capital stock has not undergone any change with the issuance of new financial assets, capital is now owned (directly and indirectly, in equity and debt) by a wider class of owners. The new claimants on wealth are entitled to a nominal return on their assets equivalent to that of the 'old' owners of wealth. But one of the best-known lessons of monetary history is that any disturbance in economic activity leads to a crisis of confidence and to a rise rather than a fall in interest rates.[49] The banking system would be induced in all probability to generate the necessary increase in liquidity. With the oil price increase under the shadow of bombs and shells in the Middle East and the effects of the oil embargo, one is hardly dealing with a tranquil neo-classical world. Rates of interest are necessarily increasing. The new financial assets will produce the same nominal yields as the 'old' ones. That is, we are faced here with a downward stickiness of nominal returns on financial assets, a phenomenon not very different from Keynes' assumption of downward rigid money wages. It follows that the increase in financial assets (liabilities) and the stickiness of the nominal returns on them will lead to a corresponding increase in the absolute nominal earnings on property titles (loosely defined as the share of profit); a fact that cannot fail to affect the structural relationships of output distribution and factor earnings.

One could be tempted to argue that the increase in loanable funds with the issuance of new financial assets would tend to suppress the nominal return on them. No conclusion could, however, be reached without reference to the initial conditions from which the new situation emerged. Starting from a quasi-equilibrium position, the increase in the oil import bill gave rise to a higher demand for loanable funds. The process of the issuance of new financial assets started, then, from a situation of financial squeeze and not of excess liquidity. It is hardly conceivable, under these circumstances, for the nominal yields of the new financial assets to settle below the prevailing yields; eventually they would be higher. In order to be able to pay the same capital returns to the new owners, prices and costs must be pushed up. In other words, with increased financial liabilities, the capital cost for production is increased.

In fact empirical investigations have shown a remarkable historical constancy in the rate of profit, capital/output ratio and the share of profit in the Gross Domestic Product (GDP) of advanced industrial countries.[50] It follows that the nominal increase in the value of capital would lead to a corresponding increase in the nominal value of output. If it is assumed then, that the rate of profit and the capital/output ratio remain constant, the value of output must go up with every increase in capital cost. A general price increase movement is set in motion. Now prices are introduced into the picture. With the increase in OPEC savings in the form of new financial assets the capital cost would increase. A general movement of price increase would be triggered off and nominal investment would be increased. Hence, in reaction to the increase in OPEC's savings there would take place a nominal increase in investment and our sacred identity between savings and investment would be rescued.

Here we find that inflation is built into the scenario. It is necessary in order to bring about the equality of savings and investment. Failing to increase real investment or to effect parallel dis-savings leaves open only the possibility of increasing nominal investment. And inflation is part and parcel of the story; it is the villain of the drama, but without it there would be no drama at all.

This is a very different approach from the much-publicized allegation that oil price increases are responsible for world inflation. It is not the oil price increase *per se* that is responsible for inflation; rather it is a particular mode of investment of oil surpluses that gives rise to the price increase. It has been found that only 2.4 per cent of the increase in prices in the United States in 1974 could be explained by oil price increases. And this should be only a one time increase. Similar conclusions have been found for other OECD countries. In other words, ours is a macro-interpretation of inflation based on the need to increase nominal — short of real — investment to match OPEC increased savings. This is different from the micro-cost-push approach to inflation which attributes the increase in general prices to the increase in energy cost. The difference between the two approaches does not stop at the diagnosis but extends to the cure. If inflation were the villain it could be controlled according to the micro-approach simply by reducing oil prices, and according to the macro-approach by increasing investment in the world.

Before proceeding any further in developing this inflation argument a word of warning is necessary. It would be a great mistake to lose a sense of proportion in discussing inflation. This is a world problem to which various factors contribute. Since I am dealing here with oil funds and the mode of their investment, it is natural to focus on their impact on inflation. Their role should not be exaggerated, however; they are not the unique cause but are merely an aggravating factor. In most industrial countries inflation has deep-rooted causes in the social, political and economic situation. We will not discuss here the hanging sterling balances or bargains between the government and the trade unions in Britain, the unsettled political situation in Italy with its continuous strikes and the flight of capital, or the monetary acquiescence (or recklessness some would say) of the Federal Reserve Board in the United States, etc. This scenario simply says that among so many factors responsible for world inflation, the placing of oil funds to increase financial assets without a parallel increase in real investment could be inflationary.

Insufficient Investment and Inflation. What I am trying to convey in Scenario III seems to be at odds with established post-Keynesian economics. Official Keynesian doctrine maintains that an increase in *ex ante* savings over investment is deflationary rather than inflationary. On the contrary, Scenario III suggests that the increase in OPEC savings, if not matched by an increase in real investment, is inflationary when we might have expected it to be demand-deflationary.[52] This is a very serious point. However, I think that the clue to this apparent contradiction lies in the origins of OPEC savings, which are realized through income redistribution and forced to some extent on the system. I have alluded earlier to this fact: I will now make use of it.

Since there has not been any major change in the distribution of income in industrial countries over short periods, the official doctrine, though recognizing the importance of income distribution, would postulate savings as a function of the level of income. This is also, more or less, a stable relation. In a nutshell we may say that Keynesian economics maintain that investment – or more precisely the ratio of investment to output – is an independent variable, invariant with respect to changes in savings.[53] Since savings depend on the level of income, if investment were then to fall short of savings, income would have to decline to reduce savings. The equality of investment-savings is maintained. The decline in income (deflation) is necessary to undo the excess savings over investment. So far so good.

But if the increase in savings is the result of a redistribution of income and not of a rise in its level, a change in the level of income would not be absolutely necessary. By analogy, one would expect that if investment fell short of savings, a reverse distribution of income would take place and so reduce the excess savings. This could be done by means of a general increase in prices, the valuation of financial assets being the triggering mechanism in this process. This price increase would eventually start to erode the new savings and a new mechanism to reverse the income distribution is set up. In a comparable argument (a neo-Pasinetti theorem) Kaldor has shown that net savings depend not only on the propensity to save but also on the investment policy.[54] The revaluation of the financial assets will be instrumental in bringing about the identity of savings and investment.

From all this it seems easy to agree with the general conclusion of the Cambridge neo-Keynesian school that 'within certain limits, there is a redistribution of income at which the system produces the required amount of savings.'[55] An isolated policy of income distribution to increase OPEC savings is bound to fail if it is not accompanied by a proper investment policy.

Having emphasized the different sources of OPEC increased savings, it remains true that savings are also a function of the level of income. The traditional Keynesian diagnosis is not altogether inaccurate. The excess of savings over investment is also deflationary. The fact that OPEC's increased savings are due to income redistribution does not deny the dependence of the savings on the level of income also. The 'income distribution' variable supplements, but does not supplant, the 'level of income' variable. This in fact accounts for the ambivalent impact of OPEC increased savings which are mainly inflationary but also partly deflationary. Undoing OPEC excess savings would require a reverse action on the distribution of income but also a decline in the level of income. The inflationary effects of OPEC savings remain prominent in this scenario.

Different Scenarios and OPEC's Interests. Before proceeding any further it might be advisable to see to what extent the various outcomes of the scenarios outlined above correspond to OPEC interests. If we accept the definition of OPEC self-interest given earlier, it seems that from the OPEC point of view, Scenario I provides the best result. 'The investment case' would in fact ensure the maintenance of the real value of OPEC assets. The oil funds would contribute to the increase in the world investment rate; the world as a whole would get richer thanks to oil funds while the probability of converting OPEC's financial assets into real assets would be greater; and in the end everybody would be better off.

'The transfer of wealth case' has an intermediate position in this order. While the real value of OPEC's accumulated assets would be maintained in this scenario, the outcome would be politically dangerous. The transfer of wealth to OPEC is real, it is true, but the world as a whole is possibly poorer, not richer. What OPEC gained under these conditions would be a loss for the others: it is a zero-sum game. Moreover, risks of the convertibility in the future of OPEC financial assets into real assets would become greater in the post-oil period.

The worst case is in fact 'the placement case', since OPEC financial assets would be losing their real value continuously through inflation. The gains accrued to OPEC through oil price increases would be eroded by general price increases and a reverse income distribution would be set in motion.

The World Economy and OPEC's Savings. In the light of observations during the past few years, world economic developments seem to suggest that the third scenario is probably the best description of the actual situation. Data on worldwide real investment rates, general prices, financial asset flows and OPEC surpluses provide ample evidence that the world respond to OPEC savings best fits the placement case.

In the 1970s, after more than two decades of unprecedented growth, the world economy faced its most serious setback for some years. At that time the world plunged into its deepest recession for a quarter of a century, which started late in 1973 and reached its low point in the first half of 1975.[56] Economic activity picked up again late in 1975 but compared to past standards the recovery was mild and growth rates remained modest. Real investment did not show any marked increase following the increase of OPEC savings, but was on the contrary disappointingly slow. It became almost a ritual with the International Monetary Fund (IMF) in its annual reports to lament the low rate of fixed investments, particularly in OECD countries.[57]

Suffice it to read the IMF annual reports:

> . . . the further deceleration or decline in the volume of private investment during the latter part of 1974 and early 1975 was the most direct and obvious manifestation of monetary restraint . . . (1975)

> Real gross fixed investment (including residential construction) declined sharply in each of the past two years . . . (1976)

> A major factor in this outturn was the disappointing behaviour of private gross fixed investment which had been showing its customary cyclical lag behind the rise in general economic activity . . . the unusual behaviour of private investment must in general be attributed to investors' cautiousness in face of inflation and other economic or political uncertainties . . . (1977)

> In most of the industrial countries levels of private fixed investment during 1977 and the first half of 1978 were very low in a medium-term perspective (1978)

IMF reports are, by no means, a lonely voice; the same message is found in OECD, IBRD, BIS, GATT as well as in central banks' reports. The rate of real investment did not show any perceptible increase after the oil price increase; in most cases it rather slackened.

As it became a world problem, inflation captured public attention and made headline news. Two-digit inflation became universal and not just the prerogative of the Latin American economies. From less than seven per cent in 1973 — which was already high by the standards of the day — the rate of inflation averaged 13.5 per cent in the industrial countries in 1974[58] and if it dropped in the following year, it still remained at twice the annual average prevailing in the sixties.[59] There were, of course, great disparities in inflation rates among nations: the Swiss did best with an inflation rate of only two per cent (at the cost, however, of a low growth rate); the Germans scored second with about 3.5 per cent. In the United Kingdom the rate was 13.5 per cent in 1977 and in Italy 21 per cent in the same year.[60] The United States, long accustomed to price stability, had to accommodate itself to an annual rate of inflation of 13 to 15 per cent and higher rates were recorded in 1979/80.

It is worth noting the behaviour of interest rates here. In the face of the huge OPEC funds looking for placement opportunities, interest rates have risen substantially instead of going down as a neo-classical approach would expect. The United States, which was the major beneficiary of OPEC funds, set the pace for interest rate increases. In the spring of 1974 that country's rates rose to a record level, for that time, of eight per cent for the discount rate, 13.5 per cent for Federal funds, about 12.5 per cent for deposits, and around 13 per cent for the bankers' prime lending rate.[61] Prime rates of 19 per cent became quite common early in 1980. As for the share of profit in total income, available data seem to suggest that they have recently tended to increase too.[62]

Against the sluggish growth in GNP and the slackness of real investment, financial assets flows have increased enormously. The spectrum of financial assets is very broad indeed. They include the all-liquid money and quasi-money, less liquid securities, and still more illiquid claims and debts. It is sufficient here to refer to simple indicators for the increase in the world's financial assets: the Eurocurrency market and the indebtedness of countries. These are incidentally related directly to OPEC surplus funds and in both cases financial claims have been soaring following the increase in OPEC savings.

Statistics on the size of the Eurocurrency market differ greatly, depending on the different definitions retained. It is estimated that the gross size of this market had surpassed the $1 trillion mark sometime between June and September 1979;[63] since then the annual average growth has been about 22 per cent. It is ironic to reflect that when the IMF met in Nairobi in the autumn of 1973 it was widely believed that the Eurocurrencies would soon disappear,[64] while in fact the Euromarket was at the time preparing its giant forward step.

The increase in public foreign debt, particularly of the LDCs, has become one of the major concerns of international organizations such as the IMF, the International Bank for Reconstruction and Development (IBRD) and the United Nations Conference for Trade and Development (UNCTAD), and has reached such alarming proportions as to need no further comment. The total debt of the LDCs increased from less than $75 billion in 1970 to over $240 billion in 1977,[65] and was projected to reach some $300 billion in 1980. The LDCs' debt represented more than 27 per cent of their GNP in 1978.[66] Given the unequal concentration of this debt among LDCs, these percentages have reached critical thresholds in some countries.

If we look now into OPEC surpluses during the past few years we come to the same conclusion. From the high figure of $60 to $65 billion in 1974, OPEC's current account balance continued to decline steadily. OPEC's surplus in 1978 was estimated at $18 billion before official transfers and at only $5 billion after these transfers.[67] This continuous decline is not only the result of real import increase, but is indeed the result of the downward trend in the real oil price.[68] In fact the dramatic changes in world income distribution brought about by the oil price increases in 1974 have been reversed by a continuous deterioration in the terms of trade of the OPEC countries since then. They have lost almost a quarter of their oil purchasing power in the last five years as Table 4.2 shows.

Table 4.2: OPEC Terms of Trade (1974 = 100)

Year	Oil Prices	Import Prices	Terms of Trade
1970–1973	20.8	70.3	29.5
1974	100.0	100.0	100.0
1975	98.4	112.8	87.2
1976	105.7	114.6	92.2
1977	113.9	125.2	91.0
1978	116.6	144.0	81.0
$1979Q_1$	116.6	151.5	77.0

Source: *World Financial Markets*, December 1978.

From this evidence it seems that in spite of OPEC's new savings there has been no parallel increase in real investment nor in real dis-savings. The emergence of OPEC's savings increased the flow of financial assets, rates of interest went up, and a general increase in prices followed. Nominal investment increased with the general price increase and a reverse process of income distribution came into play. OPEC surpluses are continuously being eroded. This seems to be accepted as a foregone conclusion. Distinguished economists seemed to take it for granted that oil fund debts would continue to erode with inflation and that 'under current and prospective conditions, such debts will actually involve a transfer of real resources, properly measured, from the lenders to the borrowers',[69] that is, with actual and prospective inflation there would be a 'kind of subsidy on borrowing'. To continue the present mode of placing of oil funds is not in the long term interest of OPEC countries but against them, and this is in broad terms 'the placement case' referred to earlier.

The situation was partially corrected in 1979 with a second major price increase and the prospects for another wave of substantial surpluses are open again. However, without a different strategy for oil funds investment there is no reason why the final outcome of the next round should be different from the previous one.

Developed and Developing Countries. The emergence from among the possible outcomes of 'the placement case' is not fortuitous. Its realization is related to the way in which economic forces have acted on the oil funds and particularly to the way they have been used. Whether the oil funds are placed in developing or in developed countries is not irrelevant to the final outcome. By and large, oil surplus funds were, and still are, placed in OECD countries. Probably no more than 20 per cent of the total funds were allocated by OPEC to the LDCs, in which they are, in fact, following the conventional wisdom.

The accumulated surpluses of OPEC are not exactly known, but there seems to be general agreement that they stood at about $180 billion at the end of 1978.[70] Of this amount only $30 billion – which is not even 20 per cent – was allocated either directly or indirectly through the World Bank and other multilateral lending institutions by OPEC to the LDCs.[71] The rest of their surpluses were channelled to the OECD countries, and it is this mode of placing oil funds that to a great extent determined the actual outcome of OPEC savings. It must be emphasized that this outcome is not due to any deliberate policy on the part of the OECD countries to set economic forces in motion with the intention of eroding OPEC financial assets. Everyone is suffering from inflation. In fact the economic structure of the OECD forbade the increase of real investment in response to the increase in OPEC savings. Unless there is a shift in effective demand towards capital goods industries it will be impossible to increase the rate of investment. The inability of OECD countries to increase their real investment triggered off inflation in response to the increased savings funds of OPEC. This is a matter of structure rather than of policy.

The situation in the LDCs is diametrically opposite in this respect to that of OECD countries. The LDCs are capital-hungry; many investment projects in the LDCs are held back for lack of finance. This does not mean, of course, that development in the LDCs is dependent only on the availability of finance. It has been shown that development is a complex process involving institutional, cultural and political changes as well as economic ones; however, it remains true that possibilities of increasing real investment in the LDCs are enormous and require finance if they are to proceed. Of course increased investment in LDCs would inevitably lead to enhanced demand for the capital goods of OECD countries. Thus it is not unrealistic that, given enough time for adjustments, capital goods industries in OECD countries would expand under the expected new demand from the LDCs.

The Surplus-Deficit Game

No conclusion can, however, be drawn from the previous section before discussing the impact of the financial institutions on the recycling process. The basic function of the financial institutions is to act as financial intermediaries.[72] OPEC surpluses placed initially in the OECD financial markets could be — and in fact are — used to finance deficits of the LDCs, thus introducing a new complicating factor that requires separate consideration. The intermediary role of the financial institutions makes it difficult to identify who lends to whom. It may well be that funds first placed in OECD financial institutions are then re-channelled to other developing countries. OPEC oil funds would then be financing deficits of the LDCs, albeit in an indirect way.

If this is the case, then one can doubt the validity of the provisional conclusions reached in the previous section. It was argued that placing OPEC funds in developed rather than in less developed countries resulted in general price increases instead of increasing real investment in the world; or in our terminology, 'the placement case' instead of 'the investment case'. If it is proved that oil funds were after all channelled to the LDCs, the argument would, if it did not collapse, suffer seriously. Thus 'the placement case' would seem independent of whether oil funds are placed in developed or less developed countries, and this would restore the conventional wisdom. If inflation is inevitable anyway, it is better for OPEC countries to place their financial assets with the more credit-worthy OECD countries and their financial institutions and let the latter assume the risks of the LDCs.

This is a very serious criticism of the whole approach used in this study. Let us first look at the facts.

Increasing Deficits of the LDCs. It seems that before the oil shock in 1973-74 there existed a relatively constant structure of trade relations. The OECD countries as a group were realizing a favourable current account, non-oil developing countries incurred a comparable deficit, and OPEC countries had an almost balanced account with a slight surplus. In 1970, OPEC countries ran a small deficit in their current account and in 1973 they had a surplus of about $5 billion. The OECD countries' surplus averaged $10 billion in the five years preceding the oil price increase, and non-oil developing countries incurred a deficit of almost the same magnitude as the OECD's surplus.

This situation was suddenly disrupted in the aftermath of the oil price increases in 1973 and 1974. The OECD countries, being the major oil importers, shifted from a surplus position of about $9.5 billion in 1973 to a deficit on current account of $28 billion in 1974. The non-oil developing countries doubled their deficit from $10 billion in 1973 to $20 billion in 1974.[73] OPEC countries were of course the beneficiaries of this new situation, with their current surplus jumping to some $60 billion in 1974.

All these figures are subject to the familiar shortcomings: errors and omissions on one hand and different definitions of surplus and deficit on the other help to explain discrepancies between figures issued by different data sources. However, it remains important that these figures trace the direction of the development in the international current account.

The immediate effect on current account observed in world trade in 1973-74 was only the first step in a long process, and subsequently evolved to a new structure. Less than five years after the initial oil price increase, OECD countries had readjusted their economies to the new situation in such a way that their combined current account reached a virtual balance in 1978.[74] The non-oil developing countries were the losers in this readjustment process. OECD countries still account for more than three quarters of world oil imports while maintaining an almost balanced account; the LDCs — without increasing their share in oil imports — ran a deficit on current account of $34 billion in 1978.[75]

In 1979 a new oil price shock not unlike that of 1973-74 occurred. After its virtual balance in 1978, the balance of payments of the OECD countries is expected to worsen. However, as with the first round, we cannot exclude the possibility that the same process will start again and that OECD countries will eventually redress their global balance of payments. It is therefore more revealing to focus our attention on the first round of oil price increases, as outlined in Table 4.3.

After the full adjustment of the first round of oil price increases, the new structure of the world's current accounts seemed to settle at a more or less balanced account for OECD countries, at a more manageable OPEC surplus and a corresponding deficit for the LDCs.[76] Under these conditions it was only natural that financial flows would be forthcoming to the LDCs and this in fact happened. It is estimated that during 1974 and 1975 commercial banks in OECD countries (either

Table 4.3: Shifts in Global Structure of Current Account Balance
($ billion)

| | 1967–72 Average | | 1977 |
	Actual current Account Balance	Rescaled to 1977 Prices and Output	
Major oil exporting countries	0.7	3	42
Industrial countries	10.2	30	—
Other non-oil countries			
more developed	−1.7	− 6	−12
less developed	−8.1	−27	−27
Total	1.1	—	3

Source: International Monetary Fund, *IMF Survey*, 16 May 1977.

mainland or offshore) financed about 45 per cent of the current deficit of the LDCs. Since 1975 the annual amount of the financing by the new banks to the LDCs has not fallen from its 1974-75 level.[77] Of OPEC's total net deposits of $30 billion in the international banking system in 1979, some $24 billion were rechannelled to the LDCs.[78]

It is clear then that OPEC surpluses are to a great extent used to offset the deficits of the LDCs and that OPEC funds initially placed in OECD's financial institutions are probably partly channelled to the LDCs. To what extent does this affect the argument about oil funds investment in developed or less developed countries?

The Economic System. In economics, no less than in other social sciences, it is difficult to distinguish between cause and effect. Relations between them are so interconnected with continuous feedbacks that it is not uncommon to confuse them. In the particular case of oil funds investment we need to keep two concepts about the economic system in mind. The first is that of process. Economic activity proceeds as a sequence of actions and reactions; every action calls for a specific set of economic forces out of which will emerge the final outcome. The second is that of a circuit; different parts or sectors are linked together through the interaction in the economy. This is the old *tableau économique*. Injecting OPEC oil funds into the world economy would necessarily call forth different economic forces and involve other parts of the world economy. The path of the economy would be different according to the economic forces involved, nor can it be indifferent to actions taken in the first place.

Scenario I ('the investment case') showed that injecting oil funds into the LDCs in the first place would enhance world demand for capital goods; this would bring about a reallocation of world resources between consumption and investment. The world would be moving along a new path with increased rates of real investment and an increase in the imports by the LDCs of capital goods would be involved, with the OECD countries being affected by oil funds indirectly through increasing capital goods trade with the LDCs. This is different from the path that would result from the initial placing of the oil funds with the OECD. Scenario III ('the placement case') showed that this would aggravate and fuel inflationary forces and pressures, with the increase in financial assets (liabilities) producing a corresponding increase in capital costs. The world would be moving along a different path with inflation *en route*. The LDCs would be affected by oil funds indirectly through imported inflation and deterioration of their current accounts, and oil funds would be rechannelled to the LDCs to finance their balance of payments deficit, not their increased investment.

It is then fair to conclude that the mere fact that oil funds are ultimately financing the LDCs does not affect our previous conclusions.

Surplus-Deficit Relations. It is always easy to overlook simple facts. The surplus-deficit situation is, after all, a zero-sum game. The surplus exists as far as the deficit is permitted to exist. This may seem a trivial fact but it is very important. OPEC surplus countries not only have a vital interest in preserving the value of their financial assets in the future, but they need also to maintain their surplus status for as long as they are unable to undertake productive domestic investment. The maintenance of the surplus status hinges upon the persistence of a corresponding deficit status. In a way, surplus and deficit countries are in the same boat.

We have seen that the initial OPEC surplus in 1974, as was to be expected, was matched with an OECD deficit. This situation could not last. Five years later, though still consuming more than three quarters of oil imports, the OECD had reached virtual current balance in 1978. The deficit of the LDCs continued to increase, in fact counterbalancing the OPEC surplus, a situation that seems to represent a new structure for world current account balances.The LDCs' deficit as a counterbalance to the OPEC surplus does not seem to be an ephemeral event but is there to stay. This is not a coincidence. It is the 'normal' outcome of economic forces ('normal' being understood in a positivistic sense), which would help bring this about.

Oil funds are not only an addition to world savings; they are also savings realized through a disequilibrium in the balance of payments. Economic forces related to disequilibria are very much in action here. Economic theory usually distinguishes between a stable and an unstable equilibrium. We need not go far to see whether or not the oil funds disequilibria are stable. It is important to keep in mind that not only can there never be a deficit without finance, but also that the ability of various economies for readjustment is different.

Broadly speaking, developed countries are in a better position than developing ones to correct any imbalances in their external accounts. In a classic article Hla Myint distinguished between two kinds of external vulnerability. The first stems from what he called 'the productivity theory of trade' where a country 'has adapted and reshaped its productive structure to meet the requirements of the export market through a genuine process of specialization'. The second is related to his theory of 'the vent for surplus' where a country 'happens to possess a sizeable surplus productive capacity which it cannot use for domestic production' and which implies 'an inelastic domestic demand for the exportable commodity and/or a considerable degree of international immobility and specificness of resources'.[79] In general developed countries exhibit the first kind of vulnerability, while the developing countries suffer from the second. The increased productivity in the first case and the high rigidity in the second explain, to a great extent, the ability of the OECD countries to adjust their external accounts in due course to the oil price shock, and the failure of the LDCs to cope with it.

In this readjustment effort, the OECD countries have greater flexibility in their relationships with other non-oil developing countries than they have with OPEC countries. Their ability to redress their external accounts with OPEC is very limited, while they maintain a tremendous economic superiority over other developing countries. The low price elasticity of the demand for oil, the limited absorptive capacity of key oil producing countries and the meagre prospects, at least in the short term, for substantially increased energy production outside OPEC, are all factors that account for the new narrow scope for the readjustment of OECD's external account with OPEC through changes in the quantities of commodities traded. Moreover, the use of foreign exchange alternations is almost denied to OECD countries in adjusting their relations with OPEC. National OPEC currencies are not in fact independent of major OECD currencies. In most cases, particularly in the Gulf area, they belong to the same currency area of major OECD importing countries. In this case the only available variable would be general price increases which normally hit more at other non-oil developing countries. This will be manifested in the increasing deterioration of the terms of trade of the non-oil LDCs. As the managing director of the IMF has noted:

> On a terms of trade basis, the cumulative loss incurred in the seven-year period 1973-79 was of the order of $80 billion. Although much stress has rightly been laid on the effect of oil price increases on the import bills of developing countries, it should be borne in mind that oil still accounts for only about one fifth of the current account deficit of the LDCs. Thus the current account deficits of LDCs have also been raised considerably by the general inflation in countries which export manufactures.[80]

It seems therefore, that given the actual world economic structure and the dominant economic status of the OECD, it is the LDCs that are bound, in the final analysis, to incur the counter deficit of the OPEC surplus. The acknowledgement of this fact is bound to be of the utmost importance to the OPEC investment policy. 'It is the poorest industrial countries and the LDCs which have had to carry the largest share of the importing countries' deficit.'[81]

The LDCs are, in fact, the ultimate debtors of OPEC's financial claims on the world economy and the real value of these claims cannot be separated from the credit-worthiness of the LDCs. OPEC countries have a definite economic interest in the prosperity of the LDCs who are the last resort guarantors for their claims. Financial institutions are so closely interwoven that any default or failure of substantial magnitude by the LDCs will undoubtedly affect OPEC financial assets. The financial institutions that receive the bulk of OPEC surplus funds are those which extend loans to the LDCs. Any disruption of the international financial market will set forth a chain reaction, similar to that known in political theory as the 'domino effect'. Indeed, OPEC countries have a direct stake in the economic health of the LDCs.

Moreover, it is likely that the OPEC countries will be called upon to assist the LDCs in case of any serious failure on their part to honour their obligations, since the world cannot afford a serious upheaval in international economic affairs. One of the possible reasons behind the so-called 'Witteveen facility' was the increase in the borrowing by some LDCs (e.g. Zaire) from the international capital market to an extent that could have affected some major international and American banks. The OPEC countries are of course *en tête* with countries contributing to this facility. Thus it is probably an illusion to think that OPEC's risks are reduced by the intermediate role played by the financial institutions in the OECD countries.

Socio-Political Constraints

Opening Remarks

The previous section of this chapter attempted to show that there exists an economic case for oil surplus countries to *invest* their oil funds in the LDCs rather than to *place* them in the developed countries. This conclusion was, however, reached according to certain assumptions. It was postulated that the long-run economic interests in preserving the real value of OPEC financial assets are paramount. Oil surplus countries were treated implicitly, moreover, as one homogenous block entertaining convergent and even coordinated objectives. This is only a device to fix ideas, a first step in an analysis by successive approximations. Further steps are needed to relax these simplifications by introducing more realism into the analysis.

Oil surplus countries are no more *Homo Economicus* than any other entity. The socio-political context of oil surplus countries, particularly in the Gulf area, is overwhelming and cannot be ignored. It is not possible to tackle the so-called financial problem dealt with earlier in terms of abstract economic analysis; there is no such thing as an 'economic rationality' — there is only rationality *tout court*.

It is my intention here to introduce other factors which affect the behaviour of the oil surplus countries. What looks like an aberration from economic rationality is perfectly justifiable, given the constraints on the oil surplus countries in the Gulf area. It should be noted here, however, that my treatment of these constraints cannot be comprehensive or complete since this would require a complete study of the political sociology of the Gulf, the international politics of oil and finance, and the problems of the absorptive capacity of the LDCs, a task beyond the scope of this work and, indeed, a forbidding area for research.

I shall limit myself to contraints within the oil surplus countries; that is, to those factors in the Gulf area which contribute to the divergence of the present investment policy from that advocated in the first part of this study. It follows that even if these constraints were removed, nothing would guarantee that oil funds would be invested in the LDCs. The international politics of oil and finance on one hand and the situation in the LDCs on the other may still hinder such a flow. It is important, nevertheless, to show that oil surplus countries are constrained from within and that the apparently economically irrational placing of oil funds is, in their own context, justifiable after all. Moreover, external factors, particularly the international politics of oil and finance, normally exert their influence through an internal mechanism. Internal factors themselves are partly the reflection of external factors.

Two sets of problems will be considered. The first concerns the particular situation *of* the oil Gulf states; the second, the situation *in* these states. The former corresponds to the morphology of these states as small, fragmented, mono-resource entities; the latter refers to the texture of the decision-making process within these countries. The one is more concerned with an outside view, the other with an inside view. However, these problems will not be treated equally. The socio-political factors affecting decision-making are so complex and intricate that only a bird's eye view can be attempted in the following section.

OPEC Financial Flows to the LDCs. Before considering these constraints we should first look at the magnitude of the oil surplus funds channelled from the Gulf area to finance the LDCs. It would be a grave mistake and an unfair conclusion to overlook or to underestimate the considerable contribution which they make. After 1973/74 OPEC members emerged as a major source of finance to be reckoned with. There is, however, considerable disparity among them in their effort to finance the LDCs. The Arab Gulf states — Saudi Arabia, Kuwait, the United Arab Emirates and Qatar — are obviously the major contributors.[82] Data on financial flows to developing countries leave much to be desired but UNCTAD and the OECD are among a number of international organizations which are currently involved in the collection of information on them.

A comparison between the Development Assistance Committee (DAC) countries and OPEC flows to the LDCs is subject to a number of reservations which bias the final picture against the contributions of the OPEC members;[83] for example, private transfers are not included in the OPEC flows, contrary to DAC flows; equity capital provided by DAC countries to investment in the LDCs is included in their Official Development Assistance (ODA) while the same is not applied to OPEC, and so on. However, regardless of these reservations, the record of OPEC and particularly the Arab Gulf states is by all standards impressive. After a fourfold increase from 1973 to 1974, total commitments of OPEC donors increased by another 22 per cent in 1975 to reach a figure in excess of $15 billion, corresponding to 7.5 per cent of the combined GNP of these countries. The volume of total disbursement from OPEC countries to other developing countries increased from about $1.6 billion in 1973 to about $11.5 billion and $9.2 billion in 1975 and 1976 respectively, corresponding to 5.6 per cent and 3.8 per cent of the donors' GNP.[84] It is reported, however, that aid from OPEC countries declined substantially in 1979. About $4.7 billion only were disbursed that year. Not only does this compare badly with the current account surplus of about $55 billion for that year but it also comprises the lowest percentage of OPEC's total GNP at any time since the 1973 oil price rise.[85]

Compared with DAC countries, the commitment of the ten OPEC donors amounted to 60 per cent of the estimated total of the DACs, although the GNP of the latter was almost 16 times the size of the former group.[86] Though it is believed that the total concessional net disbursements from OPEC countries in 1978 fell from the 1977 level of $5.9 billion to some $3.7 billion, the Gulf states (Saudi Arabia, Kuwait and the Emirates) continued to allocate a very high proportion of their GNP to these flows as compared with DAC countries.[87] The decline in concessional flows is largely due to the sharp decrease of bilateral flows from the Arab Gulf states to Egypt after the exceptionally high disbursement of the Gulf Organization for the Development of Egypt (GODE) in 1977. The net disbursement of ODA by major groups of donor countries is shown in Table 4.4.

Table 4.4: Overseas Development Aid Disbursement by Major Groups of Donor Countries

Donor group or Country	$ billion			Percentage of Total			Percentage of GNP		
	1973	1977	1978	1973	1977	1978	1973	1977	1978
DAC	9.7	14.7	19.9	78.3	68.7	81.5	0.30	0.31	0.35
OPEC	1.3	5.9	3.7	10.8	27.5	15.2	1.41	1.96	1.11
of which:									
Kuwait	0.3	1.4	0.9	2.5	6.6	3.7	5.7	10.1	4.5
Saudi Arabia	0.3	2.4	1.5	2.5	11.3	6.1	4.0	4.3	2.3
UAE	0.3	1.2	0.6	2.5	5.6	2.5	16.0	10.7	5.4
CPEa	1.3	0.8	0.8	10.8	3.7	3.2	0.09	0.04	0.04
Totalb	12.0	21.4	24.4	(100)	(100)	(100)	not applicable		

Notes: a. Centrally Planned Economies.
b. Excludes amounts provided by donors outside groups: $0.3 billion in 1978.
Source: OECD, *Review: Development Cooperation, 1979*, p. 85.

The non-concessional flows from OPEC members are channelled largely through multilateral institutions such as the World Bank and the

IMF. An emerging sector of bilateral non-concessional flows, dominated by Kuwait, is also gaining more ground in the relationship between oil surplus countries and the LDCs. In 1976 Kuwaiti non-concessional flows to the LDCs accounted for fully three quarters of all OPEC non-concessional flows, as compared with 64 per cent and 47 per cent in the two preceding years respectively. Kuwait's pre-eminence is explained by the existence of several publicly controlled investment companies willing and able to tap investment opportunities in the LDCs. The Kuwait Foreign Trading, Contracting and Investment Company (KFTCIC) is a case in point in this respect. Established in the early sixties with more than 80 per cent of public-held shares, KFTCIC is the Kuwaiti government's arm for commercial investment in the LDCs. The complementarity of KFTCIC with the Kuwait Fund for Arab Economic Development (KFAED) established in 1961 is unmistakeable; the KFAED is the main Kuwaiti instrument for aid to the LDCs.

Huge as they are, OPEC financial flows to the LDCs are only a fraction of the oil surpluses. By and large, oil surplus funds are placed in the developed countries, in spite of the spectacular increase in their financial flows to the LDCs. I intend next to deal with some factors in the Gulf oil states which are constraints on massive investment in the LDCs in general and in the Arab countries in particular.

Fragmentation and Marginality

It has been shown that the Arab Gulf oil countries have a common economic interest in investing their surpluses in the LDCs. This is not, however, the same thing as saying that *each* Gulf oil country has the same interest. There is a gap between the common and the individual interests that is not always easy to bridge. The theory of public or collective goods has helped dissipate some confusion in the matter. Moreover, though raised to world economic – or rather financial – prominence the Gulf oil states are too dependent on oil and in the long run are, after all, only peripheral economies. Fragmentation and marginality plague their investment policy and partly account for the divergence of actual oil funds placement from the otherwise collectively desirable pattern of investment.

Fragmentation of Oil Surplus Countries. We have perhaps been so much indoctrinated in recent years by the OPEC role in oil pricing that we have come to believe that OPEC really exists outside the oil pricing process. With all the fanfare that accompanies the ritual annual ministerial OPEC meetings for deciding the next round of oil price increases, nothing is easier than to lose sight of the basic facts. Outside oil pricing there is, in fact, very little indeed of OPEC concern. The investment of oil surplus funds in particular is decidedly each individual country's affair. What we have called 'the financial problem' has never been an OPEC problem, nor an Arab Gulf states' problem. Rather it is a Saudi, a Kuwaiti or a Qatari problem. One would even hesitate to speak of a UAE financial problem, since the ruler of each state in the Federation, with the possible exception of Abu Dhabi, jealously preserves his autonomy in managing his oil funds portfolio. In addition to preserving the independence in their portfolio management, the individual Gulf states even insist on making the confidentiality of their financial placement in the recipient country a *sine qua non* for the continuation of their investment in these countries.[88] Except probably for Kuwait, published information on the Gulf states' surpluses is evasive, if it exists at all. This reflects an utterly individualistic — one could even say personal — attitude towards oil funds investment that is hardly compatible with any collective investment policy for these funds.

Looked at from this angle, the problem of oil funds investment takes on completely different dimensions. The funds no longer appear as a major structural change in the world economy. Rather they are the sum of individual surpluses, each of them more or less marginal. Some countries still enjoy quite substantial surpluses. Saudi Arabia alone accounts for about half of the annual oil surpluses and Kuwait comes second. The rest of the Gulf states, though very wealthy, add only a trifle to world aggregate economic flows, each country being but an atom in the world's financial flows. Of course some countries are bigger atoms than others; the fact remains however that oil surpluses, though important in their totality, are nevertheless marginal and without economic significance once fragmented among many decision makers. In these conditions, investment in the LDCs would appear to be an extremely costly venture for each surplus country behaving independently.

Common Interest and Individual Behaviour. It is often suggested that groups of individuals, or for that matter of states, with common interests usually attempt to further them. This opinion is not only held in popular discussions but is also maintained in many scholarly writings. However, nothing seems to support this view, either logically or in practice.[89] Common interest is a necessary condition for collective action but by itself it is not sufficient to bring this about. In many cases, rational, self-interested members of a group will not act to achieve their common or group interest. Rather, rational individual behaviour can be contrary to the common interest. This is a classic problem in welfare economics, and a whole literature is devoted to the issue. It is even more central to the theory of development and industrialization of underdeveloped areas.[90]

A public or collective good is defined as one in which the consumption by one member of a group does not reduce its utility to other members of the group.[91] The distinguishing feature of a collective good is that, once provided to one member of the group it can be made available to other members at no extra cost (Samuelson's joint supply principle),[92] and/or the rest of the group cannot be excluded from benefiting from it (Musgrave's exclusion principle).[93]

A correct assessment of the nature of the costs of the collective goods is fundamental to the understanding of the principle. To be sure, they are not free goods since the production of collective goods requires the use of scarce resources and implies risks. However, once provided, a collective good appears to other members of the group as costless and they can enjoy it as free riders. In most cases the indivisibility of costs appears to reside at the heart of the collective goods problem. Whereas costs are indivisible and have to be incurred all at once, benefits can be divided among members of the group. A member of a group may not be able to incur the cost of the collective good because the initial cost exceeds its benefit to him. It is no consolation to know that the total benefit to the group could out-match the total cost. What matters to each member is the fraction of benefit that he gains from the collective good regardless of the benefits accruing to other members of the group. Without coercion and/or coordination collective goods cannot be provided, no matter how useful they may be.

Investment in the LDCs as a Collective Good. A vast literature on development has emphasized the need for a substantial investment effort to break the vicious circles in the LDCs and hence to make the effort worthwhile. Whether it is called the 'big push', 'balanced growth' or 'takeoff',[94] the message is always the same. Investment in the LDCs cannot be made profitable unless undertaken on a massive scale. While this scale could be within the reach of the oil surplus countries as a group, it is not necessarily attainable by any one country alone. Massive investment in infrastructure as well as in productive projects is, in fact, the condition to secure the profitability of investment in the LDCs. The costs of investment in the LDCs are in a way indivisible. To overcome this limitation and short of coercion being exerted by a supranational authority, coordination among countries is needed.

The situation is, to some extent, similar to that of the marketplace where structure matters a great deal. The power of and benefit for each participant differs with the types of market structure. Under atomistic competition they are 'price takers', whereas they are 'price makers' with more coordinated types of organization. The analogy with the market structure is very suggestive. Not only is it useful for a better understanding of the actual situation, but it can also shed some light on potential developments. After all, the same countries have experienced a similar situation in oil pricing. Whereas they were all losing under competitive conditions, the establishment of OPEC in 1960 and later its role in oil pricing since 1970 proved to be extremely effective in that respect.

In questioning the extent to which fragmented oil surplus countries can coordinate their investment policy, a brief review of OPEC — itself an instructive example — may be useful.

The OPEC Example. OPEC is a vivid example of the need for and the success of a collective action to bring about a common interest to a group of countries, and its history reveals both the potential and the limitations of such a collective action. What has proved to be beneficial in oil pricing matters can be equally important in oil funds investment policy.

The success of OPEC can be ascribed to a great extent to the simplicity of the problem facing its members, who confine themselves to the relatively simple task of agreeing on oil prices. In fact OPEC 'does not perform all the functions normally associated with an export cartel which usually has rigid agreements on prices, production control and market shares. Rather, OPEC ministers, during their periodic conferences, merely agree on the price of OPEC marker crude oil.'[95] There are two points to be noted here. The first concerns the perception of the need for coordinated action. It seems that, in the perception of the common interest, it is much easier to recognize losses incurred than to grasp profits foregone. The second point is that by failing to establish a collective action, the cost inflicted on the individual member who tries to act for the common good would be very high. There is something here too in the nature of a collective good.

The timing of the establishment of OPEC illustrates the first point. In spite of the advocacy of Sheikh 'Abdallah Tariqi, former Saudi oil minister, of the tremendous benefits for oil exporting countries in coordinating their oil policy, and his repeated pleas for collective action, OPEC was set up only in 1960, the 'oil consciousness' of the producing countries having been aroused by the 1959 and 1960 price cuts, unilaterally imposed by the oil companies without informing, much less consulting, the governments involved.[96] Historically OPEC was created to halt oil price cuts: it was a defensive mechanism against real losses incurred. Later on it became a powerful instrument to increase oil prices; that is, to recoup foregone profits.

Early attempts by member countries to establish their national control over the oil, which would eventually benefit all oil producing countries, were thwarted by actions from other producers. The attempts by the Mossadeq government to nationalize the Anglo-Iranian Oil Company in 1950 and 1951, and later the move by Prime Minister Qassem in 1959 to restrict severely the concession granted to the Iraq Petroleum Company, were both made pointless by the increase in oil production in other oil producing countries who competed for more markets, more production and more revenues.[97] The Iranian and Iraqi examples illustrate the high cost of an individual's failure to act for the common interest without coordinating with other members of the group. It is also true that the role of oil companies was predominant at that time and the governments concerned had little control over their oil production.

Although the first oil price increase by OPEC took place in Tehran in 1971, it was through the Libyan effort that the breakthrough was possible. The road to Tehran passed by way of Tripoli: with the advent of the Libyan revolution in 1969, a new exogeneous factor was introduced to OPEC. The new Libyan government, whether acting from naïveté or shrewdness, was an outsider to the rules of the game in the oil market. A puritan revolutionary regime, the new government was prepared in the early days — perhaps without being fully aware of the consequences — to forego some of the oil revenues and thus to incur for others, if need be, the initial cost of disrupting the prevailing situation of the oil companies working in Libya. The new military junta was obviously helped in its risk-assuming enterprise by having to deal with the weakest link in the chain of oil companies. Occidental Petroleum, the Los Angeles independent, depended almost totally on its Libyan operations with 96 per cent of its world investment concentrated there. Bunker-Hunt was in a similar situation, and these two companies were particularly vulnerable to the Libyan decisions.[98] In addition, the American Administration at the time seemed to have concluded that it could not openly assist the oil industry.[99] The success of the Libyan government paved the way for OPEC to move into the new role of collectively fixing oil prices in Tehran.

The relevance of external factors can hardly be overestimated in the two subsequent major oil price increases that followed the Tehran agreement. The October War in 1973 with the concomitant oil embargo on the one hand, and the Iranian revolution and the overthrowing of the Shah in 1979 on the other, gave OPEC valuable opportunities to increase oil prices almost with impunity. In between these two events, oil prices either increased mildly or there was a failure to reach the desired consensus (for example, the two-tier price system resulting from the OPEC meeting in Doha in December 1976). Even with OPEC, the stimulus to oil price increases was more external than internal.

It would be a grave mistake, however, to think that the growing role of OPEC in oil pricing is due only to external factors. The underlying economic and political conditions have seen dramatic changes. The role of the companies has been continuously reduced. The economics of the oil industry have also changed with the passage from easily accessible to less accessible oil fields. A parallel change took place in oil pricing principles. In a first phase, the cost of production was the main point of reference in oil prices. In a second phase, with less accessible oil fields, the cost of substitution became more relevant in oil pricing.[100]

The difficulties of achieving the common interest are obvious, but there are promising indications of a change in attitudes: new factors are emerging which call for a more coordinated investment policy by oil surplus countries.

New Prospects. New developments which are affecting the international scene could lead to a reconsideration of, and eventually to more coordination in, the investment policies of the oil surplus countries. First and foremost was the American decision to freeze the Iranian government's assets in the wake of developments that followed the seizing of American Embassy personnel in Tehran by a group of Iranian militants in November 1979. Though the American President's action under the International Emergency Act of 1977 was nothing novel — similar measures were in fact applied extensively during the Second World War — the American decision came as a revelation, or more accurately as a psychological shock, to oil surplus governments. The illusion of security was cruelly shattered. The disconcerted public statements made by OPEC officials at the time reflected their disarray and confusion. A case in point is the immediate comment of the Saudi Foreign Minister who asserted — and his assertion should not be taken literally — that the American decision 'gives us no ground for concern whatsoever, because it could never happen to us. No one could *ever* seize the American Embassy in Riyadh.'[101]

Fundamentalist Muslim rebels were apparently not interested in the American Embassy in Riyadh, but they did seize the Grand Mosque in Mecca, the holiest of all Muslim shrines, only five days after the Minister's statement.

Moreover, the Saudi Minister could not have failed to observe that the American decision to freeze Iranian assets was taken ten days *after* the seizing of the Embassy, and within hours of the Iranian Finance Minister's threat to move Iran's funds out of American banks.[102] The American Secretary of the Treasury was categorical in affirming that 'the President acted to protect American claims against Iran and not to increase pressure on Tehran to release the U.S. hostages.'[103] The Oil Minister of the United Arab Emirates perhaps reflected better the state of mind in the area when he described the American measure as 'creating doubt and anxiety in investment circles and setting a precedent for other countries to do the same whenever they have a problem.'[104]

Oil surplus countries have discovered, to their dismay, that the political risks of investment are as serious in developed as in developing countries. By way of analogy, the American 'freeze' can be compared with the oil companies' price cuts in 1959. In both cases OPEC countries stood to incur realized losses and not only forego profits. Price cuts in 1959 and in 1960 triggered a process to coordinate oil price policies, while the fear of further freezes may lead to a corresponding coordination in investment policies. The Arab Monetary Fund took the initiative in discussing '. . . the serious and dangerous precedent created by the United States' decision to freeze the deposits and assets of a particular country.'[105] This could be only a first step.

Secondly, the increasing concern among the members of the international community over the fate of the oil surpluses might eventually oblige oil surplus states to come up with something constructive. In the early days after the first oil price shock in 1973-4, the world was faced with the problem of the recycling of the oil funds. At the time the IMF came up with the Oil Facilities in 1974 and 1975, and another supplementary Facility known as the Witteveen Facility was agreed upon in late 1978. The bulk of the burden was, however, taken up by the private international commercial banks. It is recognized that although the international capital market succeeded in absorbing and rechannelling oil funds fairly efficiently, the costs to the world, and particularly to the Third World, are quite high. There is now an increasing demand for oil funds to be used for a kind of global Marshall Plan. In 1977 the Scandinavian countries proposed a scheme to the United

Nations General Assembly which involved the massive transfer of resources on a scale resembling that of the Marshall Plan. It would allow for the possibility of directing the demand created in the developing countries towards industries with excess capacity in developed countries. A similar proposal put forward by Mexico is being studied by the World Bank and the OECD is looking at a co-financing programme with OPEC to the LDCs, while similar resolutions have been submitted to the United States Congress.[106] These proposals would not necessarily take the interests of the oil surplus countries as their focal point.

More imminent is the proposal to create a substitution account within the IMF. It is true (at the time of writing) that the proposal seems for the moment to be shelved, but the message is clear enough. In their first statement, the Consultative Group on International Economic and Monetary Affairs — known as the Group of Thirty — declared that there was urgent need to reach agreement on the proposal for the establishment of a substitution account in the International Monetary Fund to issue claims denominated in Special Drawing Rights (SDRs) in exchange for official dollar reserve assets. Although the principal objective of such an account was to alleviate the pressure on the dollar, its implication for the liberty of disposal of oil surplus funds cannot be mistaken. This was explicitly stated: '. . . the need to establish this account has been lent added urgency by the prospects that members of OPEC are likely to run a substantial aggregate current account surplus for a number of years.'[107] Oil surplus countries cannot remain insensitive to these developments indefinitely.

Peripheral Economies. In a very real sense, the Gulf oil states are in the long run peripheral economies. The notion of the centre (or the core) and of the periphery has gained increasing recognition in economic and political writings. Recent literature on economic development emphasizes the notion of centre and periphery as a tool of analysis for the development of modern capitalism.[108] Domination and dependence are the salient ingredients in that notion. Political scientists are using similar notions to account for the difference in impact and influence.[109]

We are using the term 'periphery' here in a very special sense, meaning the limited potential role of oil surplus states in the post-oil era. Though promoted to world financial prominence, these countries are too dependent on oil to represent any economic significance in a post-oil period. Economically as well as culturally, they are marginal to the mainstream. No one can doubt the influence of oil and finance in present-day life. Fabulous petroleum wealth has transformed these states and their relations with other countries, yet they remain mono-resource economies, terribly lacking in endowments other than oil. In particular they lack the human resources necessary to play a real, as opposed to a financial, role. Not only is their population base very limited, but their labour policies in particular do not seem to encourage definitive settlement and assimilation of expatriate labour.

In a different context Malcolm Kerr described Egypt's failure to assume the role of Prussia, and Nasser that of Bismarck, to bring about Arab unity in the sixties.[110] It seems less plausible that the Gulf oil states, individually or collectively, can assume this sort of role in the eighties or nineties, much less maintain their leadership in the post-oil period. The role of an oil surplus country as a financier is bound to be self-liquidating after the oil era. Economic power can be expected eventually to move from financial centres to more productive centres in the future. With the depletion and/or decline in the importance of oil, this will be more than a possibility; it is virtually a certainty.

The economic marginality – in the long run – of oil surplus countries, if it does not explain the present investment policies in these countries, accounts for the lack of incentive to invest in the LDCs in general and the Arab countries in particular. Without pushing the analogy too far, nor attributing to it more of a very controversial farsightedness than really existed,[111] it could be said that the success of the Marshall Plan owed a great deal to the fact that its financial sponsor – the United States – was not only a surplus country in the financial sense, but stood particularly to assume a central, not a peripheral, place in a reconstructed Europe. With the success of the Marshall Plan, the United States consolidated rather than liquidated that position. It is very doubtful if any Gulf state envisages itself in such a role.

We will have more to say about the core and the periphery in the next section of this chapter.

Domestic Environment

Non-economic aspects of domestic environment can induce as well as constrain financial flows to the LDCs. A comprehensive catalogue of the domestic factors affecting decision-making in the Gulf goes beyond the scope of this essay, and I shall merely make a brief general mention of a few of the salient features which can influence the Gulf states in their handling of the financial problem, since it definitely takes more than an economist to deal with them.

Pan-Arabism. It might appear paradoxical to include pan-Arabism as a domestic factor in the Gulf area. It is, however, indisputable, irrespective of the ideological leanings of the observer, that particularly in the Gulf area Arab politics is not foreign policy.

Writers disagree as to the relative weight and the direction of the tide of pan-Arabism.[112] For some, the Arab states system is first and foremost a 'pan' system. It postulates the existence of a single Arab nation behind the façade of a multiplicity of sovereign states. For others, pan-Arabism is near its end, if not already a thing of the past. Still others see a continuous struggle for predominance between a 'Middle Eastern system' and an 'Arab system' or between *'raison d'état'* and 'pan-Arabism'. However all will agree that some Arab component is always present in domestic affairs.[112]

This is not an essay on pan-Arabism; we are interested in it only as it affects the Gulf states in their decisions on the financial problem. Our understanding of the problem will be enhanced if it is related to another concept to which I alluded earlier, namely the core and the periphery. For all practical purposes we can identify the Arab Gulf states with the periphery and most of the Arab recipient states with the core. It is not a coincidence that the champions of pan-Arabism came from the Arab core, while Saudi Arabia

> . . . has long been a foe of pan-Arabism and has traditionally seen itself as a guardian of the *turath*, the heritage or Islam to be more precise . . . Muslim universalism is a safer doctrine than the geographically more limited but politically more troublesome idea of pan-Arabism.[113]

The relations between the core and the periphery are not simple. If the core proclaims pan-Arabism and confers super-legitimacy over individual countries, the periphery has the power of oil wealth. Pan-Arabism and Arab money are the stick and the carrot, but in different hands, to bring about a very subtle equilibrium. The stick is in the hands of the advocates of pan-Arabism and the carrot in those of the partisans of *raison d'état*. Arab finance is not a complement to pan-Arabism; rather, it is a counterpart to it. Arab money will be forthcoming to other Arab countries in the name of Arabism, but only to a certain limit.

It is no wonder then that Arab financial flows to Arab brothers coincided with the retreat of the pan-Arab system after the war of 1967, which 'marked the Waterloo of pan-Arabism'. Far from being a triumph for pan-Arabism the Khartoum Agreement in August 1967 marked a shift of power in favour of oil wealth.

> The radical regime in Cairo would capitulate to the will of the oil states led by Saudi Arabia, but the oil states would not press their victory too far or too hard . . . Slowly and grimly, with a great deal of anguish and outright violence, a normal state system is becoming a fact of life.[114]

In the wake of the war of October 1973, it was Sadat and Assad — 'revisionists' or 'correctionists' of the pan-Arab doctrine — who obtained the Arab finance. 'The logic that triumphed in October 1973 was not the pan-Arabist one held up by Nasser and the Baath, it was the more limited notion of solidarity preferred by those states that had long opposed pan-Arabism'.[114]

Even the Baghdad Summit in April 1979 was not a break with this very subtle game. It is a game between pan-Arabism and *raison d'état*, between radicals and moderates, between the core and the periphery, or else between Arab legitimacy and Arab money. It is true that 'the oil states have wanted from Egypt an abandonment of pan-Arabist ideology and acceptance of the logic of the state system, and they got that.'[115] However, Sadat went further than his financial sponsors could accept. 'The Egyptians' urge to break out and do things on their own was precisely what Saudi Arabia did not want.' Saudi Arabia understands the political fragility that lies beneath its prosperity. 'Above and beyond particular foreign policy decisions, the oil states will continue to experience the difficulties of living in a militarized, impoverished part of the world.'[116]

Moreover, as in Khartoum where the oil money was a check to radicalism, in the final analysis the Baghdad Summit rallied the most radical Arab states to the idea of a peaceful settlement of the Arab-Israeli conflict based on the famous United Nations Resolution 242. After grooming the Sadat regime and consolidating Egypt's de-Nasserization, conservative Arab money had to appease and even to buy the more radical elements.

Institutionalization and Family Rule. The Gulf states are still largely governed along traditional lines.[117] Though oil wealth has transformed them into advanced welfare states they still remain patriarchal in a distinctly familial way.[118] The Sa'uds, the Sabahs, the Al Thanis, the Qasimis, the Al Nahyans, the Al Maktums, the Al Khalifas, are not only the ruling families: they embody the legitimacy of the existing regimes.

There are of course differences in degree among these states. Kuwait is a case in point. A more institutionalized legitimacy is obviously ingrained in Kuwait's political setting alongside, but not in place of, the traditional legitimacy. For more than two centuries this small country has been ruled by the Sabah family, generally renowned for moderation and wisdom. A long tradition of consultation between rulers and ruled (mainly the merchant community) has paved the way for the only (relatively long-lived) parliamentary experience. Traditional kinship, however, remains the basis of social life.

In varying degrees the ruling families are not only providing heads of state and political elites in the Gulf; they are also well represented in leading managerial, administrative and economic activities. In Saudi Arabia the numbers of the royal family of approximately 4,000 male members – almost a class apart – makes the House of Sa'ud the world's largest family enterprise, and causes the Rothschild banking octopus or Rockefeller's Standard Oil Complex to look like small town enterprises.[119] The same is true, though numbers are less impressive, of the rest of the Gulf oil states. Family connections loom equally in other Gulf states where the core of the political and business elite always consists of members of the ruling families. Other members of the elite are almost without exception drawn from other wealthy aristocratic families.[120]

We have seen that the pan-Arab system is retreating before the *raison d'état* system. In reality, *raison d'état* is largely quite indiscriminately mixed with *raison de famille*. Though institutionalization is progressing, *raison d'état* is, at least partially, perceived through *raison de famille*, and this perception cannot remain without effect. First a family, whatever its identification with the state, remains a collection of specific individuals with limited time horizons. This is in contrast with the metaphysical, immortal entity which is the nation. Second, family rule in the area is weighed down with a long history of family feuds. These two facts account for the more personalized outlook of the future than the otherwise more abstract *raison d'état* on the one hand, and the personal frictions – and hence limits of coordination – on the other.

In these conditions, as a high-ranking American official once observed, 'it is not possible to draw a meaningful line in the abstract between "private" and "government" investment.'[121] It seems that there is a general inclination in the Gulf area to leave the investment decisions to advisers. Very often the same individual is managing the personal investment portfolio of the ruler and that of the government. Names such as Mahdi Tajir, Fara'un (father and son) and Kamal Adham are too well-known to need any further mention; they are both public and private figures in the world of business affairs. Khalid Abu Sa'ud, investment and financial adviser to the Emir of Kuwait,[122] has long been in charge of Kuwait's investment within the Ministry of Finance. 'Usually operating behind closed doors in London, New York or a mid-East capital, the petro-dollar manager can bring cheer or gloom to the foreign exchange market.'[123] It would indeed be curious if these same advisers used different approaches to the investment of 'public' and 'private' funds. A private outlook would more likely be prevalent in these conditions.

It is interesting to note here that Kuwait's relative advance and sophistication in investment policies are not altogether unrelated to its more institutionalized system. Kuwait was not only the first Gulf state to have a parliamentary system, but also the first to have published records of its financial transactions (budgets, closing accounts), and the first to introduce the concept of a reserve fund. Compared to other ruling families, the share of the Sabah family in government public revenues is the lowest in the Gulf. During the period from 1952 to 1970/71 the family's share was only about 2.7 per cent in Kuwait compared with 32.4 per cent in Bahrain, 40.6 per cent in Qatar and 25 per cent in the Emirates.[124] Even in its investment policy, Kuwait is the largest OPEC surplus country to invest on *commercial* terms in the LDCs, which it views not only as recipients of aid for political considerations, but also as untapped opportunities for productive investment.

> There is no doubt that the increase in real investment subsequent to the availability of oil funds would have necessitated a change in world demand to make these investments profitable . . . the Third World with its untapped resources and unsatisfied needs . . . could be made the locomotive for the world increase in real investment . . . for matching available resources with investment opportunities.[125]

It is no wonder then that the more institutionalized Kuwait is the leading OPEC surplus country in non-concessional financial flows to the LDCs along with its high contribution to the concessional flows. Long-term state interests are clearer with more institutionalization.

The United Arab Emirates present yet another striking example.

The contrast between Sheikh Zaid al Nahyan, the Head of the State, and Sheikh Rashid al Maktum, his deputy, typifies two different concepts of a non-institutionalized system. To some extent this is a contrast between *raison d'état* and *raison de famille*; Sheikh Rashid is a shrewd merchant while Sheikh Zaid is more politically minded. The *raison d'état* of Abu Dhabi in its relations to other LDCs is, however, of a pre-institutionalized era. It is the largesse of an Arab ruler rather than a commitment to restructure the world economy.

The personalized nature of family rule also accounts for the continuous rivalry among the Gulf states which, in turn, puts limits to coordination among them. Political history in the area, when it is not the action of foreign powers, is a long history of feuding and disputes between ruling families.[126] Abu Dhabi was in continuous conflict with the Qawasims of Sharjah and Ras Al-Khaima for the leadership of the area,[127] while the long dispute between Al Khalifa of Bahrain and Al Thani of Qatar prevented the constitution of an enlarged United Arab Emirates which would include both of them with the other seven Sheikhdoms.[128] Frontier conflicts are a constant part of life in the Gulf area. There are − or were − frontier problems between Saudi Arabia and Abu Dhabi (Buraimi), Abu Dhabi and Dubai, Duabi and Sharjah, Ras Al-Khaima and Oman, Bahrain and Qatar, and many more.[129]

The uncertainty over the Gulf area has, however, encouraged its rulers to strengthen coordination on political, economic, oil and security matters among themselves.[130] It is not unlikely that with more awareness of the risks involved in oil funds investment, coordination among the oil Gulf states may also extend to policies of foreign investment.

The Second Stratum: Merchants and Technocrats. The second stratum, it must be remembered, is not the ruling class, but although it does not rule, it is the stratum without which the rulers cannot rule.[131] It is not our purpose here to delineate a complete social stratification of the Gulf states. It can, however, be fairly agreed that merchants and an emerging technocratic elite together constitute what could be regarded as the second stratum in the Gulf states.

In the Gulf states other than Saudi Arabia, the leading social function has been won by trading traditions. These states emerged as sedentary trading centres, although folklore and the general perception would have them only as nomadic tribes. Because of its vast territory the situation in Saudi Arabia is more complex. Since the early days of Islam trade has been highly esteemed. The society in which Islam was born — that of Mecca — was after all a centre of capitalist trade.[132] The trading traditions have accompanied most of the later history of the Arabian Peninsula, particularly the coastal states. Pearl-diving industries, sea-faring, commercial entrepots and/or smuggling all added to the increasing influence of the merchant families which grew up as trading dynasties. The merchant, or better the middleman, is a king in the Gulf area.

With the oil money, the middleman mentality was given a pronounced *rentier* content. Trade is mixed with speculation. Profits — and incomes in general — are not always related to risk-bearing or merit. Rather they are privileges of position and status. Citizenry and social status are of paramount importance here. Productivity is to a great extent an alien concept and hardly fits with an oil economy.

The situation in the Gulf oil states is so peculiar that they are in many ways economies in reverse. For them generating income is less of a problem than spending it. Everywhere else, governments are not on the whole 'income earners' and have therefore to concentrate on being tax collectors; by contrast governments in the Gulf are in fact able to distribute benefits and favours. *L'Etat Providence* if it existed at all is probably best represented in the Gulf area. As the oil sector — virtually the sole productive sector — is owned by the government, it is imperative to devise ways and means of enabling some of the oil earnings to percolate down. To the tribal tradition of buying loyalty is now added the need for the redistribution of part of these earnings to the population. As welfare states, in which the unprecedented provision of free services is second to none, the Gulf states provide their populations with a complex array of services and benefits: free education, free health care, soft (sometimes free) loans, grants, subsidies, etc. In a very real sense, there is a negative tax system whereby citizens levy various forms of impositions on governments.

The practices of the governments of the Gulf states in redistributing benefits to the population not only increased the sense of windfall profits and rentier mentality but also enhanced speculation. An early method of redistributing part of the oil revenues was through land purchases by the government. Beginning in Kuwait in the early fifties, land was bought from individuals at prices hardly related to the market value. Inversely, the government's price would set the market at exceedingly high levels. Huge fortunes were made through this mechanism. With the excessive availability of liquidity on one hand and the very thin spectrum of productive assets offered on the other, real estate prices continued to skyrocket. Governments stood to back this trend by their active role as regular purchasers in the market. In these circumstances it is quite normal to speak of a 'real estate mentality', which spread all over the Gulf area. The speculation has not, however, been confined to real estate: the stock market experienced a similar phenomenon, also with the backing of governments.[133]

We are not interested here in an in-depth analysis of the outlook and/or behaviour of the merchants. This is only relevant to our study in so far as it may affect their perception of investment opportunities outside the local market. Understandably they are attracted by easy profit-making ventures, with a marked inclination to real estate. The flourishing inter-Arab real estate investment companies illustrate this point. This does not, however, preclude a genuine businesslike attitude by the Gulf private sector towards the LDCs. Hotel building, contracting and trade are particularly favourite sectors for private investment in other Arab and developing countries. However these sectors remain limited and fall short of the investment needs of the LDCs.

Besides the merchant stratum, an emerging technocratic elite is increasingly participating in the public life of the Gulf states. The education and training of the inhabitants and the vast opportunities open to them paved the way for a growing role for the intelligentsia. Most rulers in the area have been willing to satisfy their demands for participation, and the role of the new elite has, in fact, steadily increased. While ideals of pan-Arabism are still powerful among the intelligentsia, new factors are diverting their interests towards Europe and the United States. More impressed by the technological advance of the West on one hand, but also on the other affected by the general retreat of the whole pan-Arab ideology, the new technocratic elite is more oriented to the West. Rather than Beirut or Cairo, it is London, Denver, Los Angeles or Houston which moves their memories.

Among the intelligentsia a generation gap separates those who were educated in the forties, fifties and early sixties from those of the late sixties and seventies. Not only are the latter mainly trained in Western universities but their outlook is also different. Equipped with better techniques from more prestigious universities in engineering, financial analysis and management, the new elite lacks the political perspective and commitment of the earlier generation. The new elite rests its claim for allegiance almost exclusively on the balance sheet preferring favourable facts and figures to emotional commitments.[134] The earlier generations may be at a loss with the new jargon of the Euromarket, financial analysis and/or computerized programmes, but they are more at home with political discussions and major historical trends. In other words, what they lack in technical proficiency they make up in broader perspective. With greater self-confidence, the new generation, on the other hand, is gaining in sophistication in the small what they fail to see in the large. Fluent in foreign languages, regular passengers at international airports and hotels, sharp observers of interest rate differentials, spreads and margins in the Euromarket, and expert in foreign exchange rates, spot and forward rates, etc., the new elite is very active in international business. For this new breed of technocrats, dealing with Western institutions is more professionally rewarding and also more prestigious, if not more fun. In fact, unless basically committed to Third World finance, there is a built-in bias to do business with the industrial developed countries rather than with the LDCs.

It is no wonder then that a casual look at the balance sheets of the financial institutions in the area would show the major role of foreign assets — almost exclusively assets in Western countries — among their total assets. In Kuwait, for instance, the investment companies hold as much as 60 per cent of their total assets in foreign assets: the specialized banks which have a specific domestic mandate, hold a quarter of the total in foreign assets; and this figure reaches around 50 per cent in the commercial banks.[135] The situation in other Gulf states is similar. Even development funds whose charters stipulate that their unique role is to finance projects in developing countries show the same predilection for portfolio management in Western capital markets, rather than for a committing of all their resources for financing projects in the LDCs. It was found that the share of the total assets of the Kuwait Fund for Arab Development and the Saudi Fund for Development for project finance in the LDCs never exceeded 35 per cent, the balance being invested in bank deposits or other financial securities in the international capital market.[136] It is interesting to note that the corresponding percentage for project finance in the Arab Fund for Economic and Social Development (an Arab regional institution) exceeds 70 per cent, leaving less than 30 per cent to be placed in the Western capital markets.

The charm of the West for the new elite is not confined to the more professional and prestigious types of business but is related to another phenomenon which always accompanies situations of sudden prospects for money-making. The sudden wealth accruing to governments cannot bear the strains of uncontrolled venality. The rapacity of certain elements of a new civil service entirely devoid of anything which can seriously be regarded as public spirit can hardly be overlooked. Huge development projects, joint venture partnerships, agents, tenders and awards of million — and sometimes billion — dollar contracts have provided opportunities for those in public office to use their positions for private gain.[137] Some countries are more conspicuous than others in that respect. Philby's observation in the fifties of the emergence in Saudi Arabia of 'a new bureaucracy, whose thin veneer of education has done in a couple of decades more harm to the reputation of a great country than the wild man of the desert has done in thousands of years'[138] is probably more topical now than it was a quarter of a century ago. Stories about excessive corruption in some Gulf states are attracting more attention outside the area as they arouse intense resentment inside it.[139] This can hardly be reconciled with a developmental mentality.

Conclusion

OPEC surplus countries, particularly in the Arab peninsula, emerged in 1973-74 as a world financial power. The oil price increases have introduced far-reaching financial and monetary rearrangements worldwide. There is no doubt that money and finance are powerful instruments for affecting real resources, which alone are the ultimate wealth. However, without bringing about a parallel rearrangement in real resources they risk remaining sterile.

More than two hundred years ago Adam Smith warned against the fallacy of identifying money and wealth. This was his battle with the Mercantilists. The example of Spain and England is very instructive in this regard. In the sixteenth century Spain found new riches with the influx of gold and silver from her colonies in the New World. England, with no colonies at that time, had to labour to restructure her real economy. Two different approaches are contrasted: the financial versus the real. Needless to say, it was England and not Spain that became the first world economic and sea power. Not only was the Armada defeated in a battle between the two concepts of warfare, but the defeat also represented the precursor of the triumph of the real over the monetary approach. OPEC surplus countries in the last quarter of the twentieth century are facing the same old problem of confusing finance and wealth. Smith's teaching seems to be as topical as ever.

Developed countries can only perpetuate the financial character of OPEC financial wealth. The easy façade of investing the oil funds in the rich, credit-worthy and secure OECD countries conceals the eventual erosion of the same funds. Motivated by self-interest, the placing of oil funds in the OECD countries can only be self-defeating. Developing countries, with all their shortcomings, can offer OPEC surplus countries a chance of transforming the *financial phenomenon* of oil into a *real phenomenon*. What seems to be a disinterested act of moral commitment towards brotherly poor countries is probably the only way OPEC has to preserve the value of its financial wealth.

This is not all. Regardless of what they do with their surplus funds, OPEC surplus countries will anyway be left with developing countries as the ultimate debtors of their surplus. The fate of the one depends then on the prosperity of the other.

Keynes once introduced the 'widow's cruse' and the 'Danaid jar' legends[140] into economic literature to depict situations in which entrepreneurs would stand to gain what they spent and to lose what they withheld. OPEC surplus countries seem to be in a similar situation. They gain what they 'give' to the poor and lose what they 'invest' commercially. Only an imaginative and unconventional policy for oil funds investment — to bring about a real as opposed to a financial restructuring of the economy — can promote the interests of both OPEC and the LDCs.

The new international economic order is not only the fight of non-oil developing countries; it is also the condition for the consolidation of OPEC gains in oil prices. A new oil order is not separated from it: OPEC surplus countries can in fact play a leading role in bringing about this new order. If they do not, others will do it. There is now an increasing concern in the world that oil funds should be used for a kind of global Marshall Plan that would not necessarily take OPEC interests as the focal point.

Developing countries are not, however, the promised land for oil funds investment. The development record of the LDCs — quite impressive in the sixties but less so in the seventies — leaves much to be desired. The odds against secure and successful investments in the LDCs are substantial. Not only inadequacy of infrastructure and qualified manpower, but particularly inefficient management and political instability, impede any sustained development effort in the LDCs. One country alone — even an oil rich one — cannot assume all the hazards of investment in the LDCs.

As we have shown, the oil surplus countries, led by the Arab Gulf states, are allocating unprecedented programmes of aid to the LDCs. However, this is not sufficient to bring about a restructuring of the world economic order. It would be unrealistic in fact to leave this difficult task to the oil surplus countries. They are burdened by heavy limitations of size, potential and political constraint.

It is heartening none the less that there is an increasing awareness of the seriousness of continuing the actual pattern of oil funds investment. Inflation, political risks and other factors in the developed countries are opening the eyes of the oil surplus countries to the dangers they are incurring by continuing the actual investment policy. The need for a reconsideration of and more coordination in investment policies by oil surplus countries is more and more felt in all these countries. The newly established Gulf Council for Cooperation, which includes Saudi Arabia, Kuwait, Qatar, Oman, Bahrain and the United Arab Emirates, should be looked at as a step in this direction. A more prominent role for the LDCs as recipients of investment funds cannot fail to show itself in the near future.

Notes

1. Dag Hammarskjold Foundation, *What Now: Another Development* (Uppsala, 1975), p. 6.

2. From a statement by Richard Cooper, Under Secretary of State for Economic Affairs before International Economic Policy and Trade, and International Development subcommittees, House of Representatives, *The Bonn Summit: Its Aftermath and New International Economic Initiatives* (Washington D.C.: US Government Printing Office, 1978).

3. We note here that a new global approach to the oil funds in the OECD countries emphasizing world interdependence has recently gained more ground. We shall refer later to some proposals to that effect.

4. US Senate Committee on Foreign Relations, *International Debt, The Banks and the U.S. Foreign Policy*, Sub-Committee on Foreign Economic Policy Staff Report (Washington D.C., 1977), p. 4.

5. Kenneth E. Boulding, *A Reconstruction of Economics* (New York: John Wiley, 1950).

6. Tibor Scitovsky, *Money and the Balance of Payments* (Chicago: Rand McNally, 1969).

7. Jan Tumlir, 'Oil Payments and the Oil Debt and the Problem of Adjustment', in T.M. Rybcznski (ed.), *The Economics of Oil Crisis* (New York: Holmes and Meier, 1976).

8. Arthur Lewis, 'Economic Development with Unlimited Supply of Labour . . .' in A.N. Agrawala and S.P. Singh (eds.), *The Economics of Underdevelopment* (London: Oxford University Press, 1958), p. 406.

9. Oystein Noreng, *Oil Politics in the 1980s* (New York: McGraw Hill, 1978), p. 130.

10. Bent Hansen, 'The Accumulation of Financial Capital by the Middle East Oil Exporters: Problems and Policies', in A.L. Udovitch (ed.), *The Middle East: Oil, Conflict and Hope* (Lexington, Mass.: Lexington Books, 1976).

11. Ibid.

12. Ibid.

13. Ibid.; also Thomas D. Willett, *The Oil Transfer Problem and International Stability*, Princeton University, Essays in International Finance No. 113 (1975), p. 15.

14. Saudi Arabia has chosen to invest around 85 per cent of its funds (the bulk of which are in dollars) in the United States and in deposits in Eurobanking markets. See Fred Bergsten, *U.S.-Saudi Economic Interests* (New York: American Association for Commerce and Industry Inc, 1980).

15. *World Financial Markets*, March 1980; *IMF Survey*, 5 May 1980.

16. See for example Aninda K. Bhattacharya, *The Myth of Petropower* (Lexington, Mass.: Lexington Books, 1977); Noreng, *Oil Politics*; Eric Davis, 'The Political Economy of the Arab Oil Producing Nations; Convergence with Western Interests', *Studies in International Comparative Development*, Summer 1979.

17. Noreng, *Oil Politics*.

18. Hansen, 'Accumulation of Financial Capital', p. 47.

19. From a statement by Richard Cooper, *The Bonn Summit*, p. 33.

20. For a survey of different oil funds estimates are Bhattacharya, *Petropower*, p. 13; Willett, *Oil Transfer*, p. 6.

21. See for instance Farid Abolfath et al., *The OPEC Market to 1985* (Lexington, Mass.: Lexington Books, 1977), p. 329; also Willett, *Oil Transfer*, p. 31. Willett used constant 1974 prices for future oil prices but allowing inflation to erode accumulated surpluses.

22. The figure of $40 billion annually for OPEC surpluses was quoted by Senator J. Javits in a speech 'Danger on the International Economic Front', on 8 February 1978, in *The Bonn Summit: Its Aftermath . . .*, p. 141. This was also the conclusion reached by the US Treasury. See *US Senate Committee on Foreign Relations. International Debt*, p. 33.

23. Robert Sollow, 'The Economics of Resources or the Resources of Economics', *The American Economic Review*, May 1974; H. Hotelling, 'The Economics of Exhaustible Resources', *Journal of Political Economy*, April 1931.

24. Later experience confirmed this assumption. The value of exports of the industrial countries to members of OPEC, which had represented the most rapidly expanding market since 1973, actually declined in 1979 with a 5 per cent decline in value implying a much more substantial fall in volume. General Agreement on Tariff and Trades (GATT), *International Trade in 1979 and Present Prospects*, 1980.

25. Hansen, 'Accumulation of Financial Capital', p. 104.

26. Bergsten, *US-Saudi Economic Interests*.

27. Hansen, 'Accumulation of Financial Capital', p. 113.

28. Gerald A. Pollack, 'Are the Oil Payments-Deficits Manageable?', Princeton University, *Essays in International Finance*, no. 111 (June 1975), p. 9.

29. Arthur Burns, then Chairman of the US Federal Reserve Board, reportedly suggested that OPEC's accumulative surpluses might be as large as $500 billion in 1980. See Pollack, *Oil Payments-Deficits*.

30. Joanne Salop and E. Spitaller, 'Why Does Current Account Matter?', in *Staff Papers* (IMF), vol. 27, no. 1 (March 1980), p. 106.

31. In Kuwait the propensity to save ranged in the fifties and sixties between 40 and 45 per cent of the GNP. See Ragel El Mallakh, *Economic Development or Regional Cooperation: Kuwait* (Chicago: Chicago University Press, 1968), p. 81. For the seventies the figure increased to about 60 per cent from 1974 to 1976. State of Kuwait, *Annual Statistical Abstract 1978*, p. 195.

32. W.M. Corden and Peter Oppenheimer, 'Economic Issues for the Oil Importing Countries' in Rybcznski, *Oil Crisis*, p. 27; Hansen, 'Accumulation of Financial Capital', p. 110.

33. Milton Friedman, *The Theory of Consumption Function* (Princeton: Princeton University Press, 1957).

34. James S. Deusenberry, *Income, Savings and the Theory of Consumer Behavior* (Cambridge: Harvard University Press, 1962).

35. James Tobin, 'The Consumption Function', *International Encyclopaedia of Social Science*, vol. III, 1968.

36. In particular N. Kaldor, J. Robinson, L. Pasinetti and also M. Kalecki.

37. N. Kaldor, 'Alternative Theories of Distribution', *Review of Economic Studies*, vol. XXIII, no. 2, 1955–56, and 'Capital Accumulation and Economic Growth' in F.A. Lutz and D.C. Hague (eds.), *The Theory of Capital* (London: Macmillan, 1969).

38. W.A. Ellis, *Growth and Distribution* (London: Macmillan, 1973), p. 72.

39. Joan Robinson, *The Accumulation of Capital* (London: Macmillan, 1956), p. 8.

40. Noreng, *Oil Politics*, p. 133.

41. Pollack, *Oil Payments-Deficits*, p. 12.

42. Hansen, 'Accumulation of Financial Capital', p. 112.

43. Ibid.

44. Dennis H. Robertson, 'Some Notes on the Theory of Interest' in *Money, Trade and Economic Growth, in honour of John Henry Williams* (New York: Macmillan, 1951), p. 193.

45. P. Garengni, 'Notes on Consumption, Investment and Effective Demand: Pt. II', *Cambridge Journal of Economics*, vol. III, no. 1 (March 1979), p. 29.

46. Hansen, 'Accumulation of Financial Capital', p. 112.

47. Hollis B. Chenery, 'Restructuring the World Economy', *Foreign Affairs*, January 1975, p. 247.

48. For a comparable argument see Luigi L. Pasinetti, 'Growth and Income Distribution' in his *Essays in Economic Theory* (London: Cambridge University Press, 1974), p. 106.

49. Joan Robinson, *Economic Heresies: Some Old-Fashioned Questions in Economic Theory* (New York: Basic Books, 1971), p. 84.

50. It is the merit of the Cambridge Neo-Keynesian school that it draws attention to this fact and develops growth models that account for the constancy of these ratios. See N. Kaldor, 'A Model of Economic Growth', *Economic Journal*, 1957; and 'Capital Accumulation'; also Pasinetti, *Economic Theory*; and J. Robinson, *Economic Philosophy* (Chicago: Aldine Press, 1963).

51. Helmut A. Merklein and W. Carey Hardy, *Energy Economics* (Texas: Gulf Publishing Co., 1977), p. 53. It has recently been stressed that the petroleum price increase which occurred in several steps between December 1978 and June 1979 did not cause the present resurgence of inflation in industrial countries. GATT, *Press Release*, 4 September 1979.

52. Corden and Oppenheimer, in Rybcznski, p. 29.

53. Kaldor, 'Alternative Theories; Ellis, *Growth and Distribution*.

54. N. Kaldor, 'Marginal Productivity and Macro Economic Theories and Distribution', *The Review of Economic Studies*, October 1966, p. 316.

55. Pasinetti, *Economic Theory*.

56. IMF, *Annual Report 1976*, p. 3.

57. IMF, *Annual Report 1976*, p. 8; *Annual Report 1977*, p. 3; *Annual Report 1978*, p. 3.

58. IMF, *Annual Report 1974*, p. 1.

59. IMF, *Annual Report 1976*, p. 4.

60. IMF, *Annual Report 1977*, p. 2.

61. Bank for International Settlements, *Annual Report No. 45*, June 1975.

62. IMF, *Annual Report 1978*, p. 4.

63. The Bank for International Settlement, cited in *International Herald Tribune* (25 February 1980).

64. Denis Healey, 'Oil, Money and Recession', *Foreign Affairs*, Winter 1979/80, p. 220.

65. OECD, *Development Cooperation Review 1978*.

66. Address by the Managing Director of the IMF at the Fifth Session of UNCTAD, in *IMF Survey*, 11 May 1979.

67. *World Financial Markets*, May 1979.

68. Thomas D. Willett, 'Structure of OPEC and the Outlook for International Oil Prices', *The World Economy*, vol. 2, no. 1 (January 1979), p. 51; it was estimated that OPEC prices declined in real terms by 25 per cent in constant dollar terms between 1974 and 1978, and by 40 per cent in D-marks and by 50 per cent in Yen. W. Brown and H. Kahn, 'Why OPEC is Vulnerable', *Fortune*, 14 July 1980.

69. Harry G. Johnson, 'Higher Oil Prices and the International Monetary System', in Rybcznski, *Oil Crisis*, p. 169.

70. *IMF Survey*, June 1977; *Financial Times Survey: World Banking* (22 May 1978). See also Senator J. Javits in *The Bonn Summit*.

71. *World Financial Markets*, July 1979.

72. Johnson, 'Higher Oil prices', p. 168.

73. Chenery, 'Restructuring the World Economy', p. 258.

74. *The Economist*, 17 March 1979.

75. Ibid.

76. Bhattacharya, *Petropower*, p. 11.

77. *World Financial Markets*, July 1979.

78. Bank for International Settlement, *Annual Report*, no. 50, 1980.

79. Hla Myint, 'The "Classical Theory" of International Trade and Underdeveloped Countries', *Economic Journal*, vol. LXVIII, no. 270, June 1958.

80. From an address by J. de Larosière, Managing Director of the IMF, before the Economic and Social Council of the United Nations, Geneva, 4 July 1980, and reported in *IMF Survey*, 7 July 1980.

81. See US Senate Committee on Foreign Relations, *International Debt*, p. 33.

82. Hossein Askari and John T. Cummings, *Oil, OECD and the Third World: A Vicious Triangle?* (Austin, Texas: Texas University Center for Middle East Studies, 1978), p. 37.

83. Muhammad W. Khouja, 'Some Observations on the Flow of Financial Resources to Developing Countries', *OAPEC News Bulletin*, March 1980, p. 10.

84. UNCTAD, *Financial Solidarity for Development*, 1979, p. 6.

85. *Financial Times*, 15 July 1980.

86. UNCTAD, *Financial Solidarity*.

87. OECD, *Development Cooperation Review 1979*, p. 85.

88. The Assistant Secretary of the United States Treasury stated before a Congressional Sub-Committee that 'several OPEC countries have repeatedly expressed concern about the confidentiality of their investment in the United States leaving a clear implication that they might be less inclined to invest here in the absence of such confidential treatment.' Statement of Fred Bergsten quoted in *Department of Treasury News* (Washington D.C.), 18 July 1979, p. 18. Similar views were held by Kuwait's Minister of Finance on the occasion of the American Treasury Secretary's visit to Kuwait late in 1978.

89. Mancur Olson, *The Logic of Collective Action* (Cambridge, Mass.: Harvard University Press, 1971), p. 1.

90. Tibor Scitovsky, 'Two Concepts of External Economies', *The Journal of Political Economy*, April 1954.

91. William Baumol, *Welfare Economies and the Theory of the State*, 2nd ed. (Cambridge: Harvard University Press, 1965), p. 20.

92. P. Samuelson, 'The Pure Theory of Public Expenditure', *Review of Economics and Statistics*, November 1954; November 1955; November 1958.

93. R. Musgrave, *The Theory of Public Finance* (New York: McGraw Hill, 1959).

94. See respectively D.N. Rosenstein-Rodan, 'Notes on the Theory of the Big Push' in H. Ellis and H. Wallish (eds.), *Economic Development for Latin America* (London: St Martins Press, 1966); R. Nurske, *Problems of Capital Formation in Underdeveloped Countries* (Oxford: Blackwell, 1954); W.W. Rostow, *The Stages of Economic Growth* (New York, 1952).

95. General Accounting Office, *Relationship Between Oil Companies and OPEC*, Report to the US Congress, January 1978.

96. Joe Stork, *Middle East Oil and the Energy Crisis* (London: Monthly Review Press, 1975), p. 88; Robert Stobaugh, 'After the Peak: the Threat of Imported Oil', in R. Stobaugh and D. Yergin (eds.), *Energy Future* (New York: Random, 1979), p. 59.

97. Stork, *Middle East Oil*, p. 155.

98. J.A. Bill and C. Leiden, *The Politics of the Middle East* (Boston: Little Brown, 1979), p. 375; Stork, *Middle East Oil*, p. 160; C.F. Doran, *Myth, Oil and Politics: Introduction to the Political Economy of Petroleum* (New York: The Free Press, 1977), p. 59.

99. Doran, *Myth, Oil and Politics*, p. 60.

100. Jean-Marie Chevalier, *Le Nouvel Enjeu Pétrolier* (Paris: Calmann-Levy, 1973), p. 20.

101. *Los Angeles Times*, 15 November 1979.

102. Informed at 05.45 on 14 November 1979 of Iran's intention to withdraw its funds from American banks, the President promptly invoked the International Emergency Economics Powers Act. Reported in the *Los Angeles Times* (15 November 1979).

103. Ibid.

104. *Los Angeles Times*, 27 November 1979.

105. *International Currency Review*, vol. 12, no. 1, 1980, p. 20.

106. See *The Bonn Summit*.

107. *IMF Survey*, 3 March 1980.

108. A. Emmanuel, *L'Echange Inégale* (Paris, 1969); Samir Amin, *L'Accumulation à l'Echelle Mondiale* (Paris, 1970).

109. Michael Hudson distinguishes between the pan-Arab core states and those of the periphery in his *Arab Politics: the Search for Legitimacy* (New Haven: Yale University Press, 1977).

110. A.S. Becker, B. Hansen and M. Kerr, *The Economics and Politics of the Middle East* (Amsterdam: Elsevier, 1975), p. 55.

111. John Gimbel, *The Origins of the Marshall Plan* (California: Stanford University, 1976).

112. For various views on pan-Arabism see Walid Khalidi, 'Thinking the Unthinkable: A Sovereign Palestinian State', *Foreign Affairs*, July 1978; Fouad Ajami, 'The End of Pan-Arabism', *Foreign Affairs*, Winter 1978/79; Mohamed Heikal, 'Egyptian Foreign Policy', *Foreign Affairs*, July 1978.

113. Ajami, 'Pan-Arabism', p. 364. The general resurgence of a more militant Islam encourages a climate conducive, however, to local protest movements expressing religious, nationalist, political or economic grievances. See also Valerie Yorke, *The Gulf in the 1980s* (London: The Royal Institute of International Affairs, 1980), p. 10.

114. Ajami, 'Pan-Arabism'.

115. Ajami, 'Pan-Arabism'. See also Fred Halliday, *Arabia Without Sultans* (London: Penguin Books, 1974), p. 23.

116. Fouad Ajami, 'The Struggle for Egypt's Soul', *Foreign Policy*, no. 35, Summer 1979, p. 17; and 'Pan-Arabism', p. 372.

117. Hassan Ali Al Ebraheem, 'Factors Contributing to the Emergence of the State of Kuwait' (PhD dissertation, Indiana University, 1971), p. 199.

118. Bill and Leiden, *Politics of the Middle East*.

119. *International Herald Tribune* (Supplement), February 1978. Saudi Arabia is the only state in the world that was named after a single dynasty; F. Halliday, *Arabia Without Sultans*, p. 49.

120. Bill and Leiden, *Politics of the Middle East*, p. 96.

121. *International Currency Review*, vol. 11, no. 6.

122. The first is a UAE diplomat and businessman, being Ambassador Extraordinary and Plenipotentiary to the United Kingdom; the second are respectively Rashed (father), Saudi royal adviser and Gaith (son), a businessman; the third is a Saudi politician and administrator with wide business interests. The fourth was described as 'Kuwait's money man' by the *Wall Street Journal* (9 October 1979).

123. Bill Paul, 'Playing it Safe', *Wall Street Journal* (9 May 1978).

124. Ali Al-Kawari, *Oil Revenues in the Gulf Emirates: Patterns of Allocation and Impact on Economic Development* (Durham: University of Durham, 1978), pp. 83, 105, 140, 120.

125. Address by the Kuwaiti Minister of Finance, Mr Al Atiqi on 'OPEC Funds and Opportunities for Investment in an Interdependent World' at the Ausbildungszentrum, Wolfsberg, October 1979.

126. Muhammad al-Rumaihi, 'Al-sira' wa al-ta'awun fi al-Khalij al-'Arabi' [Conflict and Cooperation in the Arab Gulf], *Al-Mustaqbal al-'Arabi*, March 1980.

127. Donald Hawley, *The Trucial States* (London: Allen and Unwin, 1970), p. 19.

128. al-Rumaihi, 'Al-sira' wa al-ta'awun fi al-Khalij al-'arabi', p. 85.

129. Buraimi is the name of only one village out of the nine forming the oasis; six belong to the ruler of Abu Dhabi and three to the Sultan of Muscat and Oman. See Hawley, *Trucial States*, p. 186; and al-Rumaihi, 'Al-sira' wa al-ta'awun', p. 85.

130. Yorke, *The Gulf in the 1980s*, p. 48.

131. Leonard Binder, *In a Moment of Enthusiasm* (Chicago: Chicago University Press, 1978), p. 26; Gaetano Mosca, *The Ruling Class* (trans.), (New York: McGraw Hill, 1939).

132. Maxine Rodinson, *Islam and Capitalism* (trans.), (Austin: Texas University Press, 1978), p. 28.

133. After an unprecedented boom in the Kuwati share market, many share prices went down by as much as 25 to 40 per cent from their 1976 peak levels. In December 1977 the Kuwaiti government was prompted to declare its readiness to buy shares at minimum purchase prices. M. Khouja and P.G. Sadler, *The Economy of Kuwait* (London: Macmillan, 1978), p. 186.

134. Robert Springborg, 'On the Rise and Fall of Arab Isms', *Australian Outlook*, April 1977, p. 93.

135. Hazem Beblawi and Erfan Shafey, *Strategic Options of Development for Kuwait* (The IBK Papers), (Kuwait: Industrial Bank of Kuwait, 1980).

136. Mahmud 'Abd al-Fadil, *Al Naft wa al-wahda al-'arabiyaa* [Oil and Arab Unity], (Beirut: Centre for Arab Unity Studies, 1979), p. 84; *Kuwait Fund Annual Report*, No. 17, 1978–79; *Saudi Fund Annual Report IV*, 1978.

137. Yorke, *The Gulf in the 1980s*, p. 19.

138. H. St. John Philby, *Saudi Arabia* (London: Ernest Benn, 1955), p. xviii.

139. Very recently, after revealing the scandal of an oil deal between the Saudi Arabian oil company Petromin and the state-owned Italian energy company ENI in November 1979, rumours of similar deals with excessive 'commissions' being made in Leichtenstein continued to appear in the mass media (*Financial Times*, 9 April 1980). When interviewed in Washington in April 1980 the Saudi Finance Minister implicitly recognizing these practices, revealed the existence of 'several laws and royal decrees outlawing payment of *excessive* commissions and limiting

the role of the middle man' (*International Herald Tribune*, 24 April 1980). Prince 'Abdallah of Saudi Arabia in an interview with the Washington Post promised a crackdown on Arab middlemen who have collected enormous commissions for placing contracts in Saudi Arabia, thereby 'presenting a distorted image of the Kingdom to the rest of the world' (*International Herald Tribune*, 26 May 1980). On the other hand, when an ex-oil marketing adviser to a Gulf oil ministry writes a novel about corruption in oil dealings in that country with accurate descriptions of almost everything else, one cannot totally dismiss the reliability of his account of such illegal dealings (Desmond Meiring, *A Foreign Body*, London: Constable Books, 1979.

140. J.M. Keynes, *A Treatise on Money*, vol. I (London: The Royal Economic Society 1971), p. 125.

5 ARAB GULF FOREIGN INVESTMENT CO-ORDINATION: NEEDS AND MODALITIES*

The Importance of Foreign Investment to the Gulf States

The similarity in economic, social and political structure of the members of the Gulf Co-operation Council (GCC) is too well-known to need any further elaboration. Culturally, historically, geographically and politically the members of the GCC present a rare example of homogeneity with a continuous landscape. Time and again these facts are stressed and repeated in every gathering on the Gulf area. I should like to emphasize here a common dilemma facing the Gulf oil states.

Promoted to world financial prominence with per capita GDP ranking them amongst the highest in the world scale, the Gulf oil states remain, none the less, structurally vulnerable. They are depleting their unique — or at least their most important — resource while unable to use productively all the proceeds of oil sales domestically. Depletion of non-renewable resources on the one hand and the limited domestic absorptive capacity on the other are the formidable twin problems plaguing the economic scenario of the Gulf. No serious economic policy can be formulated without due regard to these hard facts.

It has almost become a ritual in every discussion in the area to recall the exhaustible nature of oil. Oil extraction is not 'production' in the proper sense of adding to value; rather it is a transformation of real asset (oil) into foreign exchange. What is usually referred to as the Gulf states' 'income' is a misnomer. In fact there is little income earned; by and large there is only an exchange of assets.[1] The drawdown in oil reserves should be debited against the oil sales revenues' credit before estimating the oil income. That is, earnings from oil sales should be reduced or offset by a sum reflecting the reduced value of the remaining inventories of oil in order to reach a proper assessment of the oil value added or income.[2] Estimating the reduction in the value of oil reserves is not an easy task. It remains true, however, that oil production affects the country's assets and involves its balance sheet as much as it could affect its income statement.

* The article is adapted from an address given at the International Symposium on Oil Revenues and their Impact on Development held at the University of Exeter in October 1982 and published in the *Arab Gulf Journal*, April 1983.

129

Oil production implies, then, an act of disinvestment and unless matched by a corresponding investment the country's wealth could be seriously endangered.

There is no agreement as to the objectives of a particular society and their ranking or priority scale. Security, equity, growth are common objectives in most societies.[3] Full employment, price stability, balance of payments equilibrium, etc., are familiar policy targets in most countries. By contrast, in oil-producing countries the overwhelming concern seems to be a conservation principle understood in the widest sense. It is usually maintained that a conservation policy means, in oil producing countries, a reduction of oil production. This should not be necessarily true. A more adequate formulation of the principle should refer to a systematic effort to maintain the real value of the country's assets, be it real assets (e.g. oil) or financial assets. The real issue is not to keep as much oil as we can under the ground; it is rather to maintain or to increase the value of the country's wealth. It is perfectly consistent with the conservation principle to produce more oil rather than less if the proceeds of oil sales are put to a more productive use than just keeping oil under the ground.

Investing oil proceeds is thus the crux of all oil production policies. Oil production by itself is merely wasting depletable resources; it is an act of cannibalism. It is only through investment of the oil proceeds that oil production can be justified. Investing oil proceeds does not necessarily mean domestic investment. Foreign investments, after a discount for external risks, are no different from domestic investment.

The importance of foreign investment to the GCC members is illustrated by the second constraint on their economies — i.e. the limited domestic absorptive capacity. Sparsely populated, with few or no other complementary resources — human as well as material — the Gulf states' ability to absorb domestic investment productively, though increasing over time, falls short of their domestic savings.

It has been suggested that oil production should be determined by the absorptive capacity of the oil producing countries. This is not only an unrealistic view but also quite often unjustified. Domestic absorptive capacity is, undoubtedly, an important factor in determining the level of oil production. However, it cannot be the unique determinant; other technical, economic and political considerations must be considered. Such considerations include production reserves ratios, availability of energy substitutes (actual and potential), world demand for energy, political stability in producing and consuming countries, and prospects for foreign investment.

At the present time it seems reasonable to assume that the Gulf oil states will generally produce at a level where the oil sales proceeds exceed their domestic absorptive capacity. This will give rise to balance of payments surpluses — i.e. foreign investment. Even at the time of writing this paper (September 1982), when the prospects for oil and particularly for OPEC are so grim (the first time for OPEC as a whole to face a combined current account deficit since early 1960s),[4] it is expected that the four Gulf exporters — Saudi Arabia, Kuwait, the United Arab Emirates and Qatar — will end up with small surpluses.[5] It should also be recalled that the present exceptionally soft oil market (September 1982) is created by the alarmingly low level of world economic activity on the one hand and the liquidation of excessive stocks previously built up on the other. This is not a sustainable situation. Petro-surpluses are structural in the case of the Gulf oil producing countries and are bound to continue for some time in spite of their low level right now.

To sum up, investing oil proceeds in the case of the Gulf oil producing countries is not a matter of choice; it is not a commitment to improve the future so much as a policy necessary for preserving the national wealth. Rather than a drive for the betterment of conditions, investment in the Gulf states emanates from a survival instinct. In so far as domestic absorption capacity limits domestic investment, the issue of foreign investment becomes vital to the Gulf states. The question which then arises is how to protect the real value of these foreign investments *vis-à-vis* the vagaries of foreign exchange and inflation (political risks are not discussed in this article).

As financial assets which are claims on other economies, foreign investments risk losing their real value in the event of currency depreciations and/or inflation. In the first case there is a loss in terms of one currency when the claims are denominated in this currency *vis-à-vis* other currencies. In the second there is a loss in terms of all currencies *vis-à-vis* goods and services. The inflation risk is by and large the more serious. Moreover, with judicious distribution of investments among currencies, foreign exchange risks can be reduced to a minimum. Thus foreign exchange risks are diversifiable and can be hedged against. On the other hand, inflation is not diversifiable and remains the major economic threat to foreign investments.[6]

In what follows I shall develop an argument showing that world inflation is *not* unrelated to the way in which oil surpluses have been used. The moral is clear. To combat inflation, oil surplus countries — the Gulf states in this instance — have to follow co-ordinated foreign investment policies.

World Inflation is a Macro-Problem

Inflation in most industrial countries has, it should be emphasized, deep-rooted domestic causes in their social, political and economic structure. It would be a serious mistake to attribute inflation only to external factors — in the event, the oil shock. It is true that external factors have aggravated an already deteriorating situation, but this is different from being the dominant factor, let alone the originator. Recent world inflation had started in 1971-72, two years ahead of the first oil shock in 1973-74. Also the effect of external factors has been, I think, grossly distorted. The argument I should like to pursue here is that the inflationary impact of the oil shock is more related to a change in the world macro-aggregates, rather than to a change in commodity prices.

A vast literature has cropped up in the last few years attributing persistent inflation in industrial countries to the quadrupling of oil prices in 1973-74 and then their further doubling in 1979-80. It has been estimated, however, that only 2.4 per cent of the increase in prices in the United States in 1974 could be explained by oil price increases[7] and this was a one-time only increase. Similar conclusions have been found for other OECD countries. It was later stressed that oil price increases which occurred in several steps between December 1978 and June 1979 did not cause a resurgence of inflation in industrial countries.[8] It is also no secret that price stability has been far better attained in countries with the highest share of oil imports (Germany and Japan). The standard analysis remains, none the less, unshaken; world econonic ills, and particularly inflation, are attributed to oil price increases.

Over-emphasis on oil price increases has concealed, I am afraid, the more important change in world income distribution and its effects on the world macro-aggregates. It is true that the oil price shock increased the cost of a strategic commodity, but it is also true that it brought about a dramatic increase in oil revenues, thus changing the world income distribution. From no more than $15.2 billion in 1972, oil revenues reached more than $110 billion in 1974.[9] The change in oil terms of trade introduced a different distribution of world income, thus affecting world aggregates — e.g. savings and investment.

OPEC, and particularly the Gulf oil producing countries, were the major beneficiaries of the new redistribution of world income. Already enjoying high per capita incomes and a remarkably high propensity to save prior to the oil price shock in 1973-74, the increase in their share of world income could only further increase their propensity to save. Oil surplus funds thus appeared as an addition to world savings that could not be domestically absorbed by OPEC countries.

The addition to world savings was, moreover, quite substantial to the world economy. World oil trade increased from \$28 billion in 1970 to \$535 billion in 1980, or from seven per cent of world trade to 21 per cent. This increase was considerably larger than West Germany's or the United States' share of world trade. The change in the oil bill is equivalent to paying for all the exports of another United States or West Germany.[10] Any change of such magnitude is bound to affect the functioning of the world economy. In 1974, oil surplus funds added more than \$65 billion to world savings. Suffice it to compare this with other economic flow aggregates; for example, in the US — the largest world economy — exports and private gross fixed-capital formation were respectively \$110 billion and \$205 billion in the same year. OPEC's external savings (petro-funds) represented the equivalent of more than 50 per cent of US exports and 30 per cent of its private investment in 1974. These are not small quantities. It is true that these savings tended to decline in the following years until they reached their low point in 1978. However, these developments were the result of economic forces operating in the aftermath of the oil price increases, and can be attributed to a great extent to the mode of placement of the oil surplus funds, as will be shown.

Oil surplus funds have thus added substantially to world savings following the world redistribution of income. A new situation has emerged which needs fresh thinking.

I have analysed elsewhere[11] the impact of the initial increase in the world's savings and the financial response to it. The analysis used as a general framework was the Keynesian technique of the identity of the *ex post* savings and investments.

As I take up again the argument as presented previously, I shall try to illustrate in more detail the model for general price increase — i.e. the 'placement case'.

To sum up, it is accepted that OPEC countries have increased their savings after the oil price increase and the subsequent world redistribution of income. Yet every saving is matched *ex post* by investment. Thus three possible scenarios could have taken place in the face of

OPEC new savings, namely:

(1) a parallel increase in the rate of real investment in the world (the 'investment case');

(2) a nominal dissavings elsewhere in the world to offset the increase in OPEC savings — i.e. no change in the net savings and investment of the world (the 'transfer of wealth case'); or

(3) neither (1) nor (2), but only an increase in financial assets giving rise to an increase in nominal investment (the 'placement case').

I have argued that, by and large, a situation not very different from the 'placement case' took place in the years following the oil shock. Financial assets soared with the tremendous increase in countries' indebtedness, the huge volume of the Euromarket, etc. On the other hand, the world economy has not shown any perceptible rise in the *rate* of investment with the increase of OPEC savings, in spite of the huge surge in financial assets and liabilities. Also, nothing seems to substantiate a sizeable transfer of wealth, giving rise to nominal dissavings in the oil importing countries in favour of OPEC. It looks as if the increase in OPEC's holdings of new financial assets has not been matched by any liquidation of previously accumulated wealth in the importing countries.

In both the 'investment case' and the 'transfer of wealth case', it is assumed that the world economy would adjust to OPEC savings through changes in real aggregates; the increase in real investment in the first case and the redistribution of wealth in the second one. Financial assets would be instrumental in bringing about a real adjustment. Financial changes thus mirror real changes, and the relationships between real investment and the flow of financial assets would remain relatively constant. Financial assets would increase proportionately with the increase in real investment in the first case, and remain constant — though in different hands — in the second case.

The characteristic feature of the 'placement case', on the other hand, is that the relationship between real investment and the flow of financial assets is broken. Financial assets would increase independently of real investment and set the economy in motion. Financial assets are therefore introduced in a more fundamental way. Adjustments to OPEC savings are mainly financial rather than real.

This scenario assumes that the overall allocation of resources between investment and consumption remains by and large unaffected by the oil price increases. Also, it is assumed that there are no apparent dissavings in other parts of the world following the increase in OPEC's savings. The scenario opens a new alternative course of action through the behaviour of financial assets and their impact on the nominal aggregates rather than on the real ones.

In the face of the increase in the oil import bill and the emergence of a trade deficit on the one hand, and the reluctance of all parties to transfer wealth to OPEC and/or reduce consumption levels on the other, the deficit countries would issue new financial assets which OPEC countries would be satisfied to hold. Hence the supply of new financial assets would be matched by a new demand by OPEC to hold them. On the face of it everything seems to be in order. OPEC countries increased their savings and held a preferred form of wealth, free of political animosity, on the one hand; and on the other, oil importing countries minimized the real transfer of resources (from consumption to investment and/or property wealth from oil consuming to OPEC countries). But this cannot be the whole story. OPEC's savings seem to be increasing without a corresponding increase in real investment or offsetting dissavings. This is impossible since the accounting equality of investment and savings must hold in all cases. If real aggregates fail to react to the change in OPEC's additional savings, we shall be left with nominal changes which bring costs and prices to the forefront of the analysis.

The increase of financial assets held by OPEC surplus countries means a corresponding increase in deficit countries' financial liabilities, and if OPEC countries choose to hold their savings in the form of new financial assets, it is because they intend to own them − i.e. to receive a reasonable return on them.[12] Since we assume that the real capital stock has not undergone any change with the issuing of the new financial assets, the capital stock is now owned, in the final analysis, by a wider class of asset holders.

The new claimers on wealth are obviously entitled to a nominal return on their assets equivalent to that of the former owners of wealth − i.e. the 'new' financial assets must produce the same nominal yields as the 'old' ones.

What about these nominal returns, and how do they compare with the old nominal returns? One might be tempted to argue that the increase in loanable funds with the issuing of new financial assets would tend to suppress the nominal return on them.[13] No conclusion could, however, be reached without reference to the initial conditions from which the new situation emerged. Starting from a quasi-equilibrium position, the increase in the oil import bill gave rise to a higher demand for loanable funds.

The process of issuing new financial assets started, then, from a situation of financial squeeze and not of excess liquidity. It is hardly conceivable, under these circumstances, that the nominal yields of the new financial assets would settle below the prevailing yields; eventually they could be higher. The banking system would be induced, in all probability, to generate the required liquidity. That is, we are faced here with a downward stickiness of nominal returns on financial assets, a phenomenon not very different from Keynes' assumption of downward rigid money wages. It follows that the increase in financial assets (liabilities) and the stickiness of the nominal returns on them will lead to a corresponding increase in the absolute nominal earnings on property titles (loosely defined as the share of profit), a fact that cannot fail to affect the structural relationships of output distribution and factor earnings.

Empirical investigations have shown a remarkable historical constancy in three basic macro-ratios, *viz* the rate of profit, the capital/output ratio and the share of profit (wages) in output. It is to the credit of the Cambridge neo-Keynesian school to have drawn attention to this fact, and to have developed growth models accounting for the constancy of these ratios.[14]

The previous two assumptions (rigidity of nominal returns on financial assets and constancy of the basic macro-ratios) cannot be reconciled in one model without introducing other changes in the economic system — i.e. prices and costs. According to the first assumption, the increase in financial assets (liabilities) and the rigidity of the nominal return on them should lead to an increase in the absolute nominal earnings on property titles (share of profit). According to the second assumption, this result should in no case affect the constancy of the rate of profit, the capital/output ratio and the share of profit. The only way out is to introduce prices in such a way as to increase the nominal values of other aggregates to account for both the absolute nominal increase in financial returns on the one hand and the constancy of the ratios on the other. A general price increase can help maintain constant ratios, while at the same time servicing larger nominal returns on financial assets. Returns on financial assets are thus magnified, as are also output, wages and so forth. This is inflation. Changes in the stock of financial assets cannot remain without impact on the nominal values of output and investment.

To illustrate this point I use a simplified model similar to Marx's two departments model: Department I, producing means of production (investment), and Department II, producing consumers' goods.

Assume that there are two factors of production, labour (L) and capital (K), earning wages (w) and profits (p), respectively. Wages will comprise not only manual labour but salaries as well. By profit is meant all incomes of property owners.

$$\text{Department I} = wL_1 + pK_1 = Q_1 \qquad (1)$$
$$\text{Department II} = wL_2 + pK_2 = Q_2 \qquad (2)$$
$$\text{Total output} = Q_1 + Q_2 = Q \qquad (3)$$

Assume that wages are spent on consumers' goods (Department II) and profits on capital (Department I).

$$wL_1 + wL_2 = Q_2 \qquad (4)$$
$$pK_1 + pK_2 = Q_1 \qquad (5)$$

Assume also that the macro ratios, capital/output, the share of profit, remain constant in the economy.

$$\frac{Q_1}{Q_2} = a \qquad (6)$$

Assume finally that the rate of investment remains unchanged. Now, if the absolute nominal returns on financial assets (p) increases, from (5) it follows that the value of capital goods Q_1 will increase also. But since the ratio $Q_1 : Q_2$ is constant (6) then Q_2 must increase following the increase in Q_1, thus raising consumers' goods prices.

Prices are thus introduced into the picture as the end result in a chain of reactions to the increase in OPEC's savings. The increase in financial assets without a corresponding increase in real investment, the rigidity of nominal returns on them, and the constancy of the basic ratios of the economy, would trigger a general movement of price increases. Though real investment does not increase, nominal investment, under inflation, does grow, and the identity between saving and investment is maintained, albeit in nominal terms.

Here we find that inflation is built into the scenario. It is necessary in order to bring about the equality of savings and investment. Failing to increase real investment or to effect parallel dissavings, the only possibility open is to increase nominal investment.

The precise mechanism to propagate inflation can differ from one place to another. It can be channelled through monetary or fiscal instruments or both. The increase in financial assets (liabilities) can take the form of bank deposits, treasury bills or bonds, as well as similar instruments. In any case money supply or budget deficit will grow substantially, giving way to inflationary pressures.

The foregoing analysis would seem in flagrant contradiction with Keynesian economics. It amounts to asserting that excess savings are inflationary rather than deflationary as Keynesian economics would predict.

This is a very serious deviation indeed. I think, however, that the clue to the apparent contradiction may lie in the origin of OPEC's savings. These are savings realized through income redistribution and forced upon the system exogenously.

Since there has not been any major change in the distribution of income in industrial countries over short periods, the official doctrine, though recognizing the importance of income distribution, postulates savings as a function of the level of income. This is also more or less a stable function.

In a nutshell, Keynesian economics maintains that investment is an independent variable, invariant with respect to changes in savings. But since savings depend on the level of income, if investment were to fall short of *ex ante* savings, income would have to decline to bring savings down. The decline in income (deflation) is necessary to undo the *ex ante* excess of savings over investment. The equality of *ex post* savings and investment is always maintained.

But if the increase in savings is the result of a redistribution of income and not of a rise in its level, a deflation would not be absolutely necessary. By analogy, one would expect that if investment fell short of savings a reverse distribution of income would take place to remove the excess savings. A general price increase, particularly in non-oil commodities, could very well reverse a redistribution of income brought about by the increase in oil prices. The increase in financial assets and the revaluation of nominal returns on them could be the trigger-mechanism in this process. With inflation, a new mechanism to reverse the income redistribution is set up.

Although I have emphasized the different sources of increased OPEC savings, it remains true that savings are also a function of the level of income. The traditional Keynesian diagnosis is not altogether irrelevant here. An excess of savings over investment is also deflationary. The fact that the increased savings of OPEC are due to income redistribution does not preclude the dependence of savings on the level of income also. The 'income distribution' variable supplements, but does not supplant, the 'level of income' variable. Undoing the effect of OPEC's savings would require a reverse action on the redistribution of income and also a decline in the level of income. In this scenario, OPEC's savings may thus have a stagflationary effect with more pronounced inflationary pressures.

The emergence of the 'placement case' as the most likely of all possible outcomes is not fortuitous. It is in fact related to the way in which OPEC's savings are used; in particular, whether they are placed in developed countries or invested in developing countries. This is a basic decision with far-reaching effects on the world economy and on the sustainability of OPEC's savings themselves. What is important here, it should be emphasized at the outset, is where these savings are used in the first instance.

OPEC surplus funds have been estimated by non-OPEC sources to have reached some $180 billion by the end of 1978. Of this amount $30 billion (less than 20 per cent) seems to have been allocated directly or indirectly through the World Bank and other multilateral lending institutions to the developing countries.[15] The rest of OPEC's surpluses were channelled mainly to the OECD countries and their financial institutions.

It seems that the choice of placing the oil surpluses, in the first instance, in the industrial countries rather than in developing countries, is the principal reason for bringing about the 'placement case'. It can be argued, conversely, that investing oil surplus funds in developing countries could possibly have brought about a situation closer to the 'investment case'. The difference between the two cases is one of different responses to the availability of savings.

In industrial countries investment is almost exogenous and independent of savings, while in developing countries growth is actually constrained by the availability of savings. The opposition of Keynes' 'effective demand' to the 'Say Law' typifies the difference between developed and developing countries. That is, while Keynesian economics seems to approximate the situation in developed countries, classical economics probably provides a better description of the situation in developing countries.

In developed economies, affirms Keynes, investment is exogenous and independently determined. Savings will always adjust to investment. The whole multiplier technique is devised to show how the economy reacts to generate the necessary savings to a change in investment. If savings react to investment in developed economies, investment cannot change without a change in effective demand.

In developing countries, classical economists maintain on the contrary that savings are the limiting factor. The needs for investment are so huge that the availability of savings seems to be the only operational limit to capital accumulation. In these countries, investment would follow the availability of savings and not vice versa.

It follows from the foregoing that placing OPEC funds in OECD countries cannot increase real investment without a change in effective demand. Without a change in effective demand in favour of more capital goods industries, OECD countries cannot increase their real investment simply because financial resources happen to be available. The inability of OECD countries to increase their real investment would trigger inflation in a manner not very different from our 'placement case'. This is a matter of structure rather than policy. Investing OPEC funds in developing countries would, on the contrary, have brought the missing link to the world economy. The existence of huge needs for investment in the developing countries would have helped bring about the necessary change in effective demand using OPEC savings. Increased investment in these countries would, inevitably, lead to enhanced demand for OECD countries' capital goods. It is not unrealistic, then, to assume that given enough time, capital goods industries in OECD countries would expand under the new demand forthcoming from developing countries.

Investment in the Third World is a Collective Good

If the foregoing analysis is correct, the conclusion would be clear. There exists an economic case, as well as a political one, for oil surplus countries to *invest* their funds in the developing countries rather than to *place* them in the developed countries. It is true that, on the face of it, developed countries seem to offer Gulf oil surplus countries a wide spectrum of advantages that developing countries are unable to match. Credit-worthiness, well organized financial markets, available technology and good management are some of the attractions for oil surplus funds in developed economies. However, behind this misleading façade remain the hard facts that OPEC savings can hardly increase real investment in developed countries. Inflation would unobtrusively but persistently erode the same oil funds entrusted to highly-organized markets in developed countries. Motivated by self-interest, the Gulf oil states' investment in developed countries turns out to be self-defeating. Developing countries, with all their shortcomings, can on the contrary offer Gulf oil states a chance to transform their savings into real investment and hence protect them against erosion by inflation.

The crucial question remains, therefore, why the Gulf oil states do not invest heavily in the Third World. The reasons seem to reside in the nature of investments in the Third World. These are in the nature of public or collective goods; though reflecting the common interest of the Gulf states, they do not necessarily imply behaviour leading to that end.

It is often suggested that groups of individuals (or for that matter of states) with common interests usually attempt to further them.[16] This opinion is not only held in popular discussion but is also maintained in many scholarly writings. However, nothing seems to support this view, either logically or in practice. Common interest is a necessary condition for collective action, yet by itself it is not sufficient to bring this about. This is a classic problem in welfare economics, and a whole literature on public or collective goods is devoted to it. It is also a central theme in the theory of development and industrialization.

A public or collective good is defined as one in which the consumption by one member of a group does not reduce its utility to other members of the group. The distinguishing feature of a collective good is that, once provided to one member of the group, it can be made available to other members at no extra cost (the joint supply principle),[17] and/or the rest of the group cannot be excluded from benefiting from it (the exclusion principle).[18] Though collective goods are not free goods, since their production entails the use of scarce resources and implies risks, it remains true that once provided they appear to other members of the group as costless and they can enjoy them as free riders. In most cases the indivisibility of costs appears to reside at the heart of the collective goods problem. Whereas costs are indivisible and must be incurred all at once, benefits have to be divided among members of the group. A member of a group may not be able to incur alone the cost of the collective good because the initial cost exceeds its benefit to him. It is no consolation to know that the total benefits to all members of the group outmatch total cost. What matters to each member is the fraction of benefit that he gains from the collective goods regardless of the benefits accruing to other members of the group. Without coercion and/or co-ordination collective goods cannot be provided, no matter how important they may be.

Investment in the Third World seems to be in the nature of a collective good. Even if the Gulf states are interested in investing their savings in the developing countries, the developing countries themselves remain far from being the promised land for investment. The odds against secure and successful investment in these countries are enormous. Not only inadequacy of infrastructure and qualified manpower, but also inefficient management and political instability impede any sustainable effort to development in the Third World.[19]

A vast literature on development has emphasized the need for a substantial investment effort to break the vicious circle in developing countries and thus to make the effort worthwhile. Whether it is called the 'big push', 'balanced growth' or 'take-off', the message is always the same.[20] Investment in the Third World cannot be made profitable unless undertaken on a massive scale. While this scale could be within the reach of the Gulf states as a group for certain regions, it is not necessarily attainable by any one country alone. Here enters the nature of investment in developing countries as a collective good. There is no doubt that it is in the interests of the Gulf oil states to transform their savings into investment in developing countries. Yet one country alone – even an oil-rich one – cannot assume all the hazards of investment in developing countries. What is needed is a collective action to bring about a collective benefit.

The prerequisite for meaningful development, it has been said, is to undertake a massive investment programme. However, all the Gulf states' savings are too small to finance massive investment in all developing countries, and hence there is a need for concentration on a regional basis. Gulf states' accumulated savings, important as they are, would become largely ineffective if thinly spread out all over the Third World. In the absence of a supra-national authority able to define an investment policy by coercion, the only way to reach such a policy is through co-ordination. Without such co-ordination no investment in the Third World could bring about the desired results. It is no wonder, then, that in the absence of such co-ordination the Gulf states acting independently prefer to place their savings in developed countries rather than to assume alone all the hazards of investment in the Third World. Unfortunately, what appears as a second-best investment policy for the Gulf states' savings triggers an inflation process that would ultimately erode these very savings. On the other hand, if investing the Gulf states' savings in developing countries seems to be necessary to bring about the 'investment case' referred to earlier, this cannot be realized without a co-ordination among them.

A Gulf Dinar as Currency

Political risks apart, inflation is the number one enemy facing Gulf states' foreign investments. The analysis so far has emphasized the structural nature of inflation resulting from changes and adjustments in world macro-aggregates. The policy recommendation from the foregoing analysis, not surprisingly, required the restructuring of world macro-aggregates to favour an increase in real investment in the Third World. It was also underlined that an effective investment policy in the Third World assumed a sustained and concentrated effort. Though in the common interest of all the Gulf states as a group, the merits of investment in the Third World do not appear to each country acting individually. A co-ordinated investment policy is the only way to bring about such common interest in the absence of coercion by a supranational authority. This is a gigantic enterprise which probably needs more than co-ordination between just the Gulf oil states. It requires also co-operation and commitment on the part of the recipient developing countries.

However, inflation does not stem only from external factors; as has been mentioned, it has its internal roots. Restructuring world macro-aggregates, difficult as it may be, is not a perfect cure. Inflation would continue in industrial countries, in so far as domestic policies and attitudes would remain unchanged. Gulf states' foreign investments stand to lose from inflation regardless of its origin, internal or external.

In addition to structural changes there is a need for mechanistic devices to help hedge against inflation. These are particularly useful when inflation is caused by internal domestic consideration beyond the influence of the oil surplus countries. A new international Gulf Dinar could be one of these devices.[21]

There is, however, some confusion as to the meaning of an international Gulf currency. Very often such an international role is regarded as synonymous with an international reserve currency. This is by no means necessary. A currency can have an international role without being reserve currency.

It is useful, at this stage, to refer to the familiar distinction between the money of account and the money of payment. A currency can have an international role either if it has an international account function or an international payment function. Only in the second case is the currency used as a reserve currency.

It is not possible for Gulf states to play any role whatsoever in introducing a new reserve currency. Technically and economically the Gulf states are not in a position to assume any role in a world central bank function. On the other hand, it is not inconceivable for the Gulf states to use a new unit of account for certain transactions in so far as other reserve currencies are used for payments. It should be made clear that in the present circumstances any discussion of an international role for a Gulf currency is only referring to a unit of account function – i.e. as a 'numeraire'.

Inflation, it should be remembered, affects the Gulf oil states in two different, though related, ways. First, since the Gulf states are heavily dependent on imports, inflation reduces their real current imports. Secondly, inflation erodes the value of their nominal foreign investment.

Experience has shown that OPEC countries, through their periodic review of oil prices, do try to correct them for the effects of import price increases. However, these price corrections fail to hedge against the erosion of the value of previously accumulated nominal investment – i.e. future imports.

A device to link the price of oil with foreign investment could be the introduction of a new Gulf Dinar to be used as an accounting unit for both oil pricing and foreign lending. This amounts to the indexation of foreign lending to the oil price, thus protecting both the value of current and future imports.

It is assumed under this scheme that the Gulf states would separate the unit of account function from that of means of payment in oil pricing. Oil would continue to be paid for in different currencies, in particular the dollar, as usual. However, the price would be fixed in terms of a new accounting unit, the OPEC or the Gulf Dinar. Rather than review the price of oil, OPEC would review the exchange rate of this new currency in terms of other currencies. Changes in import prices would undoubtedly figure among the factors fixing the exchange rate of the new accounting unit.

The new accounting unit would not only be used in oil pricing, but also in foreign lending. Gulf foreign lending would thus be indexed to the real value of oil in terms of their imports.

Though the idea might look simple and straightforward, the difficulties in implementation, and particularly the resistance to it, would be enormous. A concerted effort among the Gulf oil states would be an important factor in alleviating some of these difficulties.

The members of the GCC have been considering, for some time now, the creation of a new Gulf currency. Discussions are centred around institutional and structural differences with the aim of introducing such a new common currency inside the Gulf states. A more promising outcome and probably easier to agree upon would be the creation of a new unit of account to protect the Gulf states' imports, current and future.

Conclusion

For the Gulf states, investing oil sales' proceeds is equivalent to conserving the oil wealth. Domestic and foreign investment are thus vital to their economic survival. Absorptive capacity limits the extent of domestic investment, and world inflation threatens to erode foreign investment.

World inflation is a structural problem emanating from deep-rooted internal causes as much as from distortions of external macro-aggregates.

Gulf oil states can do nothing to change internal conditions in the recipients countries. An accounting unit (the Gulf Dinar) to be used for oil pricing and lending could be a mechanistic device to hedge against inflation.

The Gulf states could also attempt to restructure the world macro aggregates to maintain their surplus position. This could be done if they were to place their oil surpluses in such a way as to increase the world real investment and not just the volume of financial assets. Investment in the Third World would seem to be a step in that direction.

In both cases, the effectiveness of each Gulf state acting alone would be very limited, if it existed at all. On the other hand, there exists a great prospect for success if the Gulf states would agree to co-ordinate their investment policies. The success of OPEC countries in price matters through co-ordination should be an example to be followed in investment policies.

Notes

1. H. Beblawi and E. Shaefey, 'Strategic Options of Development for Kuwait', *IBK Papers*, no. 1, July 1980 (Industrial Bank of Kuwait), p. 24.

2. T. Stauffer, 'The Dynamics of Petroleum Dependency: Growth in an Oil Rentier State', *Finance & Industry*, no. 2, 1981 (Industrial Bank of Kuwait), p. 10.

3. Beblawi, Shaefey, 'Strategic Options'.

4. *OPEC Bulletin*, cited in *Financial Times*, 9 September 1982.

5. Published forecasts on OPEC's current account range from a small surplus of $3 bn to a deficit of $15 bn (Chase Manhattan Bank), to a surplus of $17 bn (Marine Midland Bank) or a deficit of $9.5 bn (OPEC Bulletin). But in all cases none of the Gulf oil producers will go into the red. *Financial Times*, 11 September 1982.

6. A similar concept for risk is included in the 'capital asset pricing models'. See W.F. Sharp, 'Capital Asset Prices: Theory of Market Equilibrium under Conditions of Risk', *Journal of Finance*, 19, 42, September 1964.

7. Helmut A. Merblein and W. Cary Hardy, *Energy Economics* (Texas Gulf Publishing Co., 1971), p. 53.

8. GATT Press Release, 4 September 1979.

9. *International Petroleum Encyclopaedia* (Oklahoma Petroleum Publishing Co., 1975).

10. *World Development Report 1981* (World Bank, Washington DC, 1981), p. 20.

11. H. Beblawi, *Oil Surplus Funds: The Impact of the Mode of Placement*; the OPEC Fund, Pamphlet Series no. 16; September 1981.

12. Luigi Pasinetti, 'Growth and Income Distribution' in *Essays in Economic Theory* (Cambridge University Press, 1974), p. 106.

13. Bent Hansen, 'The Accumulation of Financial Capital by Middle East Oil Exporters: Problems and Policies', in A. Udovitch (ed.), *The Middle East: Oil, Conflict and Hope* (Lexington, Mass.: Lexington Books, 1976).

14. N. Kaldor, 'A Model of Economic Growth', *Economic Journal*, 1957.

15. *IMF Survey*, June 1977; *Financial Times*, Banking, 22 May 1978.

16. Mancur Olson, *The Logic of Collective Action* (Cambridge, Mass.: Harvard University Press, 1971), p. 1.

17. P. Samuelson, 'The Pure Theory of Public Expenditure', in *Review of Economics and Statistics*; November 1954, November 1955, November 1958.

18. R. Musgrave, *The Theory of Public Finance* (New York: McGraw Hill, 1959).

19. H. Beblawi, 'The Predicament of the Arab Gulf Oil States: Individual Gains and Collective Losses', in Malcolm Kerr and El Sayed Yassin (eds.), *Rich and Poor States in the Middle East* (Boulder: Westview Press, 1982), p. 202.

20. See respectively, D.N. Rosenstein, 'Notes on the Theory of the Big Push', in H. Ellis and H. Wallish (eds.), *Economic Development for Latin America*; (London: St Martins Press, 1966); R. Nurkse, *Problems of Capital Formation in Underdeveloped Countries* (Oxford: Blackwell, 1954); W.W. Rostow, *The Stages of Economic Growth* (New York: 1952).

21. H. Beblawi, 'The Dollar Crisis, Oil Prices and Foreign Exchange Risks: The Case for a Basket of Currencies as Numeraire', *International Journal for Middle East Studies*, II; 1980.

PART THREE:
THE KUWAITI EXAMPLE

6 KUWAIT, OR THE ART OF TIGHTROPE WALKING

Introduction

A city-state, Kuwait emerged in the last decade as a regional financial if not political centre to be reckoned with. Situated at the north-east corner of the Arabian Peninsula, Kuwait is bordered in the north-west by Iraq, in the south by Saudi Arabia and in the east by the Arabian (Persian) Gulf and Iran. The Soviet Union's southern borders are within a few hours tank drive and only a few minutes of flight by jet. British troops left the area only a decade ago, to witness the increasing dependence of Europe and Japan on the oil produced in the area. The Americans never failed to show their interest in the Gulf, elevated by the 'Carter Doctrine' to vital American interests. Survival in such a turbulent and covetous neighbourhood can only be achieved by a subtle adherence to policies of balance and evenhandedness, an art which Kuwait has mastered admirably.

Kuwait's modern origin goes back to the eighteenth century when the Al Sabah family from the Anizah tribe migrated from inner Najd to the actual location of Kuwait. The name, Kuwait, is a diminutive of 'Kut' meaning a small fort. Initially, Kuwait was part of the province of Al Hasa under the dominance of Bani Khalid. The authority of the Sheikh of Kuwait gradually asserted itself from the middle of the eighteenth century.

Though never a formal British colony, Kuwait — which was theoretically part of the Ottoman Empire but adamantly opposed to Turkish authority — ably used its British connections to counteract the Turkish influence. In 1899 the Kuwaiti ruler Sheikh Mubarak concluded with the British political resident in the Gulf a secret engagement whereby in return for 15,000 rupees, the Sheikh bound himself, his heirs and successors, not to alienate any part of his territory to foreign governments or individuals or to receive the representative of any foreign power without the prior sanction of the British Government. In 1913 the British and the Turks agreed to recognize Kuwait as an autonomous 'quza' of the Ottoman empire. This Anglo–Ottoman convention was not, however, ratified and the declaration of the 1914 war put an end to the whole arrangement. On the eve of the war, the British

Government recognized Kuwait as an independent Sheikhdom under British protection. Kuwaiti independence was granted in June 1961 when Britain formally acknowledged her independence and terminated its agreement with her.

Two major territorial conflicts set Kuwait against her neighbours in her recent history. The first arose when Saudi Arabia claimed and succeeded in amputating part of its territory in the Uqair conference in 1922. With the help of the British political representative Sir Percy Cox, Ibn Saud was compensated for the loss of territory he was forced to cede to Iraq by sharing with Kuwait equal rights of sovereignty over a neutral zone between Najd and Kuwait in the coastal hinterland to the south and which was previously allocated to Kuwait in the Anglo-Ottoman convention of 1913. Sir Percy Cox was certainly very generous towards Ibn Saud, depriving Kuwait of nearly two-thirds of her territory to Najd. Kuwait had to pay a high price and painfully swallowed the deal.

The second episode is more recent and potentially crisis-laden. No later than six days after the declaration of Kuwait's independence, General Qassim of Iraq claimed sovereignty over Kuwait, because once part of the Ottoman empire, Kuwait had been administered until 1919 as a district of the 'wilayat' of Basra. Though subsequently recognizing the independence of Kuwait and its sovereignty, Iraq has never agreed to draw the definitive frontiers between the two countries. As late as 1981, President Saddam Hussein, in a public interview given to the Kuwaiti newspaper *Al Anba*, required some modifications of the frontier to permit to Iraq a better opening on the Gulf (control over Kuwait's islands of Warbah and Bubiyan).

Kuwait's modern history is virtually no more than the history of oil: its bonanza and problems. The first shipment of oil from Kuwait was lifted on 30 June 1946. After long negotiations and rivalry between British (Anglo-Persian Oil Company, APOC) and American (Gulf Oil) interests, a new joint Anglo-American concern was incorporated, the Kuwait Oil Company (KOC), which gained concession from Kuwait on 23 December 1934. The agreement granted Sheikh Ahmed, the ruler of Kuwait, 475,000 rupees on signature, three rupees per ton 'won and saved' or 95,000 rupees per annum whichever be the greater.

Within a decade – from the late 1940s to the late 1950s – the population of Kuwait doubled from about 100,000 to over 200,000 as foreigners poured in to work and build the new Kuwait. In the last census (1980) the population of Kuwait reached 1.356 million, of which 0.794 million (59 per cent) were non-Kuwaitis.

Exported oil and imported labour with their implications are the two major concerns of modern Kuwait.

Political Outlook

Basic Political Goals

The country has been ruled for the past two centuries by a dynasty — Al Sabah — that is renowned for both moderation and wisdom. Kuwait, more than other Gulf states, is a merchant society with a long tradition in trade and exchange. Pearl-diving industries, sea-faring, commercial and entrepot trades and/or smuggling all adding to the increasing influence of the merchant families. If the Al Sabahs are the monarchs of this desert realm, the merchant families are its nobility. Rather than a nomadic tribal society, Kuwait appeared more as a federation of trading families. The merchant, or rather the middle-man, is deep-rooted in Kuwaiti traditions. Compromise and accommodation are not alien to this middle-man mentality. With oil riches, Kuwait exhibits extreme wealth side by side with extreme vulnerability. With a small population and no natural resources other than oil, Kuwait owes its wealth to the oil discovery and its revaluation. Its financial wealth was not matched by economic development of its productive capacity nor its political or military potential. A geological coincidence in a particularly favourable international juncture made the fortune of Kuwait; inherent weak economic and political structures account for its vulnerability.

In this context, the overwhelming political goal cannot be other than the maintenance of the *status quo* and accommodation. Balance of power and evenhandedness are the name of the game in Kuwait, be it in internal politics or in international relationships. With abundant financial resources and judicious use of them, Kuwait can afford to reconcile apparently conflicting claims.

An almost unprecedented welfare state where the provision of free services is second to none, Kuwait provides its population with a complex array of services and benefits: free education, free health care, soft (often free) loans, subsidies, etc. *L'Etat Providence*, if it ever existed, could be applied to modern Kuwait. In the 1950s, in his quest to redistribute part of the oil revenues to Kuwaiti families and thus create vested interests round the new oil state, Sheikh Abdullah Al Salim introduced the system of government land purchases at prices hardly related to the market value. The result is that Kuwait, as it stands now, exhibits probably the best pattern of wealth and income distribution in the region. There remains, however, much to be desired in the domain of equitable wealth distribution, though it can hardly be claimed that there exists any widespread resentment in that respect. Government expenditures continue a long tribal tradition of buying loyalty and allegiance.

In the area of distribution of power, though it remains a traditionally patriarchal and a distinctly familial society, Kuwait is also the most institutionalized state in the region. More liberal and open to various political opinions, the government labours to maintain a reasonable balance between different views.

Kuwait policy towards expatriates demonstrates it commitment to the balance of power. If assets diversification is considered the best policy for portfolio management, the same is also recommended for labour imports, thus diversifying as much as possible supply sources between Arab nationalities and Asian nationalities, as well as within different Arab nationalities. The undeclared policy for all public and semi-public institutions is to diversity as much as possible the recruitment of expatriate labour. Excessive reliance on one nationality is always looked upon as an anomaly to be rectified as soon as possible. Private business is, of course, less concerned with this balance and more sensitive to cost considerations. The government, however, through its immigration policy labours to maintain a reasonable mix among different nationalities of imported labour.

Kuwait regional policy is also heavily marked by its concern for the balance of power. A very delicate balance between brothers in Iraq, Saudi Arabia and distant cousin across the Gulf (Iran) should be maintained. But because of Arab affinities, suspicion of Iranian ambitions and fear of Iraqi reprisals, Kuwait, though formally neutral in the Iraqi-Iranian conflict, is definitely tilting towards the Iraqi position.

The complement to balance of power policy is to join forces with other similar countries. The Gulf Co-operation Council (1981) (GCC) is, in fact, a manifestation of the need to join forces among rich but weak Gulf states. In Arab politics, Kuwait is renowned for maintaining an evenhanded policy among the different tendencies in Arab politics. Though by heart and interests part and parcel of the 'moderate' group, Kuwait is one of the most outspoken for the Arab and Palestinian causes. Even in the days of Nasser, when the cleavage between 'radical' and 'conservative' or 'reactionary' groups reached its apogee, Kuwait succeeded in nourishing the best relationships with the Egyptian leader.

The same desire for balance, explains the fact that Kuwait is the only country among the Gulf states to establish diplomatic relationships with the Soviet Union and the first to recognize Maoist China. Although still investing heavily in US and European financial markets, Kuwait is tapping investment opportunities in communist countries.

The Kuwait Fund for Arab Economic Development is a case in point. Created after the Iraqi claim over Kuwait in 1961 to use financial aid as a political leverage for support and recognition, it became the very symbol of Kuwaiti policy.

A very subtle blend of political moderation and commercial shrewdness is almost second nature to all Kuwaitis. One can, however, detect signs of over-confidence which risks undermining the precarious foundation of Kuwait's fragile equilibrium. A little more vocal anti-American tone, a rather too open support for Iraq in the Iraqi-Iranian conflict, and similar stands, are more the manifestation of the increasing self-assertiveness than a typical Kuwaiti position. It is true, however, that the Kuwaiti spirit of accommodation and compromise remains its last resort.

Finally, if smallness is a physical constraint on Kuwait which, to a great extent, shaped its policy, it has, nevertheless, turned it to its advantage. Being small, Kuwait can afford to take tough positions in many instances almost with impunity. In OPEC, Kuwait is among the more militant in price and production matters. Not subject to the same political and moral pressures as Saudi Arabia nor labelled radical as Iraq or Libya, Kuwait enjoys a freedom of manoeuvrability in oil pricing and production which is the envy of others. Also what we attributed to increasing self-assuredness, is, in fact, a privilege of smallness. The contrast here between Saudi Arabia, for example, and Kuwait is very instructive. Given its size and share in world oil production, Saudi Arabia has to be more careful in its policies. With much lesser impact on world affairs, Kuwait can afford with impunity many policies that Saudi Arabia cannot.

Likely Political Developments

Political developments in Kuwait would result from changes and evolutions in the internal, regional and international environment. Three main areas of development, are liable to bring about new elements in the political situation − namely, the return to parliamentary system, the outcome of the Iraqi-Iranian war and eventually that of the Middle East conflict.

The Return to Parliamentary Life. In the Gulf area, probably Kuwait along with Bahrain has the most sophisticated political movement and an active political elite. Kuwait owes its position to its earlier independence and wealth, but also to the enlightenment of Abdullah Al Salim, its ruler at independence, and to the benevolent role of its business community. Even before independence, the Kuwaiti business community pressed for a more participatory system. In the late thirties (1938), Sheikh Ahmad Al Jaber had to concede to popular pressures and granted Kuwait its first 'Majlis'. The new 'Majlis' not surprisingly, elected Sheikh Al Salim, then the heir-apparent, as its speaker, because of his sympathetic attitude to the democratic cause. At independence, the same Sheikh Abdullah Al Salim, consistent with himself, was keen to award Kuwait a constitution and a parliamentary system (1963). Relatively liberal, parliamentary life continued in Kuwait with increased self-confidence which at times, however, proved to be outspoken. The Kuwaiti Government had to suspend the parliament and some of the Constitution's articles in the summer of 1976, when fears were aroused that political unrest *à la libanaise* could disrupt the system. The analogy between Kuwait's and Lebanon's underlying political forces was too apparent. Both are small, prosperous and relatively liberal amid totalitarian systems. Each has its contingent of foreign population not totally exempted from outside manipulation and influence. In August 1976 the government ordered the Assembly's suspension for a period of four years.

To many people's surprise the government honoured its pledge and a new Assembly was elected early in 1981. Between 1976 and 1980 the influx of oil money and the subsequent increasing interest in pecuniary gains on the one hand, the degradation of Arab politics and disillusionment with it on the other hand, relegated the claim for parliamentary rule to a secondary plan. The government's decision to resume parliamentary rule was coldly received. It should be noted, however, that the government's decision is an embarrassment to other Gulf countries, Saudi Arabia in particular. But, the lack of enthusiasm for the return of Parliamentary rule does not preclude the proper dynamics of a parliamentary life. Once restored, parliamentary rule would call for increasing public aspiration to more participation.

In February 1981, Kuwait's 43,000 registered voters (about three per cent of the total population and eight per cent of the Kuwaitis) went to the polls to elect a new 50-member assembly. The result was more comforting to the government than anticipated; moderate candidates won largely to the exclusion of radical elements and an under-representation of the Shi'ite minority (three members only). Young educated middle-class candidates won the majority of the seats. The new phenomenon is the entry of a handful of traditionalist religious representatives. Rather than representing a radical or a militant breed of new Islam, the 'Ahl Al Salaf' — the traditionalists — do not claim any global reforming system. They advocate a strict adherence to formal Islam, while lacking any socio-political perception of society. In many cases they are more of an embarrassment to the government and the Assembly. Their insistence, and the Assembly's acquiescence that Kuwaiti nationality should not be awarded to non-Muslims is an example. Notwithstanding these few embarrassments it is improbable that the actual Assembly would create problems for the Kuwaiti government; rather it is expected to work within the influence of the Emir.

During the first decade of parliamentary rule, from the mid-sixties to the mid-seventies, debate and political discussions were centred around issues of Arab nationalism and policies *vis-à-vis* oil companies. Both topics are receding in public preoccupation. Certain factors explain this development. First and foremost there is the fabulous wealth that has befallen the country. Arab nationalism as a radical movement is not so likely to thrive in the midst of increasing wealth and opportunities when, even though unequally distributed, there is a handsome stake for everyone. Secondly, the defeat of the Arab cause in the 1967 war and then the death of Gamal Abdel Nasser left the Arab arena bewildered, with no inspiring cause nor a charismatic leader. The short-lived euphoria created by the 1973 war was quickly left behind with resurgence of Arab factionalism, the Lebanon civil war, the Camp David agreements, the Syrian-Jordanian-Iraqi skirmishes, etc. Finally, the oil companies became, after the complete take-over, things of the past.

The 'grand politics' of Arab nationalism and total sovereignty over natural resources of the 1960s and early 1970s would eventually be succeeded by 'small politics' of narrow nationalism in the 1980s. Kuwaitization of civil servants and other key posts, restrictions on expatriates' activities and visa permits, strict implementation of formal precepts of Islam, and possibly also the government investment and expenditure policies are the domain of public interest and parliamentary debates.

The Iraqi–Iranian War. More relevant to the Kuwaiti political outlook are the developments on regional frontiers — in the first place the outcome of the Iraqi–Iranian war.

Kuwait is always apprehensive of any major development in either Iraq or Iran and is keeping a watchful eye on both of them. Though in different ways, both Iraq and Iran present a menace to Kuwait's tranquillity.

Iraq is the big brother of the North which has never renounced its ambitions over Kuwait nor conceded its claims over parts of its territory. Dealing with the Iraqi government is always a delicate business as the Iraqis are not particularly tactful with Kuwait. Iraq, moreover, has been run for the last 15 years by the 'Baath' party which is notorious for its unscrupulous and ruthless practices *vis-à-vis* its opponents. physical liquidation being only one glaring example. Kuwait had the privilege of actually witnessing such experiences when more than one political attempt took place on its territory. Kuwait had, of course, the tact and discretion to turn a blind eye to these 'accidents'. But the message is clear.

The situation in Iran is no more comforting. Iran under the Shah was expansionist and arrogant in its claim for hegemony over the Gulf. Iran under Khomeini is dangerous, unpredictable and irresponsible, with elusive influence over the Shi'ite minority and other Muslim fundamentalists. A revolutionary Iran is a disruption to the ideal of the *status quo* and a menace to easy-going Kuwait and other Gulf states. In December 1981, Bahraini security sources have been quoted as saying that 60 persons detained in a plot included 45 Bahrainis, 13 Saudi and one each from Oman and Kuwait. The sources said the 60 belonged to the Islamic Front for the Liberation of Bahrain and had received training and support from Iran.

In these circumstances, from Kuwait's point of view as well as that of most Gulf states, the best thing was to have the two neighbours diverting their attention away from Gulf affairs. A war between the two regional superpowers was one way to achieve this objective. The war between them has reduced their ability to meddle in Gulf affairs after the war. Both are expected to be inward looking and scarcely activist. However, the war has proved to be longer than expected and more costly to the Gulf states than anticipated.

Containing the hostilities is the major concern of Kuwait and other Gulf states. This proved to be feasible for the time being and in spite of a few accidents, the general feeling now is that the extension of hostilities is not probable. The two belligerents notwithstanding, there seems to be a general consensus that the big powers are not prepared to a generalized Gulf war which could disrupt the international order as well as oil commerce. It is remarkable that the oil trade after almost a decade of oil shortage is witnessing once again an oil glut.

In search for legitimacy, Iraq has claimed that it is waging war against Iran in the name of all the Arab nations and in particular the Gulf states. Officially, Kuwait's position is neutrality between the two belligerents, though in fact it is heavily tilting towards the Iraqi side. The news media presents, more often than not, the Iraqi view and a virtual ignorance of the Iranian version of the development of the war operations. Kuwait is also offering port and road facilities for cargo shipment destined for Iraq. Substantial financial aid is provided to Iraq by Saudi Arabia and other Gulf states, of which Kuwait's share, to date, is about $8 billion.

It is obvious now that neither Iraq nor Iran can achieve a clear victory in their fratricidal confrontation. Ironically enough, the Iranians seem to stand a better chance in the battlefield than their contenders, the Iraqis. Though the internal situation in Iran is far from satisfactory, the odds against the Iraqi regime are still higher. In a way, Iran has already known the worst, the war with Iraq is providing the Iranian regime with a rallying factor amid chaos and disintegration. The war is perhaps the most effective cohesive factor for present-day Iran. By contrast, the Iraqi army, in spite of an overwhelming edge in firepower and troop strength, seems also demoralized as financial stringency is growing. Since the initial advance of the Iraqi army in the first months, it is now either at a standstill or retreating. The Iraqi problems stem from both structural and political considerations. Iraqi Shi'ites represent about 50 per cent of the population. Though they consider themselves Arabs and do not identify themselves with Iran, they nevertheless feel uneasy waging an aggressive war against Muslim Iran with whom they share Shi'ite affinities. More serious is the nature of the Iraqi political regime as a personal regime based in no small part on repression. The image of the regime stands to loose a great deal in such an inconclusive war. While the continuation of the war helps to cement the internal regime in Iran, it erodes that of Iraq. Paradoxically, if efforts to bring an end to the fighting fail, the Iraqi regime stands to face the danger of being toppled, while the Iran regime could face a similar fate afterwards, with the restoration of peace. No wonder, the Iraqi regime is pushing for a settlement, while the Iranians are indifferent, to say the least.

Kuwait policy has been based on the assumption of a rapid settlement of the war in favour of the Iraqi regime. With the turn of the tide against Iraq, Kuwait would face the problem of mending its relations with Iran. In any case, the outcome of the war will not fail to affect Kuwait's policy externally as well as internally.

The Middle-East Conflict. Like other Arab states, Kuwait is very concerned with the Arab–Israeli conflict. The Palestinian problem has been
the focal point for Arab politics for the last thirty years. To some
extent, the legitimacy of any regime in the Arab world is a function of
its stand *vis-à-vis* this problem. Kuwait is, however, particularly sensitive
to the Palestinian problem which it sees almost as a 'domestic problem'.
With about a quarter of its population of Palestinian origin and still
more significant participation in the active labour force, Kuwait cannot
afford to be indifferent to Palestinian aspirations. Also with the Israeli
raid on the Iraqi nuclear reactor in July 1981, the feeling of relative
insulation from Israel's longer arm was cruelly shattered.

Kuwait, like other Gulf oil states would like to see an early solution
to the Palestinian problem but realises at the same time the agonizing
costs that go with it. A final settlement with the militarily powerful
Israel cannot bring about a wholly acceptable solution. A certain degree
of concession is bound to be granted in such a case which will inevitably create dissidents, particularly among the more radical movements.
Such tendencies are usually prone to destabilizing techniques – e.g.
reprisals, sabotage, terrorism, etc. Kuwait and other small and rich
states in the region are most apprehensive about such an eventuality.
Also a final settlement of the Arab-Israeli conflict would bring the
status of resident Palestinians in Kuwait, as well as in Lebanon and
other Gulf states, to the moment of truth. Though no one seriously
thinks that all the Palestinian Diaspora will ever return to Palestine,
the present situation served as an alibi to all parties that the Palestinian
residence is only 'temporary'. With a final solution, the alibi works
no more and a frontal attack on the problem will be inevitable. The
previous state of 'no war, no peace' and the distribution of roles
between 'confrontation' and 'supporting' states – though unpleasant
– was a 'second best' – short of an optimal solution – for the Arab
oil producing countries. Financial support for the 'confrontation states'
served as a well-deserved insurance policy. With the extension of the
Israeli military arm and the disengagement of Egypt after the Camp
David agreements, this scenario cannot hold anymore and a way out
should be found.

The Camp David agreements are unpopular in the whole Arab world
including the Gulf area. The Gulf governments' opposition to Camp
David is more the result of circumstances that accompanied its evolution than an opposition to the principle of a negotiated peace or to

specific arrangements of the agreements.

The Jerusalem visit was regarded in the Gulf with both stupefaction and concealed hope. However, between the visit in November 1977 and the Camp David Agreements in April 1979, dramatic changes undermined the geopolitical map of the Gulf. The Islamic Revolution in Iran brought to the forefront new facts. First, a new political phenomenon, that is, the religious fundamentalist emerged to cover the whole of the Muslim world. No prior experience was available to suggest appropriate policies to contain or counter their actions. Their sweeping victory against the most powerful and repressive regime in the area (Iran) kept traditional regimes wary of any false step that could unleash the jinnee and bring about an unnecessary confrontation. Secondly, the sad discovery of a long suspected lack of firm support from the Americans for their 'moderate' allies in the area. The impotence of the American administration to save the Shah was not comforting to 'moderate' Arab states in the Gulf.

The result was a complete paralysis in the ranks of the 'moderate' camp at the Baghdad Conference (1978) and an easy victory for the more radical elements among the Arab delegations. The off-hand rejection by Sadat to receive an investigating Arab delegation was not to help the intimidated rich 'oil rulers'. Iraq – long an outcast in Arab politics – used the conference masterfully for a spectacular come-back to Arab politics. By both appealing to the most radical by a tough stand against Egypt of Camp David, and at the same time appeasing the Saudis and moderates by accepting for the first time the UN 242 resolution, the Iraqis proved to be first-class manipulators. The Baghdad Conference was a great success for Saddam Hussein and Iraq's long aspiration for Gulf – if not Arab – leadership. The Iraqi position continued its consolidation until the unfortunate war with Iran which, with an irony of history, turned the Iraq of Saddam Hussein into one of the staunchest advocates of a return of Egypt to the Arab fold. Once the Camp David process was rejected at the Baghdad Conference, the proper dynamics of the Arab opposition resulted in the unpopularity of Camp David. Camp David became a nasty word. The dilemma for moderate Arab states, and particularly Saudi Arabia, is to come up with an alternative to Camp David. With the disengagement of Egypt, Saudi Arabia found itself in the unsolicited position of leader. The Fahd Plan is the Saudi alternative to Camp David, though a thorough reading of it reveals a striking similarity between the Plan and Sadat's speech before the Knesset. The Fahd Plan could be a first step in a long process which eventually will be another Camp David in all but name. Aware of the costs of a final settlement of the Arab–Israeli conflict, Kuwait extends a cautious support to the Fahd Plan, though preferring a wait-and-see approach. The Fez Arab Conference, held in the aftermath of a shameful PLO departure from Beirut, gave the Fahd Plan its blessing as well as its name, 'The Fez Plan'.

Socio-economic and Political Forces at Work

At the bottom of Kuwaiti society two different communities are juxtaposed, that is, the Kuwaitis and the non-Kuwaitis.

Like ancient Athens, Kuwait is a free city. Athens had, it is said, 20,000 free citizens out of a total population of more than 250,000. The former led a noble life and practised democracy, the rest performed menial work and assured production. The former exhibited the power of mind and imagination, the latter that of muscles and perseverance. In Kuwait, less than 40 per cent enjoy the privileges of citizenry while the rest of the population represents the bulk of the labour force (75 per cent). The twentieth century expatriates in Kuwait differ from their predecessors of the fifth century (BC) in material life and legal status though not quite in their state of mind. Not necessarily assuming menial and unskilled work – a large body of the expatriates is providing most of the professional work, be it in medicine, teaching, law, engineering, accounting, etc. – the expatriates are, nevertheless, marginal to the society. If legally free, expatriates are not part of the body politic no matter how long they have lived on Kuwaiti soil.

The material life of the expatriates is usually comfortable, often very comfortable and by no means comparable to the conditions of life in their home countries. More often than not their professional careers are satisfactory and fulfilling, with modern technology and sophisticated equipment at their disposal. Their emotional life is, none the less, unstable, terribly wanting in security and lacking a sense of belonging. They live in Kuwait; yet they are not part of the society though they form the major part of the labour force.

The distinction between the two communities is not only one of a political nature, it reflects two different modes of economic systems. To a large extent, the Kuwaiti community is living in a rentier economy where family connections and speculations are the name of the game. The non-Kuwaiti community is earning its living in a more productive manner though the impact of the rentier economy on it is far from negligible, giving rise to a serious corruption of the productive system itself and the ethics of work.

For the time being and save for a few incidents, no serious problems have surfaced from this dual composition of the Kuwaiti population. Kuwait's experience with imported labour − the oldest in the region − dates only from the 1950s and particularly the late 1960s. It is mainly an experience with first generation expatriates. Neither Kuwait nor any other country in the region can claim any previous experience with second generation expatriates. *A priori*, there is no evidence that the second generation will behave as the first one. Experience shows that the second generation of immigrants is more aggressive and demanding. This is more so if the expatriates are substantial in number and quality as is the case in Kuwait. A first generation is more concerned with material conditions of life and can be less interested in political and social equality if work conditions are acceptable. A second generation could aspire to a more participatory role in social life and would possibly not be content with anything short of being accepted fully into the society.

Aware of these potential problems, the government of Kuwait is increasingly concerned with the population mix − not only the equilibrium between Kuwaitis and non-Kuwaitis in general but also among non-Kuwaitis themselves since not all of them are prone to permanent residence in Kuwait.

Three categories of expatriates can be distinguished according to their country of origin; the Arab, the Asian and the European expatriates. The last category raises the least concern. Europeans are few in number, qualified for specific tasks and more importantly, always temporary. Both Arab and Asian labour is more substantial in number and can be of a permanent nature. The Arab labour is culturally integrated in the Kuwaiti society, but precisely because of this fact can be politically more conscious and demanding. The Palestinians are a case in point. The Asian labour, though culturally different, is geographically very close and has established a strong presence in other Gulf states, particularly in the United Arab Emirates.

Within the Kuwaiti community itself there exist some differences between a nucleus of old families and the newcomers. Power and wealth is concentrated in the hands of a federation of old merchant families. Around this core of the political and social kernel, layers of peripheral groups of newcomers are added to the Kuwaiti community. The situation of the Bedouins is particularly worth noting. These are nomads of the hinterland from Najd, roving all around in search of grazing and water, changing their allegiance with the change of circumstances. Their mode of life and mentality are different from urban Kuwaitis. With the flourishing of Kuwait, a great number of Bedouins were attracted by new opportunities, particularly in the army and the police. Kuwaiti nationality was then extended to them for internal political reasons. Their lot has improved tremendously since they earned Kuwaiti nationality, though they remain far less favoured compared to other Kuwaitis. The establishment of the parliamentary system gave Kuwaiti Bedouins a new awareness of their relative disadvantage.

It cannot be said that there exist signs of dissatisfaction among the Bedouins. Their relative importance in the 'Majlis' was an eye-opener to their potential political importance since, because of their numbers, they are courted by different factions. For the time being they are almost unconditional supporters of the government and especially prone to defending traditional values. They could, however, be contenders asking for a wider distribution of power and wealth in the future.

Rapid modernization with the flux of oil money and grandiose projects has produced well known social disruption. It is to the credit of Kuwait, however, that the transition to the oil era is being achieved quite smoothly. The reasons are manifold. Being a small merchant society, Kuwait was always receptive to modernizing influences; also, contrary to other Gulf states, it knew relative opulence as early as the fifties and its wealth grew gradually before the sudden rise in its revenue in the mid-seventies.

Education is eroding the traditional basis of society. The change is, however, gradual and integrative. Education started, in fact, with rich families — thus combined wealth and knowledge. Undeniably, with the spread of education to all classes an increasing demand for better distribution of wealth and power will be felt. The situation is, however, far from explosive.

Political parties are banned. It is no secret that there exist different political tendencies. The most important observation is probably the increasing depolitization of the public and particularly the young generations. Contrary to the fifties and sixties, when Arab nationalism had captured people's minds, the general mood now is more concerned with down-to-earth matters — e.g. money making in the stock exchange and through speculation in real estate. Arab nationalism, however, remains active with the nostalgic old and middle-age generations. It was quite revealing that none of the nationalist political movements' candidates could get elected in the last election. On the other hand, the increasing influence of Islamic movements is taking place in Kuwait as in most other parts of the Middle East. Kuwait has always been moderately influenced by a broad Islamic vision. A practical approach accommodating formal Islam with the needs of commerce is the general heritage of the social life in Kuwait. With the crisis of the Muslim brethren in Egypt in the 1950s and 1960s, a great number of them found refuge in Kuwait thus reinforcing the 'Islah Society' (Society for Reform). The new phenomenon is the emergence of the new fundamental Muslims — usually of the younger generation — who are more radical and militant. The appearance of the veil is but one symptom of it. Another variation of the Islamic movement is 'Ahl Al Salaf' — the followers of tradition — who made a spectacular entry in the new 'Majlis'. These are more formalistic and less radical than they appear.

The Islamic-Iranian Revolution fuelled Muslim movements in general and the Shi'ite sect in particular. The Shi'ite minority in Kuwait (20 per cent) is more identified with religious movements. Religious attachment is a defence mechanism to preserve the Shi'ite identity.

The modern institutions — e.g. the army, bureaucracy, banking, liberal professions, etc. — are more or less stabilizing forces, beneficiaries of the *status quo*, more apolitical and business-minded. Disillusioned with grand ideals, they are preoccupied with self-enhancement. They are, in the final analysis, conservative forces for the maintenance of the actual order.

The Economy

An Oil Economy

In the past two decades, Kuwait has achieved a spectacular success combining economic growth with political stability. It is estimated that total GNP has reached some KD 7 billion by the end of 1980, thus, a per capita income of KD 5,475 (equivalent to $19,900), one of the highest in the world. These figures should not, however, be taken at their face value; conceptual as well as measurement inadequacies distort the real picture.

Conventional national accounts attribute about 70 per cent of the GDP to the oil sector, with the balance of 30 per cent attributable to the non-oil sector. The distribution of the respective contribution of oil and non-oil sectors are shown in Table 6.1.

The use of conventional methods of national accounts conceal at least two basic failures. At the conceptual level, it is very doubtful if the concept of income applies at all to the oil revenues. Oil revenues are, in the final analysis, the transformation of a real asset in the ground (oil) into monetary form — i.e. the accrual of oil revenues is matched by the depletion of oil reserves. In the national economy's balance

Table 6.1: Contributions of the Oil and Non-oil Sectors to the GDP

Year	Oil GDP (%)	Non-Oil GDP (%)	GDP
1950	26.7	73.3	100.0
1960	60.8	37.2	100.0
1965	69.7	35.3	100.0
1970	57.4	42.6	100.0
1973	62.1	37.9	100.0
1975	70.6	29.4	100.0
1979	68.9	31.1	100.0
1980	69.9	30.1	100.0

sheet the increase in foreign exchange assets (oil proceeds) is accompanied by the decrease in mineral assets (oil reserves). This is hardly an income concept, it is more akin to the capital concept. The transformation of one form of assets into another form does not represent any net increase in one's net position. Calling oil revenues income is no more than a misnomer, albeit a general mistake.

At a lower level of abstraction, conventional national accounts, as applied to Kuwait, tend to over-estimate the non-oil income. Kuwait's national accounts separate, among other things, the oil sector from the government sector. This practice tends to introduce a partial double counting. Oil revenues are, in fact, counted once in the GDP as value-added accrued in the oil sector, and once again when spent by the government on current and developmental expenditures. The contribution of the non-oil sector in the GDP is, thus, over-estimated.

It appears from the foregoing that Kuwait is much less wealthy than appears from conventional national accounts. It is, none the less, a very liquid economy, since it has been liquidating its depletable natural resources for about a quarter of a century. This is a problem of the conflict between the short- and long-run perspectives.

The actual glut in the oil market is hitting Kuwait's oil revenues. From about 1.2 million b/d in 1980-1, actual production in Kuwait has declined to 0.6-0.7 million b/d (March 1983). The negative impact of the decline on Kuwait's revenues in the short-run is compensated by better conservation ratios in the long-run. This explains, to a great extent, the mixed feeling with regard to recent developments in the oil market. Given its huge financial foreign investments, Kuwait's reaction to the present situation is relatively more relaxed.

It should, however, be noted that the present oil glut situation may prove to be more than a transitory crisis. OPEC as a group of producers is facing a combination of new factors. First, it seems that conservation efforts undertaken by the OECD countries realized a substantial reduction in oil consumption (15-20 per cent). Secondly, development for alternative sources of energy (nuclear, coal) have already made important inroads. Thirdly, policies aimed at increasing oil production in the OECD countries (deregulation in the US and the development in the North Sea) proved to be effective. Finally and more importantly, production of oil outside OPEC (Mexico, Egypt) has been growing at a higher rate than in the past. OECD countries first apply to non-OPEC sources of energy and resort to OPEC only as a residual after tapping the above suppliers. This is not to comfort OPEC countries. If we add to this the slackening in economic activity, it is no wonder that oil trade of OPEC declined from about 31 million b/d in 1979 to less than 18.5 million b/d now. The prospects of a full return of both Iran and Iraq to the oil market in the more or less near future will bring to the market a fresh 3-5 million b/d, a rather depressing prospect. Saudi Arabia will remain the swing factor as it always has been. Unless it resolves to reduce its production quite substantially, the weakness of the oil market will be there for some time to come.

Inflation

Since January 1973, the Central Statistical Office has published a wholesale index. The coverage of this index is, however, open to question. Regardless of its deficiencies, the price index showed an increase of 80 per cent between 1973 and 1979, with the highest increase in 1975-6. From 117.5 per cent in 1973 (1972 = 100), the wholesale price index increased to 143.3 per cent in 1975 and 165.6 per cent in 1977. A cost-of-living index, also published by the Central Statistical Office, shows the same trend. From 108 in 1973 it reached 175 per cent in 1979. The cost-of-living index is also subject to the same objection, namely the inadequacy of basket of goods retained (based on sampling rather than systematic surveys) and the constancy of the weights used (since 1972).

Crude as they are, the cost-of-living indices show an inflation rate of about 13 to 14 per cent annually in the period 1974-7 to decline to about eight per cent in the following years. These rates seem to be quite reasonable though they remain on the low side.

Imported inflation plays a very significant role in a country almost totally dependent on imports. The sharp rise in prices in 1974-5, sustained by increased public spending after the surge of oil revenues, helped fuel the price rise in the aftermath of the oil shock. But internal bottlenecks and speculation on land have also added tremendously to the increase in prices. Land is always a privileged asset for speculation. In a country with few financial assets to invest in, land speculation is the obvious choice for new-found oil money. The stock market is another choice. However, land prices are different from stock prices in that they have a more direct relation to the general price level through their effects on housing rents. The increase in rents affects in its turn the pressure for increases in wages and salaries, and a wage-price spiral is set up. From 1977, however, the housing shortage has been substantially reduced giving rise to a sizeable surplus of house vacancies. This has not actually brought rents down, but it has stopped them from rising too much. The continuing speculation in land and real estate helped landowners to resist reducing rents even at the cost of longer vacancies. Capital gains more than make up for missed rents. Port bottlenecks were also almost completely removed by 1977.

A major factor for holding prices stable in Kuwait is the subsidy system. Though in many other developing countries subsidies are of a controversial nature whereby they hold some prices stable while adding to the budget deficit and accordingly to inflation, the situation in Kuwait is basically different. The budget is mostly in surplus, subsidies help maintain prices stable. Also with a virtually infinite elasticity of supply through imports, the government subsidies are very effective in maintaining stable prices.

The subsidy system in Kuwait includes direct subsidy to basic food items — e.g. milk, rice, sugar, butter, bread, etc. — as well as public utilities, such as gas, water, electricity. The issue of subsidizing energy in particular has raised some doubts as to its rationality. Few voices claim that these subsidies encourage waste. With an eventual decline of government oil revenues, the argument for removing or reducing subsidies on electricity, water and gas should find more support.

The Budget

The budget in Kuwait is lop-sided, representing basically an expenditure programme while the revenue side is, to a great extent, a matter-of-fact item. Revenues are overwhelmingly the oil revenues and the newly growing investment income. The tax system is conspicuous by its virtual absence. Apart from a flat customs duty of four per cent — increased in some cases to 15 per cent — income tax on corporate profits is an historical curiosity. It was first imposed in 1955 to increase the government royalties from oil companies — which were foreign companies at the time. American oil companies required, and were granted, that the increase in government royalties should take the form of a general tax law in order to get tax exemption according to American law. The result was an income tax decree (1955) still applicable to non-Kuwaiti corporate profits. The text of the law is very ambiguous and its application to foreign companies uncertain.

The first formal budget was prepared in 1955. Since this first budget, oil revenues have dominated public revenues. In a first phase, extending to 1972, the increase in oil revenues was mainly associated with an increase in oil production and export. With the oil price shock in 1973, the increase in oil revenues was mainly due to increase in prices rather than volume of production, which continues to decline from more than 3.2 million b/d in 1972 to less than 0.7 million b/d in 1983.

With the increase in oil revenues, and thus surplus funds, a new source of finance was introduced — that is, investment income. Investment income is the revenue from the investment of previous oil surplus funds. Table 6.2 shows major sources of public revenues.

Table 6.2: Public Revenues (million KD)

Year	Oil Revenues	Investment Income	Domestic Revenue	Total
1957	110.2	7.1	5.8	123.1
1960–61	159.5	9.5	14.3	183.3
1965–66	225.3	22.4	19.5	267.2
1970–71	321.1	31.8	44.4	397.3
1974–75	2534.8	152.1	63.0	2749.9
1976–77	2598.2	329.4	105.5	3033.1
1977–78	2575.3	384.2	133.9	3093.4
1978–79	3036.1	521.4	140.3	3697.8
1979–80	5940.5	880.3	147.5	6968.3
1980–81	4434.2	1743.9	225.1	6403.2

Source: Central Bank of Kuwait, *Economic Reports 1969-80*.

The most remarkable development in Kuwait in recent years is the growth in investment income which is now close to 27.2 per cent of total revenues and would increase in relative terms as the oil revenues tend to slacken with the oil glut. The government's declared objective is to reach a situation whereby investment income would cover the current expenditure; an objective which has already been realized since the 1980/81 budget.

The importance of public expenditure can hardly be overestimated. Public expenditure is, after all, the vehicle by which oil revenues are injected into the national economy. Economically speaking the oil sector is more integrated in the world economy than it is in the domestic economy with very little forward and/or backward linkage. The only major linkage to the economy is through fiscal policy by tapping the oil revenues and then injecting part of it as public expenditure. Public expenditure is thus the prime mover of the economy. It should be maintained, however, that with time the private sector grew up substantially emancipating itself from total dependence on public expenditure. Public expenditure represents about three quarters of the GDP. We have referred earlier to the implied double counting in methods of national accounts used in Kuwait.

Public expenditure grew at a rapid pace during the fifties. Development of social services and infra-structure represented an important element of total expenditures. During the sixties, public expenditure continued its growth at an average rate of 6.7 per cent per annum. With oil price increases in the early seventies, public expenditure marked a dramatic increase, with domestic public expenditure in the fiscal year 1977-78 rising roughly to ten times its level in 1970-1.

Three major categories can be distinguished in public expenditure; current expenditure, development expenditure and land purchases. The first two categories hardly need any further explanation. Land purchase is a direct transfer of wealth from government to citizen through the acquisition of land. This was a device introduced by the late Emir Abdallah Al Salim and maintained since. Table 6.3 shows the distribution of public expenditures among five categories.

The prospects for lower oil revenue in 1982 and the subsequent years increased the pressure on the Government to reduce its public expenditure. It would be difficult to reduce current expenditures in absolute terms. Development expenditures, however, can be reduced, the implementation of projects extended over longer periods.

Direct oil revenues for the 1982/83, budget are estimated at KD 3,200 million — a 40 per cent decline from the equivalent figure in the 1981/82 budget. These figures have induced the government to restrict the growth of public expenditure to only five per cent above last year's level which represents a very marked deceleration when compared with the average annual increase of 26.4 per cent over the previous decade. Even so the estimates revealed a shortfall of KD 313 million, the first such deficit since the late sixties.

However, it would be a mistake to over-dramatize the significance of this apparent deficit in assessing the overall financial position. In the first place the transfer from General Reserve to fund the shortfall of

Table 6.3: Public Expenditure (%)

	Average share 1960–1 to 1962–3	1975–6	1976–7	1977–8	1978–9	1979–80	1980–1
Current Expenditure	44.6	49.2	49.1	38.8	45.3	51.7	56.4
Development Expenditure	22.1	15.2	23.3	25.2	25.7	19.1	18.7
Land Purchase	32.2	11.0	7.1	9.6	5.5	10.9	14.9
Participation in local institution	–	18.8	13.8	15.5	13.5	9.5	–
Foreign Expenditure	–	5.8	6.7	10.9	10.0	8.8	10.0
Total Domestic Expenditure	100.0	100.0	100.0	100.0	100.0	100.0	100.0

KD 313 million is no more than the amount necessary to cover the statutory obligation to allocate KD 320 million to the Future Generations Fund. Secondly, past experience shows that actual spending, as recorded in the closing accounts, is usually less than the budget estimates. And finally, the practice of excluding investment income from the budget grossly understates annual revenues.

Amongst specific provisions of the budget, the reduction in certain government subsidies — e.g. petroleum products — may well herald a change of policy which will be developed in future years. Nevertheless, in spite of such efforts to decelerate the growth of public spending, it remains high enough to sustain a reasonable level of economic activity.

Since the preparation of the budget, however, a completely new factor has been introduced by the Stock Market crisis and the government has been obliged to inject substantial funds in order to sustain the market and to establish a Compensation Fund for the small investors.

Reserves and Foreign Investment

Technically reserves are liquid assets held by the Central Bank, while foreign investments are longer term assets held for income or capital gains. However, in common parlance the two terms are used interchangeably.

In oil producing countries the concept of reserves is different from that of other countries. Under normal conditions, equilibrium in the balance of payments is regarded to be a policy objective and any deviation (surplus or deficit) from it should be regarded as a transient phenomenon. This is not the case of oil producing countries. These, as has been mentioned earlier, are transforming their oil asset into monetary form. Thus the only way to preserve their assets intact is to reinvest the oil proceeds into productive capital. With the limited absorptive capacity of the domestic market, reinvesting oil proceeds takes the form of foreign investment. Thus balance of payments surplus is not an aberration from normal conditions — in fact, it is the only way to preserve the value of the country's assets. Hence, reserves in oil producing countries are not, in principle, a hedge against eventual balance of payments deficit nor a support for the value of local currencies.

In this respect what counts is not only foreign investment held by the government but total foreign investment, whether held by public or private entities. There is, however, little information about private foreign investment in Kuwait as well as other Gulf states. Most reserves or foreign investment refers to government possession.

Estimation of reserves on foreign investment poses an accounting problem familiar to stock valuation. Add to this a general tendency among oil producing countries to prefer to underestimate their real wealth. Few years ago, a senior official of Saudi Arabia made of the confidentiality of Saudi investment in the US a *sino quo non* for the continuation of their investment in the US. The same applies to a lesser extent to other Gulf states including Kuwait.

Therefore the estimation of Kuwait's foreign investment is subject to reservation. It seems that there exists a general agreement that Kuwait's government investment stands at some $70-80 billion.

In 1976 Kuwait introduced a new concept; the reserves for future generations. This is no more than an accounting concept. It is not a different fund managed differently. Only a certain percentage of the accumulated reserves is considered part of the reserves for future generations and accordingly cannot be disposed of for a certain period (not before the turn of the century). This is a self-limitation measure to reduce pressures for more demands on the use of the reserves. Pressures could be exerted from local interests, but more so from outside forces, particularly sister countries.

Currency

Before independence, Kuwait as well as other Gulf principalities, used the Indian rupee. Kuwait was, thus, part of the sterling area with the Bank of India as its issuing institution. After independence, Kuwait introduced its own currency, the Kuwaiti Dinar (KD), and a Currency Board was established in 1962 to monitor the monetary policy. The KD remained, none the less, on the sterling standard. After the sterling devaluation of 1967, Kuwait's authorities thought it fit to dissociate the Kuwaiti Dinar from sterling, from then on it became effectively pegged to the dollar. With the abandonment of the Bretton Woods system in late 1971, the KD remained closely linked to the dollar until the mid seventies, when the Central Bank (established in 1969) created its own basket of currencies for the KD. It is thought that the Central Bank's basket includes other than the US dollar, the DM, SF, the Yen, the Pound and probably the FF. Though these are the components of the SDR, the weights in the Kuwaiti basket are thought to be different, with higher weights for the US dollar and the Yen. The precise composition of the Central Bank basket is not made public, probably to permit a wider freedom to the Central Bank to change the weights as it sees fit. In any case, over a reasonably longer period, there is a certain stability of the KD with the US dollar. The new formula of the SDR seems to be still more stable for the KD than the old formula. The actual rate of the KD with the US $ ranges between $3.42 and $3.66 to the KD.

Monetary developments in Kuwait reflected the general economic trends of the economy and the oil revenues in particular. After a modest annual expansion in the period extended to 1969-70, a very rapid monetary expansion followed during the period 1971-6 with the increase in oil revenues and government expenditure (about 27 per cent per annum). A moderate monetary expansion characterized the period starting from 1977 (about 17 per cent), though the rate increased substantially in 1980 (about 30 per cent per annum). Following a three year period of steady progression up to 1980, monetary conditions in Kuwait were characterized by a sharply expansionary trend in 1981 with domestic liquidity rising from KD 2,857 million to KD 3,883 million, an increase of 35 per cent. The rate of growth began to slow down noticeably during the first half of 1982, however, and turned negative in the third quarter.

With the prospects for lower oil revenues it is possible that the monetary expansion will slacken still more, though the government is anxious to dissipate any idea of slackening in the economic activity following the actual oil glut.

7 THE KUWAITI STOCK MARKET*

In collaboration with Raid Fahmi

Introduction

Despite its recent origin and the limitation to trading in shares of Kuwaiti public shareholding companies, the stock market of Kuwait ranked among the biggest seven or eight stock markets in the world.[1] In some weeks, even, the daily transactions actually exceeded in value those traded in the London Stock Exchange.[2]

The importance of a study of the Kuwait stock market cannot be overestimated. This market reflects to a great extent the nature of the Kuwaiti economy, and while maintaining a pioneering lead, it represents a model for the expected development in the other Gulf countries. A number of factors, both external and domestic, gave this market its peculiar characteristics. In addition to the usual role played by stocks in the financing of the economy, the specific nature of the Kuwaiti economy helped shape the Kuwait stock market with its features — features at the same time shared by the Gulf markets in general.

In this chapter, we shall follow the development of the Kuwaiti stock market, in an attempt to trace its relations to the structure of the Kuwaiti economy while focusing on its peculiarities and the factors affecting its operations. Although the main emphasis is on the behaviour of the stock market, it must be remembered that this market did not develop in a vacuum but reflected the conditions of the Kuwaiti economy and its peculiar characteristics. In the first section, we shall discuss the structure of the Kuwaiti economy to be followed in the next section by a more detailed analysis of the trends in the Kuwaiti stock market — a survey covering the period up to the end of 1980. Later developments in the market are important enough to deserve an independent study.

* This is a revised version of a paper presented to the Conference on the Development of the Stock Market in Kuwait held in the period 14–16 November 1981, organized by the Kuwait Chamber of Commerce and Industry, The Industrial Bank of Kuwait, The Kuwait Foreign Trading, Contracting and Investment Company and the Kuwait International Investment Company.

173

The Structure of the Kuwaiti Economy: Excess Savings

Financial Assets

Stocks are a form of financial assets used for the financing of the modern economy. An important feature of modern economies is the divergence in expenditure and income earning patterns giving rise to surplus and deficit units. Surplus units earn more than they spend, while deficit units spend more.[3] As a result, the need arises to transfer the surplus from the surplus units to finance the deficit units, while providing the former with adequate security and reasonable return. Financial assets, in their different forms, represent legal means to facilitate the movement of the surplus from surplus units to deficit units. In other terms, financial assets are claims or obligations on the deficit units held by the surplus ones.

Wealth is accordingly divided into real assets, which represent goods and services, and financial assets, which are obligations on these real assets. The more forms and types of the financial assets are available, the more efficient the financing system of the economy.[4] Different forms – maturities, yields, risks, etc. – of financial assets accommodate the varying needs of both surplus and deficit units.

As a result of the sophistication of the financial systems in modern economies, several types of financial assets and new procedures and rules have been developed for each and every type.

Although all societies have known for quite a long time in their history, some forms of financial assets, such as money, the diversity in the forms and types of financial assets is a relatively modern phenomenon. With the development of commercial capitalism and the growth in the international trade in the sixteenth and seventeenth centuries, and later the rise of the industrial revolution since the end of the eighteenth century, financial assets flourished considerably, and were helped by new forms of financial and commercial papers. The emergence of these new financial assets helped to boost growth and international trade by providing the means for their financing.

The concept of shareholding companies was, in particular, a landmark in the development of modern societies. This new form of company helped to accumulate large capitals transcending thus human life and their limited resources. With the emergence of this new form of company, projects became larger than the financial capabilities of one individual and the time horizon of these projects was longer than his life span. In addition, this new form of company has led to yet another major transformation in the capitalist system, that is, the separation between ownership and management.[5] This is a development that has been at the root of the development of management as a new art or science.

The importance of shareholding companies and the concept of stock as financial assets cannot be assessed properly in isolation from other financial assets. In fact, the stock concept as a form of financial assets gains its importance and significance only within a framework of a complete array of financial assets at the disposal of the investors.

The diversity and scope of the financial assets have helped to increase the efficiency of the economic calculus by providing investors and savers with a matrix of costs and yields of the different financial assets. A study of the stock market cannot be complete without reference to other available financial assets.

In most countries a gradual and long process took place for the emergence and development of different financial assets usually reflecting a corresponding interaction between real and financial realities.

In Kuwait this development has been brisk and sudden. External factors overshadowed the domestic productive forces in shaping the characteristic features of the market. Kuwait stock market was thus characterized by the unusual speed at which the stock market and the financial assets in general have developed on the one hand, and on the other by the minimal, or non-existent, relationship between the domestic productive structure and the financial markets. The first financial institution to operate in Kuwait was a branch of the British Bank of the Middle East opened in 1941, while the first Kuwaiti shareholding company was established in 1952 (National Bank of Kuwait). Less than three decades later, the Kuwaiti financial market has become one of the most active in the world. This remarkable development owes much to the forces behind the Kuwaiti economy and its specific peculiarities.

The Oil Sector and the World Economy

It has become almost a ritual in discussing any problem in Kuwait to emphasize the fact that it is an oil-based economy. But then again, it is impossible to grasp the development and growth of financial assets — including stocks — in Kuwait without pointing to the nature of the oil sector in its relation to both the world and national economies. Though geographically and geopolitically part of the national territory, economically the oil sector is related to the international economy. The oil sector is not, to be sure, integrated in the domestic economy as much as it is an extension of the world economy though attached geographically and politically to the national economy. It is natural, then, that the growth and development of the oil sector reflect changes in the world economy and in particular the balance of power between the oil exporting and the consuming countries. The impact of oil on the domestic economy remained minimal, almost confined to the contribution of the oil revenues to the budget and public expenditure.

Oil prices remained stable for almost seventy years, and only started to increase from 1970 and in particular in 1973–4. At the beginning of the century, the price of a barrel of oil was about $1.2 and reached about $1.6 at the end of the 1960s.[6] By the late 1970s it was already over $32.

Although the increase in the oil price could be attributed to pure economics, reflecting the increase in the prices of other commodities on the one hand, and the need to raise prices of depletable commodities, on the other,[7] the real reasons remain, however, outside the realm of economics. A more realistic interpretation resides probably in the change of the world balance of power, thus giving rise to a new distribution of the world income between the oil exporting countries and the consuming countries. There was not, to be sure, any major change in the underlying production and consumption patterns before and after the increase in the prices of oil, only the bargaining power of the OPEC countries has been enhanced dramatically increasing their share of the world income. The increase in the oil prices in 1973–4 has led to an increase in the share of the oil producing countries in the world income from about $15 billion in 1972 to more than $110 billion in 1974.[8] In 1980 Saudi Arabia's revenue alone surpassed the $110 billion threshold. The huge increases in the oil producing countries' revenues led to a parallel increase in their propensities to save (particularly the Arab Gulf countries). In Kuwait, for example, the propensity to save during the 1950s and 1960s was about 40–50 per cent of GDP.[9] With the redistribution of the world income, the propensity to save in Kuwait and other oil-producing countries increased accordingly − that is, their ability to demand and accumulate financial assets increased also.

From the above, it does not seem unreasonable to assert that the increase in Kuwait's savings, i.e. its ability to finance, reflected the relation of the Kuwaiti oil-based economy with the world economy and was independent from any domestic need for finance. While the increase in the ability to finance could be attributed to the change in the international balance of power, the need for domestic finance has remained related to the structure of the domestic economy, that is, its 'absorptive capacity'. Domestic absorptive capacity usually grows at a continuous but gradual pace.

The contrast between the ability to finance and the domestic need for finance is thus, glaring. Not only did the ability to finance dramatically outpace the domestic needs for finance, but the factors lying behind each of them are different. The ability to finance is related to the increase in the oil prices, which in turn is a result of the change in the balance of power between the oil exporting and consuming countries. This is an area liable to sudden change. The need for finance on the other hand, represents a change in the domestic production and consumption patterns which has by its nature a more stable pattern and generally changes gradually.

Moreover, the relationship between the ability to finance and the oil revenues had clear effects on the link between foreign financial assets and domestic financial assets. In most cases, foreign financial assets are not perfect substitutes for domestic financial assets. Different currency areas to which each of these two types of assets belongs, entail different exchange rate risks, interest rate differentials and more generally different monetary policies. It follows, then, that domestic financial assets are relatively imperfect substitutes for foreign financial assets. It remains, however, true that the integration and/or independence of the financial assets' markets is a topic of great controversy among economists.[10]

In the case of Kuwait, this is by no means clear. It can hardly be maintained that Kuwait represents an independent currency area. We have previously referred to the predominant role of the oil sector in the economy of Kuwait. Two-thirds of Kuwait GDP is produced in this sector. Moreover, the remaining third is not wholly independent domestic production. It has been demonstrated that conventional national income accounts result in serious distortion of income measurements in the oil producing countries overstating the allegedly non-oil-sector.[11]

The oil sector is not only an overwhelming sector of the economy, but it is also a foreign-exchange earner. This is a fact of far reaching consequences. Oil is marketed in the international markets and is paid for in foreign currencies, generally in dollars. It appears then that the major part of Kuwait GDP is in fact realized in a foreign currency area (the Dollar Area), to be partially transformed into local currency (the Dinar), to facilitate local transactions. The conversion takes place from foreign assets into domestic assets and not vice versa, as in most other countries. It does not seem far fetched, then, to argue that financial assets in Kuwait are not independent of foreign currency areas. The sensitivity of the Kuwait domestic financial market to foreign financial assets should then be very high. This should not preclude, however, the existence of important barriers for substitutability of domestic and foreign assets.

Although the Central Bank of Kuwait fixes on a daily basis the exchange rate of the Dinar *vis-à-vis* foreign currencies, it remains true that the foreign exchange components – mainly dollars – in the GDP (the income from the oil sector plus the incomes from foreign investments) is very high. The dinar area is, to a large extent, part of a larger foreign area (mainly the dollar area). The relationship between domestic financial assets and foreign assets can thus hardly be overestimated. This has been amply illustrated when interest rates increase abroad (particularly on the dollar), while the local rates were maintained at low level, leading in most cases to an outflow of local capital.

The Imbalance between the Supply of and Demand for Domestic Financial Assets

It has been pointed out that the growth in the ability to finance (savings) in Kuwait largely surpassed the domestic need for financing (investment), or in other terms the demand for financial assets outmatched their supply. Since the supply of financial assets reflects a need for finance while the demand represents an ability to finance, the former is lagging behind, and the latter is abundant. Kuwait thus showed an increase in demand for financial assets, that is, too much money chasing too few assets, leading to the increase in their prices.

The supply of and demand for financial assets are supply of and demand for stock variables rather than flow variables – i.e. elements of wealth. It is natural that all the other elements of wealth will be substitutes for them; in particular, with the shortage of financial securities, land will be looked upon as a form of financial assets. Land is not in itself an income earner, and the return from holding land is usually realized from capital gains with the appreciation of its value. Therefore, the inclusion of land in the financial assets array introduces a new anticipatory factor calling for capital appreciation and hence pushing prices of other competing financial assets up; thus investors and speculators buy land as a form of financial assets, expecting their prices to go up. An anticipation wave for land prices increase cements the future prospects for further increases. Price increases are immediately transmitted to other financial assets. Thus the entry of land as a competing asset in the financial market, fuels price increases and speculation.

The surge of international and domestic inflation in the mid-1970s pushed individuals to switch from fixed-income securities to other forms of wealth, especially land, thus confirming the trend of price increases. This, in turn, affected the general level of prices as a result of the increase in rents and their effect on wages. Moreover, the increase in the price of land and real estate increased profits of real estate investment companies and those companies which speculate in the real estate market. Therefore the increase in their share prices is not only indirectly related to the increase in land prices, but also due to direct profits realized by many companies speculating in real estate and in shares of companies speculating in real estate. A chain reaction followed with everyone speculating on everyone else's shares pushing up all the share prices at once.

Also some government actions, in their turn, have helped speculation continue. It is no secret that the government's expenditure policies have, for good or bad, provided support and sometimes protection to speculators. Land acquisition policies, adopted in the 1950s as a means of distributing wealth, have in time turned to become an inflationary vehicle for land prices affirming the speculative trends in the financial assets.

Since the expenditure by the government on land purchases is regarded by recipients as capital and addition to their wealth rather than an income, they place it to acquire alternative forms of wealth; land or stocks. The financial assets market is thus affected by government expenditure in general, and by expenditure on land acquisition in particular.

Further to this indirect effect, the government (as we shall see later) took direct measure to bail out the market when it faced difficulties following overheated speculation.

Speculation and Forward Transactions

Two extreme types of explanation are available for the pricing of securities. They are, none the less, only limiting cases. Real life is somewhere between them.[12]

According to the first type of analysis, share prices tend generally to be set systematically and rationally according to the economic value of the real resources held by the company representing the stock. That is, the share price is determined, ultimately, by the prospective earnings of the company, or in other words it is measured by the present value of its future earnings. This type of analysis inserts, in fact, the prices of securities in familiar competitive equilibrium models.

The second limiting approach envisions the determination of share prices, essentially, as a speculative and anticipatory phenomenon. The share prices reflect the psychological state in the stock market. Earnings prospects could be one factor affecting the market sense but only as much as it is reflected in the market perception of the future prices of securities. Keynes in a famous passage described this mentality when the market has

> . . . reached the third degree where we devote our intelligence to anticipating what average opinion expects the average opinion to be. And, there are some, I believe, who practise the fourth, fifth and high degrees.[13]

It seems that the Kuwait stock market is best approximated by the latter model with speculation at its root.

Speculation could, however, be a healthy phenomenon benefiting the economy as long as it is kept within reasonable limits. In a world of uncertainties and expectations, it is useful to have a group of individuals specializing in hedging against uncertainties and bearing risks. A speculator is a person who consents to bear risks and assume uncertainties for others thus relieving them from future hazards. But if speculation exceeds its natural limits to become the fulcrum of the market turning investors into speculators, it becomes an evil and leads to instability and chaos in the economy.[14]

It is feared that speculation in Kuwait has exceeded these reasonable limits and that it threatens to become the very basis of the financial assets market. This could undermine the ability of the stock market to fulfil its natural function as a vehicle to finance the economy.

In Kuwait the financial assets market behaves so independently that it appears quite remote from other real markets. The situation in other Gulf countries does not seem very different, even though they are lagging behind a little. The entry of the Kuwaiti capital into the Gulf countries and the growing interest in this new-found market have helped provide the financial assets markets with another long breathing space for speculation.

Some practices and measures used in the Kuwait stock market have helped to sustain the speculative trends in the market. Commercial banks credit policies, especially overdraft, on the one hand, and the widespread practice of forward deals, on the other, have helped inflating demand for financial assets by adding fresh liquidity in excess of owned resources. Forward deals in Kuwait dominate the stock market and as such warrant a closer look.

Kuwait forward deals differ, it should be realized, from the usual forward transactions known in other markets. Rather than an agreement to sell and buy at a prearranged price on a designated date in the future, Kuwait forward sales are spot sales with credit. The seller delivers the buyer the shares on the spot and the buyer will hold them immediately; only payment is deferred to a future date (usually a post-dated cheque). For all practical purposes, forward deals in Kuwait are spot deals on credit and without collateral. The forward price is not independent of the spot price; it is invariably the spot price with a premium (an interest rate or rather a usury rate) which varies between 50–150 per cent for one-year delivery. Forward deals are used in fact as a means of finance at usury rates.

The relationship between the forward practices and speculation is obvious. A speculative market cannot continue upwards indefinitely even with persistent bullish anticipations. There should be a continuous injection of new liquidity to match the increased prices. Even a liquid economy like Kuwait, with excess savings, would face liquidity shortage sooner or later. Forward transaction (Kuwaiti type) provided the market with a new instrument for credit creation, by-passing, to a great extent, the banking system. After all the banking facilities could not match the insatiable need of the stock market for liquidity. The forward market in Kuwait came to fill the gap by providing an almost limitless mechanism for credit creation, but also exponentially increasing the risks.

In the final analysis, liquidity is created through bank intermediation in the exchange of obligations. With forward transactions and the continuous flow of post-dated cheques, dealers in the stock market introduced a new form of credit bypassing completely the banking intermediations. With everyone issuing and receiving at the same time, post-dated cheques, prices of shares continue to rise, and, the cheques are rolled over without even passing through the banks. This is a new mechanism for liquidity creation. Though generally accepted, the post-dated cheques are usually used in the stock market and eventually in the real estate market. They represent a new form of liquidity, though with a restricted acceptability to the financial assets markets. In permitting a continuous increase in the share prices, forward deals, backed by post-dated cheques, at the same time increased the market illiquidity. The new post-dated cheques thus injected, are no more than a theoretical or accounting money in a barter share-exchange market. Shares are exchanged among themselves at growing prices. The new share prices can hardly be liquidated and leave the system. Fortunes are ever-growing in the stock market, yet they are locked in. These are the rules of the mirage-wealth creation game. The relative acceptability of this new form of liquidity helped to limit the effect of the increase in the share prices to the stock market with no or little leakage to the rest of the economy. It remains true, however, that the continuous increase in the share prices cannot be held absolutely insulated from the rest of the economy. An increase in house rents necessarily follows a rise in land prices and eventually affects the general price level. Also a wealth-effect on income expenditures (Pigou effect) cannot fail to materialize. An increase in the sales of Rolls-Royce cars, for example, was not totally unassociated with the new wealth realized in the stock market. By and large, however, the inflationary effects of the stock market remain limited.

The fact that the same people are buying and selling among themselves with post-dated cheques has increased clearing situations and subsequently the interdependence of the market.

The forward transactions, while introducing a powerful mechanism to sustain ever rising share prices, have also increased the instability and uncertainty of the market. Should over-optimistic anticipations be halted for any reason, reverse movement will follow and the forward transactions could be of little help.

Finally, as mentioned earlier, the extension of the securities of the Kuwait market to the Gulf region has brought new dimension for speculation.

Capital inflows from neighbouring countries contributed to these new wonderful riches. Demand for shares increased and also wealth, for a time.

Institutional Framework

In addition to the structural imbalance of the economy, it is important to pin-point also the inadequacy of the institutional set-up in the Kuwait stock market. For, although the size of the stock market has expanded enormously, the organizational and institutional aspects have lagged behind.

The first law governing securities in Kuwait was issued in October 1962, and was intended to regulate dealings in foreign securities, as domestic securities were negligible at the time.[15]

The promulgation of the commercial law in 1960 established the legal framework for financial assets. A new Commercial and Companies Law was promulgated in 1980, but it is too early to evaluate the effects of this new law. Law No. 32 of 1970 reflected the need and laid the foundations to regulate the securities market. In accordance with this law, a committee was set up (1977) to supervise the dealings of the stock exchange and to draw up a draft law for its functioning. Consequently, the role of the Ministry of Commerce and Industry in regulating and organizing trading activities in securities has increased.

It is important to point out also that the organizational and institutional features are not only limited to legal organization but also include the need for establishing new institutions capable of rationalizing the investment behaviour. It is not enough to have a law regulating securities trading. Also, there is a need to regulate and promote alongside the primary market or the issue market an adequate secondary market. This is an area of almost complete void.

Furthermore, the development of the market cannot be maintained without the necessary data and information. There exists a compelling need for further institutions that are able to compile, classify and analyze data and relevant information. At present, daily statements on shares, combined with monthly, quarterly and annual bulletins are issued by the Securities and Investment Department of the Ministry of Commerce and Industry. These constitute the main authoritative sources on stock movements in the Kuwaiti market. Besides this the Ministry compiles trading price indices on the basis of the above-mentioned sources.

So far no specialized institutions have come into being to process relevant information professionally. Study and research that monitor and analyze development trends are also conspicuous by their absence in the Kuwait stock market. Naturally, future development of the stock market will depend on the availability of institutions and regulations providing relevant and reliable information.

Terminology could be misleading. The term 'recession', with all its undertones as used in Kuwait, helped pressurize the government to intervene in support of speculative trends. Since recession is bad, while a recovery is a good thing, every time a decline takes place in the stock or real estate market prices, everyone is alarmed, the mass media cries wolf and the government is called upon to intervene. The government has unfailingly intervened by increasing expenditure, especially with land purchases to inject new liquidity into the market. Once the government's intervention even took the form of an open-ended buyer in the market at a minimum price. The government – big brother – is always there to help bail out the stock market in moments of difficulty – an insurance policy for speculation.

The Development of the Stock Market in Kuwait

The emergence of the Kuwaiti financial market did not take place until after World War II, when the financial resources of the country started to grow rapidly as a result of the increase in oil production and export. In the pre-oil era, the Kuwaiti economy was entirely based on three economic activities: trade — particularly re-export trade — fishing and boat building, and pearling. Pearling, however, steadily diminished in importance since the beginning of the twentieth century.

All these economic activities were based on small individual ownerships with very limited capital and technical requirements. Therefore, they were completely self-financed and there was no actual need for external financing. On the other hand, the then prevailing low income levels could hardly provide a substantial amount of savings in the domestic economy that may be used for intermediation purposes. The opening of a branch of the British Bank of the Middle East (BBME)[16] in 1941, signalled the birth of the financial sector in Kuwait.[17] The establishment of the first bank came when the first signs of oil wealth potential became apparent following the major oil discoveries in 1937.

From 1946 onwards, the oil sector became the dominant sector in the Kuwaiti economy. This transformation led to the elimination of traditional activities, and the introduction of drastic structural changes in the economic fabric of the country, while providing at the same time opportunities for accelerated economic growth and development.

The rapid economic expansion and continuous increase in financial resources generated a growing demand for financial assets and gave strong impetus to monetary and financial development. Domestic financial markets were actively promoted by state and private sectors as a means of enhancing Kuwait's position as a financial centre, investing more efficiently the abundant domestic savings and contributing to the diversification of national income sources. Over the past decade, the Kuwait stock market grew spectacularly to become one of the world's biggest in terms of turnover. At the same time, stock trading became the investment activity number one for the majority of Kuwaiti investors.

The purpose of this part of the chapter is to trace the development of the Kuwaiti stock market since the first appearance of domestic equity stocks in the economy, with particular emphasis on market developments in the 1970s when organized stock dealing came into existence. The historical period was divided into three main intervals. The limits for each interval were defined on the basis of the main trends of change in the volume of publicly issued shares by new and existing Kuwaiti shareholding companies for the period preceding the emergence of an organized secondary market. For the latter period − i.e. the 1970s the distinction was based on the state of activity in the trading market.

The Transitional Period to the Oil Economy from World War II until 1960

This period witnessed the formation of the first public shareholding companies and the appearance of corporate equity issues as the first type of tradable securities in the Kuwaiti economy.

During this period, four Kuwaiti shareholding companies were incorporated − the National Bank of Kuwait (1952), the Kuwait National Cinema Company (1954), Kuwait National Airways (1956)[18] and the Kuwait Oil Tankers Company (1960) − with an initial cumulative capital of 103,857,800 rupees (1 rupee = KD 0.075) and their total issued shares amounted to over one million shares. This amount of capital represented only 1.9 per cent of oil revenues for this period and 8.7 per cent of the value of land acquisitions.

The small size of the issued shares and the very narrow base of shareholders did not allow any significant stock trading. Besides, the rapid growth of the companies' assets and their high profitability during this period, made share ownership a lucrative investment. Speculative activities were mainly concentrated in the real estate market which offered what seemed then, limitless opportunities for quick profits. Land prices were shooting up as a result of intensified demand generated by government construction and land acquisition programmes. Hence, land and real estate became the main form of wealth holding in this period, absorbing a large proportion of the capital funds transferred to the private sector by the government.

The Emergence of the Stock Market 1960–70

This period can further be divided into two sub periods: the first one, extending from 1960 to 1962, witnessed a large expansion in the formation of new shareholding companies and the issue of shares to the public; while the second, extending from 1963 to 1970 was characterized, by relative recession in both new stock issues and dealings in existing stocks.

The Period 1960–2. This period witnessed the actual emergence of the shareholding companies sector as an effective and important sector in the Kuwaiti economy. The economic and financial activities of the stock market developed to become one of the major fields of economic activity in the newly created state. In the period 1960-2, and after the promulgation of the Commercial Companies Law in May 1960, the creation of new shareholding companies gained a new impulse that resulted in the establishment of 13 new public shareholding companies[19] with a total capital of KD 35.8 million. The shares of the new companies were denominated in Kuwaiti dinars following the freeing of the monetary sector from foreign ties with the establishment of the Kuwait Currency Board and the issuance of the Kuwaiti currency.

The government played a major role in the establishment of shareholding companies and promoted their development. Out of the 13 companies which were established, the government had a substantial equity participation in seven of them totalling about KD 15.4 million, 43 per cent of the companies' total capital.

No adequate information is available to determine the exact amount of the total paid-up capital during this period. However, it is estimated that it amounted to KD 20 million, or about 55 per cent of the total capital of the new companies.

Although the shareholding companies sector was able over this short period to multiply the volume of capital inflow into the sector, yet the amount of funds absorbed by the newly established companies was only a small proportion of the private sector investible funds. This was reflected to some extent, in the heavy oversubscription by the general public in the newly issued shares.

The establishment of new companies, coupled with the increase in the capital of existing ones mainly through the issue of bonus shares, led to a large expansion in the shares' issue base. Between 1959 and 1962, the overall volume of issued shares in the market rose from 0.985 million to 5.3 million, out of which 3.6 million are in the private sector hands. Although the bulk of these shares were of newly founded companies which had barely started operation, they were all legally tradable according to the Commercial Law. This loophole in the law provided the opportunity for speculation to flourish through trading in the shares of newly established companies even before their actual performance could be monitored and evaluated.

The purposes and activities of the established companies covered three economic sectors: financial, manufacturing and the transport and services sector. The financial sector, which included banks, investment and insurance companies, had the largest share of newly established companies and their subscribed capital. During this period, two banks, three insurance companies and one investment company were established. The government's participation in this sector was limited to the investment companies, the ownership of which was equally divided between the government and the private sector. The total capital of these companies amounted to KD 20.5 million, that is 58 per cent of the total capital of the newly approved companies. As far as the total capital of all shareholding companies is concerned, the cumulative capital of the financial sector companies amounted to KD 23.4 million or 52 per cent of the total nominal value of companies' capital amounting to KD 45.48 million.

Manufacturing companies, on the other hand, included the Kuwait National Petroleum Company, the National Industries Company and the Kuwait Flour Mills Company. Their total capital amounted to KD 11 million or 31 per cent of the cumulative capital of the companies established during this period about 24 per cent of the total nominal capital value of the market.

In the transport and services group, two companies were established with the participation of the government. Their total capital amounted to KD 4 million or 11 per cent of the cumulative capital of newly established companies. If, however, the Kuwait Oil Tanker Company and the Kuwait National Cinema Company are included within this sector, then its share of the total nominal value of the market capital will amount to 18 per cent. It is worth noting that the Kuwait Oil Tankers Company was, up to that date, fully owned by the private sector.

Secondary Market Activities. [20] The absence of any regulatory and legal framework organizing stock trading activities did not hinder fervent dealing taking place in the stocks of the newly established companies. Trading was carried out either directly between traders and stock owners or through unofficial brokers – often land and real estate agents. There is no available data on the volume of trading, the number of deals and their values, to give full account of the stock trading activity that took place in this period; however, stock price records of transactions concluded at brokers' offices reflect, to a significant extent, the state of the market. Prices for individual stocks differed from one broker's office to another according to the stock demand and supply situation with each broker.

A study undertaken by the Kuwait Investment Company (KIC) on stock price movements during the years 1962-3 [21] indicates that during 1962 the market was very active and that it reached its peak towards the end of the year. The stock price index took a steep and steady upward course until December 1962 recording a 43 per cent increase within less than a year. Considering that a large number of shareholding companies were established in 1962, it becomes clear that speculative motives were a major factor behind the sharp price increases.

Lack of detailed data makes it difficult to draw conclusions as to the total trading and which companies or sectors attracted most traders, and the velocity of turnover of stocks among traders.

Among the factors contributing to the expansion of the activities of the stock market during 1961 and 1962 are the increase in domestic liquidity resulting from Government land acquisition payments which amounted to KD 148 million during the fiscal years 1960/61 and 1961/62 and the increase in bank credits to the private sector during this period. On the other hand, the slackening of the building and construction activities may also have helped in diverting some of the injected liquidity to the stock market.

The Period 1963-70. The shareholding companies' sector continued to grow and expand during these years, but at a lower rate than the previous period. While nine shareholding companies were established during the years 1961-62, only eight public and two closed shareholding companies were incorporated in the period 1963-70. Trading activities slackened markedly and stock prices went on the decline.

The downward trend in primary and secondary market activity seems to have started at the beginning of 1963. This was evidenced by the lukewarm reception of newly floated companies and the general drop in stock prices.

The ten companies which were incorporated during this period were all established in the years 1963-8 and none was founded during 1969-70. The cumulative capital of the newly established companies amounted to KD 43.75 million, 96 per cent of which was paid-up. The government participation in these companies was very high and amounted to nearly KD 26.3 million, or 60 per cent of the total authorized capital. Out of the ten companies, six could be classified as industrial, one as an investment company — where the government had a 98.72 per cent participation — two classified within the transport and services sector, and the tenth was the Al Ahli Bank of Kuwait which was fully owned by the private sector. By the end of 1968, the number of shareholding companies in Kuwait was 25, with a total nominal capital of KD 100 million, of which the government's share was 43 per cent and that of the private sector was 57 per cent.

It is worth noting here that all the capital increases of the existing companies came from the reserves and the issuance of bonus shares. In other words the net long-term external funds absorbed by the shareholding companies' sector during the period 1963-70 did not exceed KD 42.2 million — which represents the value of the paid-up capital in the newly established companies.

The companies' sectoral composition underwent a substantial change compared to the previous period. The financial sector companies lost their predominant position to the industrial companies, whose total capital increased to KD 47.4 million, accounting for 47 per cent of the total market nominal capital. On the other hand, the share of the financial sector has declined to 31 per cent although their total capital rose to 31 million KD. The increase in the industrial sector's share is attributed to the appearance and expansion of the petrochemicals industry which is characterized by its capital intensive nature. The transport and services sector also witnessed an impressive expansion with the incorporation of the Kuwait Transport Company and the Kuwait Food Company, and its share in the total market capital rose to 22 per cent.

Trading Activities and Stock Price Development. The incorporation of new companies and the increase in the capital of existing ones led to the expansion of the new issues base. By the end of 1968 the number of shares of the shareholding companies has reached 11,841,045. But if we exclude the shares of the government and the stocks of the closed companies, these will decrease to 6,026,118 shares. Lack of information on the exact number of stockholders makes it difficult to assess the expansion of the shareholders' base. However, it is unlikely that it expanded substantially, since many of the newly established companies had large participation by the National Industries Company and the Petrochemical Industries Company.

As regards trading activities and the levels of prices, this is difficult to discuss in detail due to the continued absence of systematic regulations to organize trading operations, and the unavailability of information regarding the volume of transactions, their values and price movements. However, the general trend of stock prices for the period 1961-6 could be traced on Figure 7.1 which depicts the movement of the stock price index prepared by the Kuwait Investment Company.

As the exhibit shows, stock prices seem to have been in continuing decline in the period between the beginning of 1963 and early 1966. But prices picked up substantially in 1966 registering a 23 per cent increase on the index. However, this spell of activity did not last long. With the

Figure 7.1: Shares Price Movement for Kuwaiti Shareholding Companies during the Period 1961–6 (Dec. 1961 = 100)

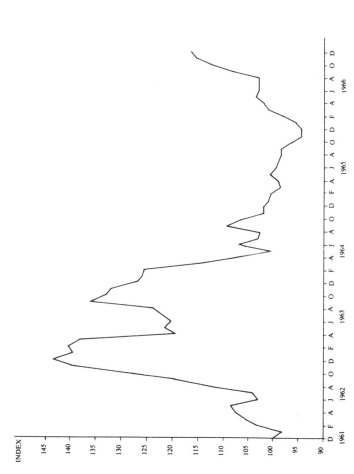

Source: Annual Reports of the Kuwait Investment Company 1963–6.

advent of 1967, trading activity contracted visibly and an acute recession set-in, which continued till the end of the decade. As stock prices
dropped and trading activities shrunk the enthusiasm of Kuwaiti
investors for stock trading subsided considerably. According to some
estimates the average monthly volume of trading in 1969 amounted to
only 40,000-50,000 shares, the equivalent of the daily average volume
of trading in 1965.

Another indicator of the extent of market contraction during that
period is the available figures on the annual turnover in the stocks of
four main companies during 1969, which totalled 41,935 shares, only
about 8.4 per cent of their total issued shares. A study conducted in
1974,[22] estimated the average price of all shares to be KD 17.8 at the
end of 1970, 26 per cent higher than the average book value. Average
price/earnings ratio was also estimated at 8.5.

Main Features of the Stock Market in the Period 1960-70. The
growth achieved during these years in the number of Kuwaiti shareholding companies and in the volume of shares distributed to the public
through public subscription was not accompanied by any development
in the legal and organizational framework of share issuing and trading.
The issue of new shares remained governed by Law No. 15 of 1960,
which severely limits the base of stock traders and contains a number
of loopholes. The Law restricts the right of subscription in the capital
of Kuwaiti shareholding companies to Kuwaitis only, except in rare and
limited cases. The Law stipulates also that the nominal value of companies' shares should not be less than KD 7.5 Under this Law, trading
in the shares of newly established companies was allowed even before
they commenced operations specified in their articles of association.
Apart from a few articles in Law No. 27 of 1962 dealing with transaction procedures in foreign shares, there were practically no explicit
legal rules governing stock trading operations.

The absence of a proper legal framework for the issue and trading of
stocks gave rise to widespread acts of fraudulence and encouraged
harmful speculative activity, such as founders' selling their stocks
immediately after the incorporation of their companies at prices higher
than the par value by as much as 40 per cent. In addition, the high par
value of shares fixed by the law put stockholding beyond the reach of
small and medium investors. No doubt, lack of proper legal and
organizational framework was one of the main reasons accounting for
the excessive speculation that usually occurred when new companies
were floated. Considering the generally low level of dealing activity in

the secondary market through the greater part of this period, investment in stocks tended to be illiquid and represented therefore, a long term commitment of funds. This, of course, increased the risks involved in buying stocks, and made yield considerations the major criterium in taking stock positions. It is noteworthy that all companies established during this period proved to be economically sound.

Trading activities did not only lack the legal and regulatory framework but also lacked basic market characteristics of a single market. Share transactions were carried out either directly between traders by negotiation or through the scattered brokers. With no information dissemination system in the market and poor communication channels, share prices usually differed from one broker's office to another according to the demand and supply orders placed with each broker. In actual fact, there was not a unified market but a fragmented one. On the other hand, companies annual reports provided the only public source of financial data relevant for investment decisions. Stock investors largely relied on their private sources of information, and naturally not all traders had the same access to such relevant information. However, the small size of the Kuwaiti commercial and financial community and the close links among its members made such information widely shared and hence effectively reducing the real need for extensive additional company disclosures.

Although the law tried to ensure wide participation in shareholding companies by requiring that every Kuwaiti subscriber should be allotted some shares, the shareholders base was still very narrow at the end of the decade. According to some estimates,[23] the number of active traders in the market did not exceed 300 individuals in 1970, and the number of shareholders of the National Bank of Kuwait, the oldest Kuwaiti Shareholding Company, was only 192. In addition, government control of more than 45 per cent of the total shares outstanding then, limited considerably the volume of tradable stocks.

Stock Market Conditions at the End of 1960s. The market recovery that characterized trading activities during 1965/66 did not last long because of the austerity measures which the government was forced to take after the 1967 war and which led to the contraction of all domestic economic activities. The general fall in economic activity has reflected itself in stock-trading activities. The decline was further intensified as the investors' initial enthusiasm for holding and trading stocks faltered when they became disappointed by their low returns compared to other forms of investment. This was mainly due to the fact that most of the companies were in their initial stages of operations and had not yet started distributing profits to the shareholders. Towards the end of the decade, the stock market was in a state of stagnation. No new public companies were established between 1968-70, and whatever stock-trading took place was mainly due to investors seeking to improve their liquidity position.

The combined effect of these factors coupled with the absence of regulatory and legal framework organizing stock-issuing trading activity rocked the confidence of Kuwaiti investors in the stock market. This attitude was reinforced by the decline experienced in the major world stock exchanges in New York, London and Tokyo. Thus, the prevailing market conditions thence did not provide attractive alternative invest-ment outlets capable of absorbing the influx of Kuwaiti funds seeking refuge from the losses they incurred in international financial and money markets.

Therefore, when the government decided to develop the role of the securities market, as part of its overall policy of expanding the domestic investment channels, the first task it had was to inspire the investors with some confidence in the market. A number of measures were intro-duced to improve the organization of the market and to provide basic controls and regulations that guaranteed the safety of transactions. As a result, 1970 could well be considered the actual beginning of the organized market for stock-trading.

The Growth of the Stock Market 1971–80

During the 1970s the stock market underwent important developments and changes that resulted in increasing its capacity to absorb and cir-culate funds. This included the issuing of a number of laws and resolu-tions which laid the organizational basis for the trading operations of Kuwaiti shareholding companies, and which paved the way for the emergence of the Stock Exchange. These developments greatly en-hanced the role of the stock market in the economic life of Kuwait, and contributed also to bring about a significant change in the indivi-dual attitudes and inclinations towards financial and economic activities. Thus, the last ten years may be considered the actual history of the Kuwait stock market, when its peculiar features and characteris-tics became evident.

In the light of available information and data, we can notice a number of distinct periods in the process of the market development, over the last decade, whether from the point of view of trading activity or as far as its organizational and regulatory framework is concerned. Being a newly born dynamic market in its early stages of development organizational changes are introduced in piecemeal fashion and usually in response to particular problems and short-comings that become fully apparent during periods of unusual market activity, such as booms and crises. For the purposes of this study, we distinguished between the various periods on the basis of the trend movement of stock prices and volume of trading in the secondary market.

Period I: The Beginning of Market Organization and the Emergence of Speculation (end 1970-beginning 1974). This period was in general characterized by the upward trend of stock prices and the volume of trading: an unprecedented expansion in the new issues base, and the introduction of a number of laws regulating trading activities in domestic securities. In November 1970, Law No. 32 was promulgated. It substituted Law No. 27 of 1962, on the organization of foreign securities, and established the basis for trading the securities of Kuwaiti companies.

On 8 August 1971 the Minister of Commerce and Industry issued a resolution entrusting to the Companies and Insurance Supervision Section in the Ministry the task of regulating trade in securities, to compile statistical analysis of stock movements and profits of Kuwaiti shareholding companies and to publish an official daily statement on the prices of stocks. Stockbrokers were also obliged to register with the Ministry of Commerce and Industry and to report daily on all stock transactions as well as on trading prices. In February 1972 the Bureau of Securities commenced its activities in the Commercial Centre, in the city of Kuwait.

The Developments of the New Issues Market. After subjecting the stock market to legal organization and government supervision, especially after the emergence of the Stock Exchange, trading in the official market was limited to the shares of public Kuwaiti shareholding companies.

At the end of 1973, the total number of public shareholding companies numbered 31, as a result of the incorporation of eleven companies during the period 1971-3 most of which were established in 1973. Total nominal value of the public companies' capital rose to KD 140 million at the end of 1972 and to KD 184 million in 1973 — that is, an increase of 52 per cent and 100 per cent respectively in comparison with the total cumulative capital of the public shareholding

Table 7.1: Shareholding Companies Classified by Sectors

Sector	No. of Companies	1970 Cumulative Capital (KD)	Capital Distribution According to Category (%)	No. of Companies	1973 Cumulative Capital (KD)	Capital Distribution According to Category (%)
Banks	4	11,412,500	12.4	6	23,670,000	12.8
Insurance Companies	3	2,250,000	2.4	3	2,500,000	1.4
Investment Companies	2	17,500,000	19.0	3	38,347,500	20.8
Industrial Companies	7	39,800,000	43.1	9	70,400,000	38.2
Transport Companies	2	13,752,690	14.9	2	20,502,690	11.1
Commercial and Services Companies	4	7,576,442	8.2	5	15,576,442	8.5
Real Estate Companies	—	—	—	3	13,306,900	7.2
Total	22	92,291,632	100,0	31	184,303,532	100.0

companies in 1968. A large proportion of the companies' capital increases was internally financed through reserves and profit capitalization. The external amounts absorbed by the shareholding companies did not exceed KD 55 million, of which the government contributed KD 9.6 million.

The expansion in the number of the shareholding companies produced a basic change in the structural composition of the market. As may be noticed from Table 7.1, the most important change was the emergence for the first time of the real estate companies sector and the substantial decline of the relative weight of the industrial companies sector. The banking sector maintained its relative importance, while the investment companies sector showed a moderate increase.

As shown also in Table 7.2, the number of stocks issued increased from 11.05 million at the end of 1970 to about 21.33 million in 1973. At the same time, the number of government-owned stocks increased from 5.03 million to 8.2 million in the same period. However, the government's share in the total decreased from 45.5 per cent to 38.4 per cent as a result of its low participation in the capitals of the newly established companies. The total number of tradable stocks increased from 6.02 million to about 13.14 million, an increase of 118 per cent.

The most significant expansionary feature characterizing the shareholding companies sector during this period was the appearance of real estate companies. During the years 1972/73 and 1973/74 eight companies were established with a cumulative capital of about KD 42 million. The establishment of these companies introduced a qualitative and quantitative change to the Kuwait stock market. Their inclusion in the market and the public trading of their stocks added a new and important depth to the market. This has created also a direct link between the price of stocks, as financial assets, and the price of land. In addition, the public issuing and trading of the stocks of real estate companies has allowed small investors to have access to the highly profitable land and real estate market, since direct individual investment was beyond their resources.

The floating of the new companies attracted unprecedented demand. For example, the stocks of the Kuwait International Investment Company were over-subscribed by 136 times, those of the National Automotive Manufacturing and Trading Company 109 times, and those of the Refrigeration Company 43 times. The non-existence of limits on individual subscriptions and the availability of cheap credit facilities were the major factors contributing to the excessive demand for subscription.

Table 7.2: Issued Shares of Kuwaiti Shareholding Companies during 1970 and 1973

Group of Companies	1970			1973		
	No. of Companies	Total Issued Shares	Government's Share (%)	No. of Companies	Total Issued Shares	Government's Share (%)
Banks	4	1,455,030	–	6	2,856,000	3.4
Investment Companies	2	1,750,000	77.9	3	4,087,875	49.3
Insurance Companies	3	260,000	–	3	292,500	–
Industrial Companies	7	4,940,000	64.7	9	8,520,000	65.0
Transport Companies	3	2,033,692	16.0	3	2,633,692	30.0
Commercial and Services Companies	3	612,153	23.5	4	1,612,153	7.0
Real Estate Companies	–	–	–	3	1,330,650	29.2
Total	22	11,050,845	45.5	31	21,332,870	38.4

Table 7.3: Share Prices of Kuwaiti Shareholding Companies, Sept. 1970–Dec. 1973 (in Kuwaiti Dinars)

Group of Companies[a]	1970 Sept.	1971 March	1971 June	1971 Sept.	1971 Dec.	1972 March	1972 June	1972 Sept.	1972 Dec.	1973 March	1973 June	1973 Sept.	1973 Dec.	Percent change Sept. 70–Dec. 73
Banks	24.500	27.380	30.750	34.380	39.310	50.380	46.233	56.545	65.586	60.818	58.000	76.760	71.867	193
Investment and Insurance Companies	11.660	12.880	14.940	16.230	17.750	22.060	19.366	26.740	29.815	30.186	30.640	42.520	42.070	266
Industrial Companies	14.250	16.130	16.880	18.000	18.250	21.130	19.709	26.273	32.904	30.910	26.172	34.389	39.830	178
Real Estate Companies	—	—	—	—	—	—	11.000	12.594	17.000	24.861	24.400	35.250	38.583	251[b]
Others	12.420	13.580	14.830	17.330	18.420[c]	21.930	17.100	21.365	24.572	24.764	25.233	35.750	32.400	161
General Average	15.025	16.741	18.400	20.393	22.012	26.878	23.706	30.245	34.414	33.565	33.030	45.107	45.626	204
No. of Companies whose Shares are traded	22	22	22	22	22	22	24[d]	24	25[e]	24	26[f]	27	319	

Notes: a. The composition of each group is shown in Table 7.4 and it is the same classification used then by the Central Bank.
b. Percentage change in Prices during the period June 1972–December 1973.
c. Average Prices of Shares in January 1972.
d. Shares of Kuwait Real Estate Co. and Bank of Kuwait and the Middle East are traded.
e. Shares of United Fisheries Co. are traded.
f. Shares of United Real Estate Co. and Kuwait Refrigeration Co. are traded.
g. Shares of Kuwait International Investment Co., Real Estate Bank, National Automotive Manufacturing and Trading Co., and the National Real Estate Co. are traded.
Source: Reports of the Central Bank of Kuwait.

The Development of Stock Prices and Trading Movement. The relative depression in stock trading activity and stock prices, which was prevailing at the end of the 1960s, started to disappear towards the end of 1970, when stock prices and trading started an upward trend which continued until the beginning of 1973. The surge in prices and trading volume did not follow a gradual course but proceeded in sudden leaps.

As illustrated in Table 7.3, the general price average of stocks increased from about KD 15 in September 1970 to KD 20.4 in September 1971, and to more than KD 45 at the end of 1973 — that is, an increase of more than 200 per cent over the period 1971-3. However, it is worth of noting here that the general price average is only a crude indicator that has many serious shortcomings. It gives equal relative weight to all companies irrespective of their size and is not appropriately adjusted to take into account companies bonus issues or the coming of new companies to the market. In this instance, the indicator grossly understates the real magnitude of the price increases, since it includes the stocks of nine newly established companies.

The table indicates also that the leap in prices was general, yet increase was very sharp in the case of the real estate stocks, which rose by more than 250 per cent in less than two years after the floating of the companies. This accelerated price increase reflected the heated wave of speculation that ran through the lands and real estate market and the tremendous increase in the market value of the companies' assets. However, the acute general price increases was not matched by a similar growth in the assets and profits of the companies, or a qualitative change in their performance. In the period between the end of 1970 and the end of 1972 average profits increased by a mere 7.1 per cent, and book value per share by 4 per cent. In addition, the average price/earning ratio at the end of 1972 and 1973 was about 29 per cent and 47 per cent respectively.[24] This was also reflected in the ratio of average market prices to the average book value per share, which increased from 2.53 at the end of 1972 to 3.74 at the end of 1973.

It is worth noting that the rise in the stock prices included also the stocks of newly established companies that had not started their operations yet and hence have no measurable indicator for the future earnings of their operations.

With the sharp upsurge in prices, the market value of the outstanding shares multiplied six-fold in the period 1970-3, about four times the total shareholders' equity at the end of 1973.

Available figures on the value and volume of trading during the years 1972-3 (see Table 7.5) and 1973-4 show even more clearly the

Table 7.4: Kuwaiti Shareholding Companies with Traded Shares
Classified by Sectors

1970–1	1973–4
Banks	**Banks**
(1) National Bank of Kuwait	(1) National Bank of Kuwait
(2) Commercial Bank of Kuwait	(2) Commercial Bank of Kuwait
(3) Al Ahli Bank of Kuwait	(3) Al Ahli Bank of Kuwait
(4) Gulf Bank	(4) Gulf Bank
	(5) Bank of Kuwait and the Middle East
Insurance and Investment Companies	(6) Real Estate Bank of Kuwait
(5) Kuwait Investment Co.	
(6) Kuwait Foreign Trading, Contracting and Investment Co.	**Insurance and Investment Companies**
(7) Kuwait Insurance Co.	(7) Kuwait Investment Co.
(8) Al-Ahleia Insurance Co.	(8) Kuwait Foreign Trading, Contracting and Investment Co.
(9) Gulf Insurance Co.	(9) Kuwait International Investment Co.
	(10) Kuwait Insurance Co.
Industrial Companies	(11) Al Ahleia Insurance Co.
(10) Kuwait National Petroleum Co.	(12) Gulf Insurance Co.
(11) Kuwait Petrochemical Industries Co.	
(12) Kuwait National Industries Co.	**Industrial Companies**
(13) Kuwait Flour Mills Co.	(13) Kuwait National Petroleum Co.
(14) Kuwait Metal Pipes Co.	(14) Kuwait Petrochemical Industries Co.
(15) Kuwait Cement Co.	(15) Kuwait National Industries Co.
(16) Kuwait United Fisheries Co.	(16) Kuwait Flour Mills Co.
	(17) Kuwait Metal Pipes Co.
Other Companies	(18) Kuwait Cement Co.
(17) Kuwait Transport Co.	(19) Kuwait National Fisheries Co.
(18) Kuwait Oil Tankers Co.	(20) Kuwait United Fisheries Co.
(19) Kuwait Shipping Co.	(21) Refrigeration Industry and Cold Storage Co.
(20) Kuwait Cinema Co.	(22) National Automotive Manufacturing and Trading Co.
(21) Kuwait Hotels Co.	
(22) Kuwait Food Co.	**Other Companies**
	(23) Kuwait Transport Co.
	(24) Kuwait Oil Tankers Co.
	(25) Kuwait Shipping Co.
	(26) Kuwait Cinema Co.
	(27) Kuwait Hotels Co.
	(28) Kuwait Food Co.
	Real Estate Companies
	(29) Kuwait Real Estate Co.
	(30) United Real Estate Co.
	(31) National Real Estate Co.

Table 7.5: Quantities and Values of Shares Traded, Second quarter 1972–Fourth Quarter 1973 (value in thousands of KDs and quantities in thousands of shares)

Group of Companies	1972								1973							
	April		2nd Quarter		3rd Quarter		4th Quarter		1st Quarter		2nd Quarter		3rd Quarter		4th Quarter	
	Qty	Value	Qty	Value	Qty	Value	Qty	Value	Qty	Value	Qty	Value	Qty	Value	Qty	Value
Banks	28.7	1,175	58.1	2,462	75.0	4,072	190.9	3,411	122	7,134	225	13,117	96.7	7,488	114	7,049
Investment and Insurance Companies	29.8	449	89.0	1,253	246.5	5,117	402.5	10,450	150.3	2,825	1,717	28,773	2,056	55,243	459	10,818
Industrial Companies	55.9	1,195	226	5,578	148	3,653	474.9	17,167	214.4	8,164	554	19,268	1,084	49,547	512	30,961
Real Estate Companies	—	—	—	—	2.1	26	2.6	43.8	20.3	473	83	1,915	247	8,190	146	4,785
Others	29.3	573	114.4	2,579	362.4	10,755	411.3	13,902	184.6	6,582	620	20,004	926	41,382	419	20,495
Total	144.1	3,520	492.5	11,867	834	22,047	1,480.3	54,974	681	25,178	3,201	83,077	4,409	161,850	1,665	74,108

Source: Reports of the Central Bank of Kuwait.

tremendous changes that took place in the market during this period. The total number of traded shares rose from 3.48 million in 1972-3 to 10.8 million during 1973-4, recording an increase of 2.4 per cent, as it reached about KD 357 million in 1973-4. Trading activities achieved their peak during the period extending from April to September 1973, when 7.6 million shares were traded for a value of KD 242 million. This was also accompanied by a sharp upturn in stock prices and the incorporation of five new companies and the offering of their stocks for public subscription. Between October 1973 and March 1974, the volume of trading declined enormously and the monthly volume of trading dropped from 1.3 million shares to 0.5 million.

During this share boom, the annual value of total traded shares as a percentage of GDP rose from 6.7 per cent to about 17 per cent. This provides an indication also to the substantial expansion in the stock market capacity to attract funds.

Features of the First Boom Period (1971-3). The consecutive leaps and bounds in stock prices and the unrealistic levels they have reached fuelled a strong wave of speculation, which in turn reinforced the price movement in its upward trend. In 1973, total share turnover amounted to about 70 per cent of the total shares owned by the private sector. The continuous increase in prices provided ample opportunities for making quick profits, thus attracting new traders and more funds to the stock market. The intensive wave of speculation and the exceptional profits that could be obtained from share trading led to the establishment of a number of new companies with the intention of making capital gains from selling the new shares in the secondary market. Under the then prevailing legal arrangements, official trading in the shares of new companies could begin immediately after their establishment. Absence of official regulation obviously gave additional impetus to speculative trading in new shares. No doubt, a major feature of the stock market during this period and one which had serious effects on its operations is the appearance of forward deals.

Although forward trading is known in one form or another in security markets elsewhere in the world, however it has some unique aspects in Kuwait. In the forward deal in the Kuwaiti stock market, the buyer takes immediate possession of the shares and gives the seller by return a post-dated cheque for the whole amount due. The period of the deals ranges between one month and two years and their price always carries a premium on the current market price of the share transacted. The premium rate depends mainly on the liquidity situation

Table 7.6: Commercial Banks, Credit Facilities and Liquidity Position (KD million)

Year	Credit Facilities (1)	% Change	Commercial Banks total claims on Private Sector (2)	% Change	Commercial Banks Private Sectors deposits in local currency (3)	% Change	Claims on the Private Sector Deposits % (2/3)
1971	146.9	7.1	161.4	—	307.7	—	52.5
1972	175.7	19.6	187.4	16.1	389.2	26.4	48.2
1973	246.6	40.4	266.3	42.1	407.4	4.7	65.4
1974	351.7	42.6	361.9	35.9	465.8	14.3	77.7
1975	462.5	31.5	506.7	40.0	667.9	43.4	75.9
1976	849.3	83.6	934.3	84.3	925.5	38.6	101.0
1977	1072.6	26.3	1238.5	32.6	1345.3	45.3	92.0
1978	1374.5	28.1	1559.4	15.9	1592.0	18.3	98.0
1979	1917.5	39.5	2119.3	35.9	1718.2	7.9	123.3
1980	2418.6	26.1	2671.4	26.0	2018.3	17.5	132.4

Source: Central Bank Economic Reports.

in the market, the intensity of trading activity and rates of share prices increases. This peculiar form of forward transaction is more in the nature of a personal credit extended from the seller to the buyer rather than a means of hedging or covering against market volatility and share price fluctuations. Hence it contributes greatly to fuel speculative trading and exert strong upward pressure on share prices during the boom. More dangerously, a large outstanding volume of forward deals may precipitate a collapse if the market falters. It seems that the market created this form of non-institutional credit to supplement the credit facilities provided by the financial system which despite its rapid expansion, did not keep pace with the tremendous increase in the total value of transactions in the stock and the real estate markets. As Table 7.6 shows, banks credit facilities increased by about 68 per cent during the period 1971-3, against a 20 per cent increase only in the bank's KD deposits. This clearly indicates that commercial banks pursued very expansionary credit policies. None the less, total bank credit represented only 72 per cent of the total value of shares traded in 1973, compared to 198 per cent in 1972. This rough indicator gives some idea to what extent bank credit expansion failed to accommodate fully the liquidity requirements of the frenetic activity in the stock market and the land and real estate market.

The surge in speculative activities in the domestic assets markets coincided with a large expansion in government expenditure following the sizeable increase in oil revenues after the Tehran Agreement in 1971, and the return of funds from abroad caused by the uncertain conditions of the international markets.

Period II: Weakening of the Market (beginning 1974-end March 1975). There was a marked decline in overall stock market activity during this relatively short period. The continuing increase in share prices and volume of trading came to a stop towards the end of 1973, when both began to drop steadily. Between January 1974 and the end of March 1975, the average monthly trading decreased 58 per cent in volume and 68 per cent in value terms. The decrease in the value was greater although there was only a marginal drop in stock prices because of the change in the composition of the traded shares. Trading activity concentrated in this period on low priced stocks.

The drop in stock prices, which accompanied the trading contraction, was of lower magnitude. Average stock prices registered a decrease of 8.2 per cent between the fourth quarter of 1973 and the first quarter of 1975. The turnover ratio also witnessed a drop compared with 1973.

Monthly average volume of trading during the period was only 1.9 per cent of the total stock issued and only 3.2 per cent of the total tradable stocks. The comparable figures for 1973 were 3.9 per cent and 6.3 per cent, respectively. This indicates the shrinkage of the speculation phenomenon which reached its peak in 1973.

This contraction in the market activities was a natural reaction to the intensive activity which characterized the market in 1973 and to the continuous rise in stock prices. Therefore, this was a period of adjustment by the market to restore balance to price levels which rose to unrealistic levels in the previous period. Leading investors had also to withdraw temporarily from the market in order to reassess their port-folios and evaluate their financial position in the light of the results of the hectic trading of the previous period.

Another important factor contributing to the decline in market activity was the sharp drop in forward transactions. This came after the issuing of the ministerial decision No. 52 of 1974 by the Minister of Commerce and Industry which made forward transactions in securities illegal. The measure was intended to prevent the deflationary conse-quences of forward deals from building up and to avoid the downward pressures on share prices that arise from forced sales by traders short of liquidity when the deals are due for payment.

During 1974, the market base expanded by the incorporation of two new shareholding companies thus increasing the number of sharehold-ing companies to 33. The total cumulative capital of these companies increased to KD 214 million, in which the government had a 41 per cent stake.

The stock issues base expanded also to reach 23,342 million, an increase of 9.4 per cent. The share of the government in these stocks was 9,660 million, and consequently the tradable stocks were 13,682 million. By the end of 1974, the market value of the total outstanding shares reached about KD 895.7 million, or 2.41 times the shareholders equity. The comparable figure for 1973 was 4 times.

The decline in the stock market activity coincided with the outflow of funds abroad attracted by the increased interest rates differential between domestic and international assets. The curve of market activity did not resume its upward trend until the second quarter of 1975.

Period III: The Peak — the Runaway Boom (April 1975–end 1976). This period is considered one of the most important stages in the development of the stock market. It witnessed an unprecedented outburst of trading activities and an unbridled surge in prices, which also affected the new issues market. This period witnessed also major amendments in the Companies' Law aimed at closing some of the legal loopholes relating to the regulation of issuing and subscription procedures in public companies stock, which were widely exploited by speculators and undermined the orderly behaviour of the market.

An Emiri Decree was issued, promulgating Law No. 3 of 1975, which introduced amendments to some articles of Law No. 15 of 1960 concerning shareholding companies. According to these amendments, company founders were required to examine subscription applications before making the share allotment, as a measure to prevent the practice of subscribing with fictitious and duplicated names. Trading in the stocks of newly created companies was not allowed before the elapse of one year from the establishment of the new companies and after the publication of their first balance sheet. The amendments also stipulated setting the minimum nominal price of stocks at KD 1 and reduced the maximum limit for subscription in order to expand the subscribers base.

It is worth noting that these amendments aimed mainly at improving the regulation of new issues offered for public subscription and dealt only marginally with trading operations. However, it affected of course the supply of stocks offered for trading.

Developments in the New Issues Market. During 1975-6, the Kuwaiti stock market experienced a large expansion similar to that which took place in 1973. In the period from April 1975 to November 1976, seven new public shareholding companies were incorporated with a total capital of KD 45.75 million, divided into 42.15 million shares, out of which KD 32.7 million was actually paid-up. But on the other hand, the shares of the two biggest industrial companies – the Kuwait National Petroleum Company and the Petrochemical Industries Company – were withdrawn from the market following their full acquisition by the government.

The overall outcome of these developments was a substantial expansion in the new issues base and fundamental changes in their sectoral distribution, as reflected in Table 7.7. The government's share in the market dropped enormously as a result of the nationalization of the Kuwait National Petroleum Company (KNPC) and the Petrochemical Industries Company (PIC), which represented a major government participation in the shareholding companies sector. With the withdrawal of the oil sector companies from the stock market – with the exception of the Kuwait Oil Tankers Company – the relative importance of the

Table 7.7: Major Shareholding Companies at the end of 1976, Classified According to Main Activities (in Kuwaiti Dinars)

Group	No.	Authorized Capital	Per cent of Total Capital (%)	Paid-up Capital	Per cent of Total Paid-up Capital (%)	Number of Shares	Per cent of Total Market (%)
Banks	7	44,671,312	16.8	44,394,522	18.4	14,106,175	20.9
Insurance Companies	4	8,233,327	3.1	6,233,327	2.3	4,507,777	6.7
Investment Companies	3	46,294,130	17.4	46,294,130	19.2	4,880,038	7.2
Industrial Companies	13	68,390,000	25.8	52,055,446	21.6	24,202,000	35.8
Transport and Communication Companies	4	56,936,605	21.4	56,810,469	23.5	6,758,214	10.0
Commercial and Services Companies	4	15,456,442	5.8	10,456,442	4.3	10,622,153	15.7
Real Estate Companies	3	25,500,000	9.6	25,179,646	10.4	2,550,000	3.8
Total	38	265,481,816	100.0[a]	241,423,982	100.0[a]	67,626,357	100.0[a]

Note: a. Totals not exact due to rounding.

industrial companies sector declined substantially.

Table 7.7 shows that each sector's share in the issued stocks differs markedly from its share of the total market capitalization. This is attributed to the difference in the nominal value of the different companies' stocks, especially those incorporated during 1976 which predominantly had a nominal share value of KD 1. These companies contributed significantly to the broadening of the issued base.

As a reflection to the revival of the economic activity during the years 1975 and 1976, the closed companies sector achieved an enormous growth represented in the establishment of more than 50 companies with a total capital of KD 92 million, of which about KD 58 million was paid-up. The shareholding companies were therefore able during that period to absorb a total of about KD 164 million.

The Development in the Movement of Trading and Prices. After the relative contraction in the activities of the market during 1974, the market revived again during 1975 and 1976 with trading and price movement registering new peaks. During the fourth quarter of 1975, the volume of traded stocks increased steadily to surpass the high levels they reached in 1973. The total number of traded shares amounted to 18.4 million in 1974, with a total value of KD 449 million, an increase of 338 per cent over 1974.

Although intensified trading covered almost all companies, the sharp increase in the volume of traded shares was not accompanied by a similar increase in price movement. Prices rose moderately in comparison with the increase in the volume of trading. Between the first and fourth quarters of 1975, the stock price average increased by 20 per cent, with the highest increase recorded by the stocks of real estate companies which jumped by 80 per cent. This was a reflection of the speculation fever that caught the real estate market since the beginning of 1975.

In 1976, active trading continued, but was associated with a sharper movement in prices which recorded a spectacular leap against a moderate increase in the volume of trading. The volume of traded stocks amounted to 19.8 million with a total market value of KD 952 million, that is an increase of 7.5 per cent and 112 per cent respectively on the corresponding figures in the previous year. The sharp upturn in the prices started from the beginning of the second quarter of 1976, and continued until November. The average price of shares went up in the course of this short period by 135 per cent. Consequently, the gap between the market value and book value of stocks widened still further, as the proportion between them reached 8.8 times. The extra-ordinary increases in the stock prices of Kuwaiti companies made them reach unrealistic levels from the point of view of standard economic and financial criteria. The average stock price amounted to as much as 11 times its average nominal value, and as much as six times its book value. The absence of a meaningful relationship between the market price of shares and the underlying companies financial and earning position was evidenced by the excessive levels reached by the market capitalization rate, which averaged about 70 by the end of 1976. Speculation waves during 1975 and 1976 exceeded the levels they reached during 1973. The shares turnover increased to 8.6 per cent of total tradable shares compared with only 6.3 per cent in the previous period. Demand was particularly high for the stocks of newly estab-lished companies because of their low par value fixed at KD 1.

The fervent speculation wave that hit the market in 1976 also had some peculiar features that made it differ from the previous wave, above all its origin in the real estate market. As a result of the huge increase in oil revenues during 1974-5 and the ensuing economic boom, demand for residential quarters, commercial offices and lands increased to unprecedented magnitude and led to sharp increases in rents and land and real estate prices. This was accompanied by an easing of credit facilities by the banking system for real estate investment and construction activities. In addition, the government aiming at easing the housing problem, distributed housing plots to citizens at nominal prices and increased the amounts of social and housing loans provided by the Credit and Savings Bank. The combined effects of these develop-ments helped in bringing about a wild wave of speculation in the land and real estate market, starting from the second half of 1975, which pushed the price of land to exaggerated levels. This wave peaked in the second half of 1976, when suddenly the price upsurge stopped and demand began to shrink.

The bounce in the price of land and real estate led to the fast and continuous appreciation of assets of real estate and investment com-panies and was consequently reflected in their stocks. This situation tempted also a number of shareholding companies to enter the land and real estate market although such an activity was completely remote from their line of work and did not figure in the companies' objectives as stated in their articles of association. As a result, many companies achieved quick profits that led to more than proportional increases in the market prices of their stocks.

The sequence of events during this period indicates that the wave of speculation initially started in the land and real estate market and passed over to the stock market. That is to say, the stock price developments followed the price movement trends of land and real estates.

Expansionary trends in the domestic liquidity and banks' credit contributed to exacerbate inflationary pressures on the prices of shares, land and real estate by allowing the financing of speculation activities. During the years 1975 and 1976 domestic liquidity increased at the rate of 24 per cent and 37 per cent respectively, while short term credit facilities for the same period registered record levels of 31.5 per cent and 83.6 per cent respectively. In 1976 credit facilities classified under 'personal loans', which are normally used to finance speculative activities, registered a rate of growth of 135 per cent. It seems that the credit expansionary policies of the commercial banks deviated to such an extent from normal prudent banking practices that they prompted the Central Bank to intervene. It issued a number of instructions and directives to commercial banks requiring them to tighten their credit policies and limit the facilities used to finance speculation. An indicator that illustrates the pressures that were exerted on the domestic liquidity held by banks is the increase in the ratio between claims on the private sector and deposits in KD, which increased in 1976 to 101 per cent compared with 76 per cent and 78 per cent in 1974 and 1975 respectively (Table 7.6).

Another important feature of the market boom in 1975 and 1976 is the forward deals which the Ministry of Commerce and Industry failed to limit and control, and which were a major factor fuelling speculative trends and feverish stock trading. The drastic increase in the average share deal and the excessive premiums offered on forward transactions (the premium rate was around 30 per cent for one year deferred payment) reflected to a large extent, the growing gap that was emerging between the market's demand for liquidity and the banking system ability to supply it as their credit expansion capacity neared its maximum acceptable limits.

The malpractices and irregular operations observed in the market during 1973 reappeared again at a larger scale in 1976. Such as subscription in new issues with imaginary names, unofficial transactions, and manipulation of share prices by big traders at the expense of small investors.

The Looming of the Crisis. With the advent of the final quarter of 1976, the first signs of sharp market reversal began to appear on the horizon, and the authorities began to fear the possibility of the total collapse of the market. The upward share prices movement reached extravagant levels making many shares virtually unmarketable while putting increasing strains on dealers resources. Another major dampening factor was the loss of momentum of speculative activities in the real estate market and the downward trend in land and real estate prices which commenced from the middle of the year. At the same time forward deals accumulated in the hands of speculators and amounted to hundreds of millions of KDs. Some of these obligations were due within close intervals of time. Thus, the possibility of the contraction of the market and the decrease in prices threatened the successful conclusion of these deals, especially that the extraordinary activity of the stock market attracted many small and medium-size investors who entered the market with mainly borrowed money and had very little extra resources to maintain a depreciating portfolio for a long period. Malpractices further-intensified this precarious situation.

In an effort to cure the situation and develop the organizational framework of the market, the Ministry of Commerce and Industry issued in November a resolution establishing the Securities Committee with broad authority for the organization of securities trading in the market. In addition, the Central Bank tightened its control on the commercial banks in order to curb their credit facilities which went to fuel speculation. In confirmation of the fears expressed earlier by the authorities and other market observers, the general trend of prices took a sharp down-turn plunge towards the end of 1976 that put the market on the verge of collapse.

Period IV: The Crisis (end 1976–end 1977). The stock market went during this period, through a severe crisis that shook the investors' confidence in the market and threatened to have more serious consequences, were it not for the government intervention which supported the market to get over its difficulties. The issue base however continued to expand, increasing the market capitalization. The total number of outstanding stocks amounted by end of 1977 to approximately 95 million, covering 40 companies, with a total nominal value of about KD 347 million, of which KD 319 million was paid-up. Excluding the share of the government, amounting to 22.8 million shares (24 per cent of the total issued stocks), and the share of the private sector in companies which had not published their first balance sheets yet, the volume of the legally tradable stocks was reduced to approximately 27.7 million, an increase of 28.8 per cent over the corresponding figure at the end of 1976.

Developments in the Secondary Market. Towards the end of 1976, the signs of a strong and general reversal movement affecting trading and prices began to appear and the downward trend confirmed itself in the beginning of 1977. The steep decline in prices created a wave of confusion and disarray among traders and particularly the small and medium investors.

On the trading level, the volume of traded stocks exhibited a sharp decline amounting to 31 per cent compared to 1976 and the stock turnover decreased from 19.8 million in 1976 to about 13.7 million in 1977 despite the increase in the number of outstanding stocks. The full extent of the market contraction becomes clearer if we excluded the traded stocks of the Kuwait Sanitaryware Industries Company which alone accounted for 57 per cent of the total turnover in 1977. The rate of decline then reaches 70 per cent of the previous year's level. The rate of decline was higher in the sectors which experienced the largest volume of trading during 1976, that is, the real estate companies and the unclassified companies which come under 'the other companies' category.

Lower trading activity was also accompanied by a general decrease in the stock price estimated at 19 per cent according to the adjusted stock price index prepared by the Ministry of Commerce and Industry. But on the basis of the simple price average of all shares, the rate of decline was about 38 per cent during the year. However, since price changes are recorded only when dealing takes place, the true extent of the price fall is not fully reflected by these percentages.

The shrinking in total turnover value was much more acute at 64 per cent due to the combined effect of lower volume of trading and lower prices.

During 1977, the Government took several measures and issued a number of resolutions that had deep effects on the stock market and its subsequent development. In April 1977, the stock exchange and the Securities Market was established, and a Ministerial resolution was issued regulating forward transactions, defining the basis for concluding such deals, and making them fall under the direct control and supervision of the Ministry itself. In August 1977, further resolutions were issued suspending the establishment of new public-subscription shareholding companies and prohibiting the increase in capitals of existing companies except within the minimum limits possible. Later, in December 1977, the Government decided to intervene more forcefully in support of the market, so it issued a resolution taking effect from 24 December 1977 authorizing the Kuwait Foreign Trading, Contracting and Investment Company (KFTCIC) to purchase on its behalf any shares offered by the private sector at the lowest price prevailing in the market in the period 1 October 1977 to 17 December 1977. As for the stocks which were not traded during this period, another floor price reference would be set. In order also to ease the burden of debt obligations on the traders, the government issued instructions to the banking system to reduce the interest rate charged on outstanding loans and extend the repayment period for an additional two years with possibility of further extension depending on the financial conditions of individual borrowers. It was hoped that these measures would reduce pressures on borrowers to liquidate their stocks at a loss and thus choke off the oversupply of stocks in the market.

Major Factors Contributing to the Market Reaction. The price decline and the contraction of market activity was to a large extent the natural consequence of over-speculation and the escalation of prices to unreasonable levels during 1976.

However, several additional factors contributed to reinforce the recessionary and weakening trend in the market. We deal briefly in what follows with what we consider the most important of them.

Forward Deals: A large proportion of the forward deals concluded during 1976 were for periods ranging from six months to one year, with maturity dates falling in the first half of 1977. Many of these transactions carried a premium of 25–30 per cent on the share prices ruling in 1976.

But by the end of 1976 and early 1977, the market had fallen by about 30 per cent below that level thus forcing many investors, particularly the unwary buyers who failed to cover their positions, to liquidate their portfolio at a loss to meet their obligations. The clustering of forward deals payments dates within narrow time intervals resulted in hard-pressed investors swamping the market with their sale offers, thus depressing it still further. Moreover only a trickle of the total value of these deals was reinvested in stocks, hence draining liquidity from the market. Shortage of liquidity led many traders to finance themselves expensively by concluding new forward deals at high premiums and selling the share spot, incurring in the process substantial losses as well as worsening the market supply situation.

There is little doubt that the large volume of forward deals and their excessive rates greatly magnified the effects of the drop in prices. The liquidity problem also hit the major shareholding companies which were actively involved in the real estate and stock markets. Many of them chose to improve their financial position by proposing substantial capital increases. The improper timing of the new rights issues caused additional strains on an already weakening market.

Domestic Liquidity Situation: A number of reasons and developments helped in contracting the rate of domestic liquidity directed towards the stock market. The growth rate of the private sector's domestic liquidity decreased to 30 per cent from 37 per cent in 1976 to 25 per cent in 1977. This was attributed basically to the imposition of tighter rules by banks on private sector credit, and the increase in the interest rates on loans. As a result the growth rate of commercial banks' claims on the private sector dropped to 33 per cent from 84 per cent in the previous year. However, government expenditure continued to exercise an expansionary role growing by 30 per cent and effectively eased the market liquidity problem by injecting about KD 150 million into the system through its stock purchases.

The Appearance of New Financial Assets: Another major factor that affected the level of liquidity directed towards the secondary stock market and enhanced its recessionary trends was new stock issues which absorbed a large portion (KD 94 million) of private investors' liquidity. Added to that are the amounts of money (KD 30 million) transferred abroad to participate in Arab and Gulf companies, whose stocks were offered for subscription in the domestic market. The establishment of the offshore Gulf companies with Kuwaiti capital started at the end of 1976 and gained momentum after the ban on the establishment of new shareholding companies introduced in August 1977.

Psychological Factors: The optimistic expectations that prevailed among traders during 1976, especially in the last quarter, were based on the anticipation of good company results and also boosted by the continuing upward trend of prices since 1975. The optimistic mood of the market began to dissipate rapidly after a disappointing profit distribution and a sharp reverse in prices giving rise instead to feelings of insecurity and precaution. These attitudes were further consolidated with the successive decreases in prices and the views that were being spread in some economic circles in Kuwait that Kuwait's oil revenues might decrease — and consequently public expenditure contract — as a result of the failure of the OPEC conference in Doha to reach a unified policy on oil pricing.

The 1977 developments of the market underlined the risks involved in a market boom based on excessive speculation and the ignoring of basic relevant economic, financial and other investment considerations relating to securities investment and trading. It also emphasized the fragile foundations on which the market was based and the vulnerability of the majority of small and medium investors to the manipulations and speculative manoeuvres of the big traders.

Although the measures and actions undertaken by the government to rescue the market, averted a total collapse of investors' confidence and contributed to reduce the losses incurred by a large sector of stockholders, yet it had a negative long-term impact on the efforts to curb speculation. The government intervention to support the market helped in one form or another to plant the feeling that the government will underwrite and bear part of the exceptional speculation risks. In doing so, the government has established a precedent that may be interpreted as government readiness to accept responsibility of intervening to protect speculators. This, we think, has far-reaching effects on the nature of traders' expectations and consequently on their investment behaviour in the direction of strengthening speculation tendencies.

Period V: Idolization of the Market, 1978–80. During these years the Kuwaiti stock market consolidated its position in the domestic economy and enhanced its importance to become a major feature of local economic activities. Many of the companies formed during the boom period proved to be economically viable while others, mainly the industrials, remained in operation by deviating from their basic purpose. Total market capitalization, represented in 1980 2.5 times the non-oil GDP against 1.25 times in 1977 (Table 7.8) which reflects the growing relative size of the market. Even more significant was the expansion of the stockholders base, particularly after the share split. However, this was not coupled with a parallel development in the market's organizational and institutional arrangements. Hence, the expansion in the market activities was not accompanied by a substantial change in its main characteristics which remained unaltered throughout the previous periods, namely its relative narrowness in comparison to the country's investible funds and sensitivity to world political, financial and economic events and developments and the predominance of speculation. The market has however acquired certain new features, some of which are positive related to the improvement of the market's organizational and regulatory aspects; while others are an outcome of the developments in the market structure and changes in

Table 7.8: The Stock Market and the Non-oil GDP

Year	Ratio of Market Nominal Value to non-oil GDP %	Ratio of Total Market Value to non-oil GDP %	Ratio of Total Trading Value to Total Market Value of Stocks %
1970	21.3	N.A.	N.A.
1973	N.A.	N.A.	32.4
1975	21.4	109.3	40.3
1976	20.2	177.2	40.7
1977	22.0	125.4	17.5
1978	22.0	177.0	46.2
1979	21.4	222.1	41.2
1980	33.4	248.1	30.0

the domestic securities market following the appearance of the unofficial parallel market where the stocks of Gulf companies and unlisted
Kuwaiti companies are traded.

Development in the Primary Market and the New Issues Base. The
main features of the growth and development of the domestic stock
market and its issue base, during this period, were determined by the
government measures taken in August 1977, the decision to split the
shares of Kuwaiti companies to a value of KD 1 nominal instead of
their previous par values of KD 7.5 and KD 10 and the government
support operation to the market in the period December 1977 to
April 1978 during which it purchased shares to a total value of KD 150
million. Although these government actions were intended to overcome
and treat a temporary crisis affecting the market, yet some of these
measures went beyond that and affected the structure of the market
and its role in domestic economic activity. They produced also certain
developments that were probably not initially envisioned by the authorities when they issued them. This applies particularly to the decision
to stop the establishment of new public shareholding companies.

The share split and the decision of the government to enter the
market as a purchaser of stocks resulted in structural and statistical
changes in the issue base during 1978. The structural change was manifested in the increase in the government share in the total stocks issued
to approximately 35.4 per cent at the end of 1978 compared with 24
per cent in 1977. The share splits, on the other hand, multiplied the
number of issued shares by seven and a half or ten times.

Since the decision to suspend the establishment of new companies remained effective until mid-1979, the expansion of the issue base during 1978 and 1979 came basically from capital increases of existing companies. At the end of 1978 the issue base consisted of some 373 million shares, 7.5 per cent higher than the previous year, and increased to 430 million in 1979. The latter increase came from about 27.6 million rights issues by existing companies and the distribution of 30.9 million bonus shares. Premiums on the rights issues totalled about KD 63 million. In June 1979 the market witnessed the withdrawal of the stocks of the Kuwaiti Oil Tankers Company (approximately 25.9 million shares) after its nationalization and the inclusion of the General Warehouses Company. In 1980 the issue base experienced a significant expansion as a result of the lifting of the ban on the establishment of new companies. The net increase in the total number of shares outstanding amounted to nearly 165 million, an increase of 38 per cent over the previous year. By the end of 1980 there were about 595 million shares outstanding in the market, spread over 41 domestic public shareholding companies of which the government had 256 million shares or 43 per cent of the total number issued.

Table 7.9 illustrates the main changes that took place in the sectoral distribution of the stocks of the Kuwaiti shareholding companies during the years 1977-80. Industrial companies replaced banks as the companies with the highest percentage of the total stocks' issue base and of the total capital of the companies listed in the Stock Exchange.

The imposition of a government ban on new shareholding companies in Kuwait for a period of two years led Kuwaiti investors to seek alternative outlets with features similar to the domestic market, which they found in the Gulf shareholding companies. During the ban period, several companies were incorporated in the neighbouring Arab Gulf states with only minor non-Kuwaiti participation. In actual fact, these companies became a form of Kuwaiti off-shore company.

Development of the Secondary Market (Trading and Prices Movement). Despite the fact that the Kuwaiti stock market surpassed during 1978-80 the record levels reached in the previous periods in forms of turnover volume and value, recession periods were of a longer duration, especially during the last two years when the market was stagnant for most of the period, while bullish periods were short and limited to only a few months of each year.

On the level of trading activities, the market began to recover from its 1977 slide toward the end of the first quarter and the beginning of the second quarter of 1978. The surge in activity was largely in anticipation

Table 7.9: Stocks of Kuwaiti Shareholding Companies — Public Subscriptions

Group	Issued Stocks						Government Stocks			Untraded Private Sector Stock			Legally Tradeable Stocks					
	1977	%	1978	%	1980	%	1977	1978	1980	1977	1978	1980	1977	%	1978	%	1980	%
Banks	26,802,130	28.4	88,138,800	23.7	120,381,907	20.2	10,392,000	12,942,903	16,778,329	10,000,000	5,100,000	—	6,410,130	22.7	70,095,897	32.3	103,603,218	34.5
Investment Companies[a]	5,130,663	5.4	49,426,040	13.3	70,383,494	11.8	2,563,457	27,907,250	37,669,326	—	—	—	2,567,206	9.1	21,518,790	9.9	32,714,168	10.9
Insurance Companies[b]	4,800,110	5.1	12,821,988	3.4	19,774,000	3.3	2,040,000	4,252,500	5,753,413	1,960,000	1,960,000	—	800,110	2.8	6,609,488	3	14,020,587	4.7
Industrial Companies[c]	24,700,000	26.2	76,380,000	20.5	211,470,634	35.5	2,977,900	22,662,393	103,379,436	12,000,000	8,000,000	32,100,000	9,722,100	34.5	45,717,607	21.1	75,911,198	25.3
Transport Companies[d]	18,584,236	19.7	84,704,781	22.7	65,306,185	11	3,306,932	42,655,153	47,385,618	10,000,000	10,000,000	—	5,277,304	18.7	32,049,928	14.8	17,920,567	6.0
Services Companies[e]	10,677,153	11.3	16,880,679	4.5	45,755,692	7.7	144,118	1,744,699	17,298,366	10,000,000	—	10,000,000	533,035	1.9	15,135,980	7	18,457,326	6.2
Real Estate Companies	3,760,000	4.0	44,233,100	11.9	61,846,000	10.4	882,000	18,819,567	34,629,931	—	—	—	2,878,000	10.2	25,413,533	11.7	37,216,069	12.4
Total	94,454,292	100	372,585,388	100	594,917,912	100	22,306,407	131,984,495	252,894,419	43,960,000	25,060,000	42,100,000	28,187,885	100	261,540,923	100	299,923,133	100

Notes: a. Kuwait Financial House was established in 1977 and was listed in the Stock Exchange in 1978.

b. Warbah Insurance Company with a capital of KD 4 million was listed in the Stock Exchange in 1979.

c. Kuwait Tyres Company with a capital of KD 8 million was listed in the Stock Exchange in 1979.

While the stock of Kuwait Pharmaceuticals Company, with a capital of KD 6 million, and the Kuwait International Petroleum Investment Company, with a capital of KD 100 million, were not tradeable until the end of 1980.

d. The stocks of the Kuwait Land Transport Company, with a capital of KD 10 million, were not tradeable until 1979.

e. The stocks of Kuwait General Warehouses Company, with a capital of KD 25 million, was not tradeable until the beginning of 1981.

of government decisions sanctioning the share splits. The relatively intensive trading activities continued throughout the second and third quarters of the year and weakened in the fourth quarter when the market entered a period of calm trading that lasted several months.

The total volume of trading during 1978 amounted to approximately 165 million shares compared with 60 million, and 176 million respectively (adjusted figures based on a standardized share par value) during the years 1977 and 1976, an increase of 175 per cent on 1977 and 94 per cent on 1976. However, in terms of total turnover value, the market achieved in 1978 a record level when the value of total traded stocks jumped to KD 1,385 million compared to KD 346 million and KD 946 million respectively during 1977 and 1976. For most of 1979 recession took grip of the market, and especially in the last months of the year. However, an exception to this was the third quarter which witnessed a sharp upsurge of activity, and about 71 million shares, the total value of which amounted to about KD 800 million, were traded. This represented 43.5 per cent of the total turnover value for the whole of the year, which amounted to KD 1,837 million, and 42 per cent of the total traded stocks during the year (169 million shares). In the fourth quarter market activity shrank markedly with the shares turnover dropping by 74 per cent relative to the third quarter level.

In 1980 the market continued its weak performance with a significant decline in trading activities which led to a fall of 14.8 per cent in annual turnover compared to the 1979 level. The drop was larger in value terms approximating 29 per cent on the previous year's level. The market was weak for most of the year apart from a short lived recovery in the months of June and July. Activity dropped to its lowest level for several years in the last quarter when the total volume of stocks traded did not exceed 11 million, compared with 61 million and 50 million traded during the second and third quarters respectively.

Examining the trends of the Kuwait stock market and its trading activities during the last three years, one can notice that periods of low activity were more numerous than the high periods, and that a marked change took place in its previously experienced seasonal pattern. The market thrived during the summer season, while it slumped during the last months of the year, when activity was supposed to surge because of the companies' dividend announcements. Although this unusual pattern may be partially attributed to the advent of the Holy Month of Ramadan in the summer season, which is usually accompanied by heavier activity in the stock market for social reasons related to the way Kuwaiti Society celebrates this Holy Month. But there are

Table 7.10: Kuwaiti Shareholding Companies Volume of Traded Stocks (in thousands)

Group	1974	%	1975	%	1976	%	1977	%	1978	%	1979	%	1980	%
Banks	2,686	7.2	6,708	3.9	7,806	4.4	2,431	4.0	59,973	58.0	81,388	48.0	47,686	33.0
Investment Companies	8,332	22.4	26,190	15.2	50,658	28.7	15,436	25.7	42,175	25.6	24,379	14.4	24,537	17.1
Insurance Companies	65	0.2	368	0.2	695	0.4	179	0.3	684	0.4	3,452	2.0	1,048	0.7
Industrial Companies	10,325	27.7	73,760	42.8	63,775	36.0	16,030	26.7	27,207	16.5	22,619	13.4	14,833	10.3
Transport Companies	9,182	24.6	26,509	15.4	23,635	13.4	18,749	31.2	6,382	3.9	8,427	5.0	23,607	16.4
Services Companies	358	1.0	734	0.4	613	0.3	72	0.1	7,732	4.7	6,071	3.6	9,264	6.4
Real Estate Companies	6,320	17.0	37,904	22.0	29,115	16.5	7,104	11.8	20,618	12.5	22,884	13.5	22,734	15.8
Total	37,268	100.0	172,173	100.0	176,297	100.0	60,001	100.0	164,771	100.0	169,220	100.0	143,709	100.0

Source: Figures were derived from Ministry of Commerce and Industry Bulletins.
NB. The nominal prices of stocks have been adjusted to KD 1 in 1978; for comparison reasons, the volume of stocks for previous years has been divided accordingly.

more influential contributing factors, such as the wide fluctuations in the international interest rates and the grave political developments in the region, especially the Iran-Iraq war. Our earlier discussion indicates also that the share splits have to an extent increased trading activity, in particular in the years 1978 and 1979, by attracting to the market new small investors. This was reflected in the increased number of transactions compared to previous years. However, the impact of the splits may be assessed better when analyzing the sectoral distribution of the stocks traded in the years 1978-80. Until 1977, banks shares represented only a small proportion, ranging between four and seven per cent of the total volume of stocks traded, because of their high price levels. But since 1978, bank shares formed the biggest component of the total traded shares in the market. They accounted for 58 per cent, 48 per cent and 33 per cent of the total turnover during the years 1978, 1979 and 1980 respectively (see Table 7.10). The increase in demand for bank shares was reflected on their prices, which rose considerably.

Judging by the high turnover ratios of the various company groups, the shares of investment and real estate companies were the most heavily traded. The ratio was for the former 196 per cent and 75 per cent in 1978 and 1979 respectively and 81 per cent and 61 per cent for the latter in respective years. This also indicates that the shares of these companies were very much in demand by speculators.

The renewed confidence and hope of investors in the Kuwaiti stock market and the growth of its ability to accommodate the domestic and external economic and political shocks during the last years was clearly reflected on the stock prices movement, which showed a general upward trend causing prices to reach new record levels (see Tables 7.11 and 7.12 below). The increase in the general stock price index in the period end 1977 and end 1980 amounted to more than 63 per cent.

The stock prices movement during the years 1978-80, and in particular after the share splits and up to the third quarter of 1979, led to a sharp increase in the market value of the companies' outstanding shares. Market capitalization rose from KD 1,976 million at the end of 1977 to about KD 2,000 million at the end of 1978 and to KD 4,460 million in December 1979, registering annual increases of 52 per cent and 49 per cent respectively. However, the depressed state of the market in 1980 led to a drop in the total market value of stocks by 1 per cent compared with the previous year. The decline in market capitalization was mainly the result of the fall in the stock prices of the financial sector companies (banks, investment and insurance), which represent 43 per

Table 7.11: Kuwaiti Shareholding Companies, Share Price Index (100 = Jan. 1976)

Group	1976	1977	1978	1979	1980
Banks	221.9	195.1	315.3	496.6	469.7
Investment Companies	276.2	194.1	248.1	258.8	241.8
Insurance Companies	301.1	279.1	569.8	774.9	693.8
Industrial Companies	224.4	172.7	226.8	236.0	211.9
Transport Companies	149.0	121.7	101.2	113.0	140.2
Services Companies	243.6	231.9	298.5	272.5	359.2
Real Estate Companies	356.3	280.1	384.0	444.5	464.5
General Index	235.8	191.8	258.9	311.4	313.3

cent of the total outstanding shares in the market.

The majority of listed companies produced good financial results and steadily improved their performance during the years 1978-80. The companies total net profits increased from about KD 80 million in 1978 to KD 119 million in 1980. However, despite the improved earning powers of the shares, the link between prices and earning remained as weak as before. This was manifested in the extravagant values of the price/earnings ratios for most of the listed companies, which averaged well over 50 in December 1980.

Excessive speculation remained a major feature of the Kuwaiti stock market, particularly during the market take offs in 1978 and 1979. The market share turnover ratio increased from 50 per cent in 1977 to 76 per cent in 1978, and 63 per cent in 1979. The difference between the market value and book value widened further, as the ratio between them rose from 3.3 in December 1977 to 4.9 at the end of 1978 and to 5.8 in 1979. However, in did not reach the level it recorded during the run away boom in 1976 when the rate was six-fold. It should be noted however that speculation activity during this period was based on a sounder basis than in 1976, since it was mainly concentrated on the shares of companies with strong and reliable financial positions, such as banks, investment and real estate companies.

The daily data on the movement of the price index prepared by the Ministry of Commerce show that the extent of the price fluctuations has steadily decreased in the years 1978, 1979 and 1980. The annual range of fluctuation (highest point to lowest point of the index during the year) contracted markedly from 102.3 points in 1978 to 97 points in 1979 and 90.0 points in 1980. The coefficient of variation, which is a measure of the monthly fluctuations of the price index[25] decreased during the same years from 15.3 per cent to 9.8 per cent and thence

Table 7.12: Kuwaiti Shareholding Companies, Share Price Index (Quarterly Figures) (100 = 1st Jan. 1976)

End of Period	Banks	Investment	Shareholding Companies			Services	Real Estate	General Index	% Change
			Insurance	Industrial	Transport				
1979									
1st Quarter	398.1	273.0	520.0	233.2	87.6	267.9	403.1	274.4	6.0
2nd Quarter	437.3	272.9	694.2	245.9	117.1	252.6	429.8	304.6	11.0
3rd Quarter	548.3	292.9	818.7	246.7	121.7	319.3	493.3	339.8	11.6
4th Quarter	496.6	258.8	774.9	236.0	113.0	272.5	444.5	311.4	(8.4)
1980									
1st Quarter	442.6	231.8	741.6	218.8	111.4	259.6	438.0	290.0	(6.9)
2nd Quarter	550.9	257.2	767.0	226.0	140.4	398.3	522.4	342.4	18.0
3rd Quarter	512.5	273.7	718.0	225.3	149.9	380.6	486.7	335.3	(2.1)
4th Quarter	469.7	241.8	693.8	211.9	140.2	359.2	464.5	313.3	(6.6)

Note: Figures between parentheses are negative.
Source: Ministry of Commerce and Industry.

Table 7.13: Monthly Rate of Trading in the Kuwaiti Stock Market

Month	1978					1979					1980				
	Number of shares	Value (KD, 000)	No. of trans-actions	Average volume of trans-action	Average value of trans-action (KD, 000)	Number of shares	Value (KD, 000)	No. of trans-actions	Average volume of trans-action	Average value of trans-action (KD, 000)	Number of shares	Value (KD, 000)	No. of trans-actions	Average volume of trans-action	Average value of trans-action (KD, 000)
	(1)	(2)	(3)	(1/3)	(2/3)	(1)	(2)	(3)	(1/3)	(2/3)	(1)	(2)	(3)	(1/3)	(2/3)
January	729,163	32,316	384	1,899	84	8,292,072	85,508	1,619	5,122	53	3,461,355	37,477	782	4,426	48
February	833,128	43,871	529	1,575	83	12,778,910	152,405	2,280	5,605	67	12,834,208	141,986	2,013	6,376	71
March	2,788,903	169,813	2,277	1,225	75	22,313,969	275,949	3,009	7,416	92	6,097,072	55,802	917	6,279	58
April	10,690,222	108,674	1,933	5,530	56	7,837,579	75,589	1,557	5,034	49	6,717,368	57,812	1,213	5,982	52
May	8,907,521	72,958	1,891	4,710	39	14,915,091	102,343	3,131	4,764	33	25,330,606	257,269	3,936	6,436	65
June	15,502,009	126,108	4,498	3,447	28	12,760,550	129,341	2,873	4,442	45	28,914,475	259,833	4,141	6,983	63
July	26,906,123	205,204	6,094	4,415	34	41,156,659	455,548	8,023	5,130	57	36,717,819	315,736	4,717	7,784	67
August	21,463,996	149,849	5,468	3,925	27	13,904,431	182,358	2,502	5,557	73	8,717,155	81,610	1,122	7,769	73
September	20,478,654	187,626	4,147	4,938	45	16,687,561	161,612	3,531	4,726	46	4,172,574	35,949	738	5,654	49
October	16,945,964	166,625	3,284	5,160	51	8,560,134	87,281	1,658	5,163	53	3,825,298	23,706	621	1,160	38
November	4,288,319	40,106	915	4,687	44	4,071,469	55,141	724	5,624	76	3,219,203	26,675	391	8,233	68
December	8,297,672	91,631	1,643	4,996	56	5,664,858	73,103	1,095	5,173	67	3,701,970	31,632	559	6,622	57
Total	173,750,433	1,394,459	33,065	5,255	42	168,943,283	1,836,975	32,002	5,279	57	143,709,103	1,325,523	21,114	6,806	63
(April & Dec.) Average	14,821,498	116,232	2,755		52	14,078,607	153,015	2,667	5,313	59	11,975,759	110,457	1,760	6,559	59
Standard Deviation	6,943,246	57,922	1,840		19	9,512,392	108,605	1,816	822	15.6	11,165,252	102,155	1,507	997	10
Coefficient of Variation	47%	50%	67%		37%	68%	71%	68%	14%	26%	93%	92%	86%	15%	17%

to 7 per cent. Although it is difficult to reach firm conclusions about the stability of this trend of development, it does point, however, to a less volatile trend in the prices of Kuwaiti stocks. By contrast, the monthly figures for the volume of trading during the same period, reflected an increasing dispersion in the pattern of yearly trading. The coefficient of variation of the monthly volume of trading increased from 48 per cent in 1978 to 68 per cent in 1979 and to 93 per cent in 1980 (see Table 7.13).

It seems therefore that the market continues to move in spurts whereby heavier than usual trading activity is concentrated in a few months of the year. The trend in the price movement may be considered positive since it implies a lower degree of risk and if confirmed means also fewer opportunities for speculative gains. We do not think however that the market movement over the period 1978-80 is sufficiently long to make strong generalizations. But there is little doubt that improved regulation of the Kuwaiti stock market had a positive impact in ridding the market of some of its harmful speculation.

Conclusion

In the preceding discussion, we have traced the development of the economic and institutional framework which determines the process of the issuing and trading of the shares of Kuwaiti shareholding companies. We have presented a detailed historical account of the development of the Kuwaiti stock market through its different stages. (This is also summarized in Tables 7.8, 7.14 and 7.15 and also Figures 7.2 and 7.3.)

This historical review of the stock market has highlighted the peculiar characteristics of the Kuwaiti economy on the one hand and the inadequacy of the market's organizational arrangements on the other. While it is difficult to overcome the restrictions imposed by the nature of the Kuwaiti economy, there is wide room for further improvement in the spheres of controls and regulations governing the market and this calls for continual intervention by official and private bodies supervising the market. However, rules and regulations will not be effective unless the specific nature of the Kuwaiti economy is taken into due consideration.

It is clear from our study that an officially organized secondary securities market came into existence only in the last few years. That is when the Securities Committee was formed and started performing its

Table 7.14: The Stock Market in the National Economy

Year	Total Capital of the Market in Nominal Values (KD,000) 1	Market Value of Total Stocks listed in Stock Exchange (KD,000) 2	Gross Domestic Product (KD,000) 3	Domestic Liquidity (KD,000) 4	Total Issued Stock (KD,000) 5	Government Share %	Tradeable Stocks ('000) 6	No. of Stocks traded annually ('000) 7	Value of Traded Stocks (KD,000) 8	8/3 %	1/4 %	2/4 %	1/3 %	2/3 %	Stock turnover ratio f %
1970	92,292	N.A.	1,013,400	362,100	11,050	45.5	6,020	N.A.	N.A.	25.5	N.A.	9.1	9.1	N.A.	N.A.
1972	184,304	1,000,000a	2,111,000c	571,900	21,330	38.4	13,140	9,955	324,010	15.3c	32.2	174.9	8.7c	47.4	82.0
1974	214,000	895,700	3,229,000d	720,500	23,322	41.5	13,681	4,255	102,511	3.2d	29.7	124.3	6.6d	27.7	31.0
1975b	218,456	1,114,964	3,476,800	891,200	30,740	35.7	19,765	18,409	449,194	12.9	24.5	125.0	6.3	32.1	93.0
1976	265,482	2,325,178	3,834,400	1,220,300	67,600	25.4	21,500	19,800	946,000	24.7	21.8	190.5	6.9	60.1	92.0
1977	347,000	1,976,400	4,053,500	1,583,300	95,000	24.0	27,700	13,700	346,000	8.5	21.9	124.8	8.6	48.8	49.5
1978	382,585	2,999,841	4,209,500	1,950,300	372,585	35.4	216,541	164,771	1,385,000	33.0	19.1	153.8	8.9	71.3	76.0
1979	429,560	4,460,000	6,435,600	2,289,700	429,560	35.0	267,560	169,220	1,837,000	28.5	18.8	194.8	6.7	69.3	63.0
1980	594,918	4,417,033	7,373,700e	2,857,500	594,918	43.0	299,923	143,709	1,325,000	18.0	20.8	154.6	8.1	59.9	48.0

Notes: a. Estimates

b. Burgan Bank was not included in 1975, because it was established on 24 Dec. 1975, with a capital of KD 10 million divided into 10 million shares.
c. National Income for the fiscal year 1973/74 was used, therefore figures should be considered approximations for the year.
d. National Income for the fiscal year 1974/75 was used, therefore figures should be considered approximations for the year.
e. Central Bank estimates.

$$\text{f. Turnover Ratio} = \frac{\text{Quantity of traded stocks} \times 100}{\text{Quantity of tradeable stocks}}$$

Table 7.15: Profits of Kuwaiti Shareholding Companies, Classified According to Groups (in thousands of KDs)

Group	1978			1979			1980		
	Paid-up Capital	Net Profits	%	Paid-up Capital	Net Profits	%	Paid-up Capital	Net Profits[a]	%
Banks	80,639	25,487	32	90,747	33,973	37	182,775	48,864	43
Investment Companies	49,426	12,023	24	66,712	15,610	23	70,368	11,736	17
Insurance Companies	12,822	7,488	58	16,059	9,244	58	19,736	9,653	49
Industrial Companies	67,980	13,567	20	94,441	14,937	16	104,566[c]	19,600	19
Transport Companies[b]	49,768	1,273	3	53,601	3,095	6	60,229	4,503	7
Services Companies	11,881	3,499	29	25,599	2,725	11	28,256	5,076	18
Real Estate Companies	44,233	16,413	37	50,738	19,168	38	61,700	19,150	31
Total	316,749	79,749	25	397,897	98,752	25	457,700	118,583	26

Notes: a. Some figures are not very accurate because they are derived from the statistical analyses prepared by the Ministry of Commerce and Industry.

b. The Kuwait Oil Tanker Company and the Kuwait Transport Company were excluded from the 1978 figures because the stocks of the two companies were later withdrawn from the market.

c. The figure does not include the paid-up capital of the Kuwait Pharmaceutical Industries Company and the Kuwait International Petroleum Investment Company because they have not commenced their operations as yet.

Figure 7.2: Total Capital of Kuwaiti Public Shareholding Companies

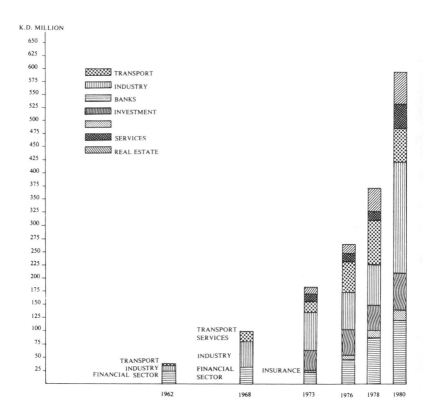

duties and when the stock exchange was opened in 1977. But unofficial trading activities in Kuwaiti shares conducted either through unlicensed scattered middle-men or directly between stock owners, dates back to the first appearance of ownership rights in the Kuwaiti economy during the 1950s.

We have found that excessive speculation and inflated share prices have been continuous features of the market and a major source of public concern. As we have indicated in various parts of our study, share prices bear little relation to the companies' underlying financial and productive conditions or to share yield, instead they mainly reflect the exaggerated expectations of big speculators. The persistence of these trends seriously undermines the economic functions of the

Figure 7.3: Shares Price Movement for Kuwaiti Shareholding Companies during the period Jan. 1978-Dec. 1980 (Jan. 1978 = 100)

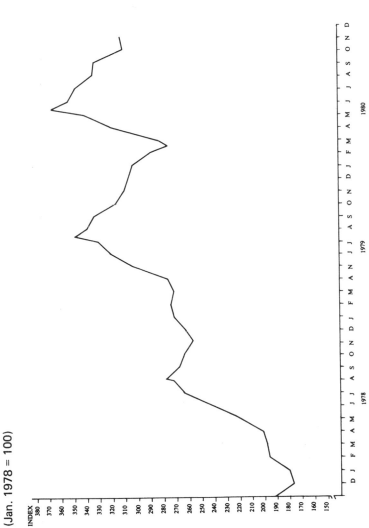

Source: Ministry of Commerce and Industry

securities market, namely to mobilize domestic savings and allocate them to efficient economic enterprises. Improving the organizational and institutional framework of the market is undoubtedly a prerequisite for its more efficient working. One would expect however that the objectively imposed scarcity of domestic real and financial assets relative to available investible funds will tend always to make then overvalued.

Despite its rapid growth over the past decade, the market for Kuwaiti shares remains narrow. By the end of 1980, there were only 41 public Kuwaiti shareholding companies, 39 of which were listed on the Bourse. Table 7.14 shows that the nominal value of listed shares at the end of 1980 was only eight per cent of the GDP. To broaden the market, the Government allowed recently the listing of sound closed Kuwaiti shareholding companies and well established Gulf companies with good performance records.[26] It is unlikely that these new rules will have substantial impact on the market since the spectacular growth of the unofficial market since 1979, has already provided an active secondary market for the different types and cateogories of unlisted Kuwaiti and Gulf companies.

Although Kuwaiti law entitles each Kuwaiti citizen to be a shareholder in publicly floated new shareholding companies, the market remained dominated by a few active traders with large shareholdings. The big dealers have a strong influence on the market and set the tone for its movement. Some of them act also as market-makers for some shares. The heavy concentration of share ownership allows individual dealers to induce share price movement artificially to make speculative gains. It is hoped that the recent establishment of securities companies, whose main function is to act as market-makers, will reduce the dominance of individual big speculators and lessen price volatility. The relaxation of legal restrictions on non-Kuwaiti share-ownership in Kuwaiti shareholding companies is an obvious possible way of enlarging the market's traders base.

The narrowness of the market is of course to a large extent structural, mirroring the smallness of the local economy. But government restrictions on new entries to the market and the limitations imposed on private investment in the oil sector have been additional constraints on the deepening and broadening of the securities market. The latter constraint has been eased lately with the formation of the hundred million dinars Kuwait International Petroleum Investment Company and the offering of 30 per cent of its shares for public subscription. The new company represented a substantial new addition to the market and became the largest industrial company listed in the market.

It appears from our study that the stock market is a secondary source of financing, particularly for non-financial companies. Usually, internal resources (retained earning) or loans provided by the banking system form more important sources of finance for existing companies. But equity financing remains more important in relative terms than in other countries because of Kuwait's booming secondary market and the general popularity of shares with investors. It has been suggested that the stock market might play a bigger role in supplying the capital needs of public companies if new share issues were priced closer to their market value in the secondary market, instead of being offered at low premiums to the existing shareholders.[27] The services of specialized institutions such as investment banks, are in this respect indispensable to ensure the proper economic pricing of new share issues which is currently governed in the Kuwaiti stock market by legal considerations and *ad hoc* criteria.

In all cases, however, the stock market will remain a minor source of funds for private enterprise as a whole in view of the limited number of companies listed on the stock exchange and the availability of access-ible alternative sources of finance.

In addition to the organizational and institutional shortcomings of the markets, many of the present undesired features of the Kuwaiti stock market seem to be due also to insufficient control of liquidity and credit directed to the market. The problem assumed new dimen-sions with the appearance of forward deals which represent an informal type of credit created by the market to finance its dealings beyond the reach of official controls. The Central Bank has achieved some measure of success in tightening controls over banks credits used to finance share speculation, but more needs to be done to close the various loop-holes that are used to circumvent the Central Bank lending rules. Forward transactions are less amenable to controls by the monetary authorities, but the involvement of the financial system in these risky transactions needs to be closely watched. Recent moves to organize this form of transaction on a sounder financial and regulatory basis are over-due considering the large outstanding volume of these deals on both the official and unofficial markets. This study has shown in ample detail how these deals undermine the stability of the market and expose it to the danger of collapse in the case of prices levelling off or declining.

Epilogue

A few months after this last chapter was written (November 1981), the Kuwaiti stock market collapsed (August 1982) making world headline news. The *Souk Al Manakh*, along with oil had made Kuwait's worldwide reputation.

It is true that this was a time when we were particularly well served in news of bull markets. Paradoxically, since August 1982, that is, when the Kuwait stock market collapsed, bulls were in evidence in all expected places and also in some unexpected ones. News of crises are not lacking either. The Tel Aviv stock exchange was described as 'Israel Las Vegas' (*Financial Times*, 21 January 1983). In Canada the Vancouver stock exchange became the best game in town for those who wanted to gamble (*Financial Times*, 9 February 1983). The boom on the Swedish stock market surprised all observers — 'nobody living today has ever seen anything like this', observed one trader in the Stockholm stock market in February 1983 (*Financial Times*, 18 February 1983). Subsequently, the Swedish stock market, which had been booming for more than two years, was forced to close its doors for a week from 29 April 1983 (*The Economist*, 30 April 1983). The Dow Jones and *Financial Times* indexes attained new highs in the first half of 1983 after the long depression in the previous two years. The same is true for Tokyo, Hong Kong, Taiwan, Singapore as well as other places.

But all this was nothing compared to the Kuwait stock market crisis when the bubble finally burst sometime in July–August 1982. The gross value of unpaid cheques registered in September 1982 reached KD 26.6 billion ($90 billion) — a higher figure than Mexico's total external debt ($80 billion). Of that amount eight individual traders — 'the eight magnificents' — owed some KD 18.5 billion ($63 billion).

Our previous paper was mainly concerned with shares in Kuwaiti public shareholding companies leaving aside transactions on the unofficial stock market — *Souk Al Manakh* — which includes shares of both closed companies and Gulf offshore companies. The experience of the last two years proved that the official stock market was only the tip of the iceberg. Of the total forward cheques registered in September 1982, (KD 26.6 billion) forward contracts in the official Kuwait stock market were estimated at KD 4.5 billion between August 1981 and September, 1982.

The ingenuity of Kuwaiti traders to evade regulations in order to practice the national sport of speculation on the stock market can hardly be surpassed. The restriction on banks' facilities gave rise — it has been seen — to a parallel unofficial credit facility through post-dated cheques. Also, the government's restrictions on establishing new public shareholding companies were bypassed by the establishment of closed and Gulf offshore companies. While the government strictly controlled the creation of public shareholding companies, no such regulations inhibited the establishment of closed companies. Also Kuwaiti 'investors' found many Gulf states more than ready to grant them licence to form 'Gulf' companies on their territories. These are Kuwaiti companies in all but name.

Though officially banned from trading in the Kuwait stock market, closed companies' and Gulf companies' shares were hotly traded in the informal *Souk Al Manakh*. The government turned a blind eye to this 'illegal' market. The prospects of huge fortunes induced speculators to establish new companies — closed or offshore — and trade them on a 200-500 per cent price increase in the forward market. Prices soared, while circulating post-dated cheques also increased. It was possible in that happy time for a more or less penniless 'investor' to borrow KD millions by buying stocks forward and cashing them spot to start his 'financial' business. That was all right while prices continued rising, but when the boom came to an end; many people found themselves with almost worthless papers while heavily burdened with grossly inflated debts.

Since what goes up —artificially — must come down, the Kuwait stock market was out of steam by the second half of 1982. In July 1982 some dealers, sensing the imminent difficulties of the market, began to cash their cheques ahead of the due dates — a practice permitted by Kuwaiti law. A minor crisis was thus turned into a full-scale crash. The rest of the events is only a classic story in such circumstances.

The government's first act was to ban all forward contracts. On 20 September 1982 a decree was issued to suspend the right of citizens to sue for debt in respect of unsettled forward transactions. The decree also set up an arbitration panel and required the registration of all post-dated cheques related to forward dealings in the stock market. The government also established a compensation fund for the smaller investors — defined as one owed not more than KD 2 million ($6.75 m). The fund had an initial capital of KD 500 million. It is estimated to have issued, as of May 1983, bonds of face value of about KD 640 million.

In spite of declared refusal to put more cash into the market, the government has been compelled since early 1982 to support the market through stocks purchase by one of the government's investment companies (KFTCIC). The government's support was limited to Kuwaiti stocks in the official market. It was estimated that the government has injected some KD 570 million as of May 1983.

Notes

1. Central Bank of Kuwait, *The Kuwaiti Economy in Ten Years*, the economic report for the period 1969–79, p. 106.

2. Kuwait, *Financial Times Survey*, 25 February 1977.

3. John G. Gurley and Edward S. Shaw, *Money in a Theory of Finance* (The Brookings Institution, Washington DC, 1962).

4. Ibid.

5. For example see A. Berle and Means, *The Modern Corporation and Private Property* (New York, 1932), p. 356.

6. Jean-Jacques Servan-Schreiber, *Le Défi Mondial* (Fayard, Paris, 1980).

7. Robert Solow, 'The Economics of Resources or the Resources of Economics', *The American Economic Review*, May 1979.

8. *International Petroleum Encyclopaedia* (Petroleum Publishing Co., Oklahoma, 1975).

9. Ragaei El Mallakh, *Economic Development or Regional Cooperation: Kuwait* (Chicago University Press, 1968), p. 81.

10. Robert S. Aliber, 'The Integration of National Financial Markets: A Review of Theory and Findings', *Weltwirtschaftliches Archiv*, vol. 114, no. 3 (1978).

11. Thomas Stauffer, 'The Dynamics of Petroleum Dependency: Growth in an oil rentier state', *Finance and Industry*, no. 2 (1981), pp. 7–28.

12. William J. Baumol, *The Stock Market and Economic Efficiency* (Fordham University Press, N.Y., 1956), p. 37.

13. John M. Keynes, *The General Theory of Employment, Interest and Money* (Harcourt-Brace, New York, 1936), p. 150.

14. Hazem El-Beblawi, *The Economic Bulletin* (Ministry of Finance, Kuwait, 1977) (in Arabic).

15. Central Bank of Kuwait, *The Kuwaiti Economy in Ten Years*, the economic report for the period 1969–79, p. 106.

16. BBME was replaced in 1971 by Bank of Kuwait and the Middle East, which is fully owned by Kuwaitis.

17. For more details about this period see: M.W. Khouja and P.G. Sadler, *The Economy of Kuwait, Development and Role in International Finance* (Macmillan Press, London, 1979; R. El-Mallakh, *Kuwait, Trade and Investment* (Westview Press, Boulder, Colorado, 1979).

18. Kuwait National Airways was initially established as a shareholding company with Government equity participation. A few years later it was nationalized and became the Kuwait Airways Corporation.

19. In addition to that, a number of closed shareholding companies were also incorporated during this period.

20. The analysis and evaluation of the development of the stock market during this period is based on the annual reports of the shareholding companies and the reports by the World Bank experts.

21. The company established an index number, based on stock prices of ten leading companies, on the basis of December 1961 = 100.

22. M. Khouja and W. Said, *The Kuwait Stock Market, Performance and Prospects* (Kuwait Economic Society, 1974).

23. Report presented by a British Consultancy group to the Ministry of Commerce and Industry in 1970 on the establishment of a Kuwait Stock Exchange.

24. Khouja and Said, *The Kuwait Stock Market*.

25. Coefficient of Variation =

$$\frac{\text{Standard Deviation}}{\text{Monthly average of the Price Index}}$$

26. Until mid-1982, only six closed shareholding companies and two Gulf companies have qualified for listing. There is little evidence to suggest many more have shown interest to be quoted on the stock exchange.

27. Basil Al-Nakib, *The Role of Specialized Institution in Developing the Kuwaiti Stock Market*, (paper presented at the Conference on 'the Development of the Stock Market in Kuwait', Kuwait November 1981).

INDEX